MIKOYAN
MiG-29 'FULCRUM'

1981 to present

COVER IMAGE: Mikoyan MiG-29.
(Mike Badrocke)

© David Baker 2017

All rights reserved. No part of this publication may be reproduced or stored in a retrieval system or transmitted, in any form or by any means, electronic, mechanical, photocopying, recording or otherwise, without prior permission in writing from Haynes Publishing.

First published in June 2017

A catalogue record for this book is available from the British Library.

ISBN 978 0 85733 397 1

Library of Congress control no. 2014957456

Published by Haynes Publishing,
Sparkford, Yeovil,
Somerset BA22 7JJ, UK.
Tel: 01963 440635
Int. tel: +44 1963 440635
Website: www.haynes.com

Haynes North America Inc.
859 Lawrence Drive,
Newbury Park, California 91320, USA.

Printed in Malaysia.

Acknowledgements

This book would not have been possible without the help and assistance of many people in the Russian aviation industry who have provided support over several decades, unravelling detailed aspects of aircraft engineering and design as practised by leading manufacturing and machine-building factories. In particular, I would like to acknowledge the assistance of members of the former TsAGI, the Central Aerohydrodynamic Institute in Moscow, who were extremely helpful during many hours of discussion during the 1980s, which informed a better understanding of the principles and protocols laid down in Russian aeronautical design and engineering.

I would also like to thank several senior ranking officers of the German Air Force which helped unravel various aspects of MiG-29 operation as well as its engineering and maintenance. Their help has been enormous and has complemented much of the information that came from the Russian manufacturers of engine and airframe. In addition several individuals from countries still operating the MiG-29, but who have elected to remain anonymous, have helped in no small way to bring this aircraft out of the shadows.

But no book is the product of the author's efforts alone and unseen to the reader lies a group of skilled and talented people involved in design, layout and in editing the author's original text. To those at Haynes Publishing who have worked on this book, and others written by this author for that publisher, heartfelt gratitude for a job well done.

I would particularly like to thank Jonathan Falconer of Haynes Publishing for having placed me under contract to write this book, for the ongoing support of editor Steve Rendle, for the attentive eye of copy editor Ian Heath, and James Robertson for his scrupulous attention to the detailed design of this book.

I would also take this opportunity to express my continuing high regard for what, for an author, is one the world's most outstanding publishing houses today. In an industry challenged by the surfeit of 'free' web-based information, they hold fast to the good principles of old-fashioned publishing, quality bookbinding and an understanding, respect and courtesy for authors enduring what can at times be a very lonely profession.

About which I would also like the reader to know that, like previous books, this one was made possible by the most important person in my life – my dear wife Ann – for her continuous support and forbearance.

MIKOYAN MiG-29 'FULCRUM'

1981 to present

Owners' Workshop Manual

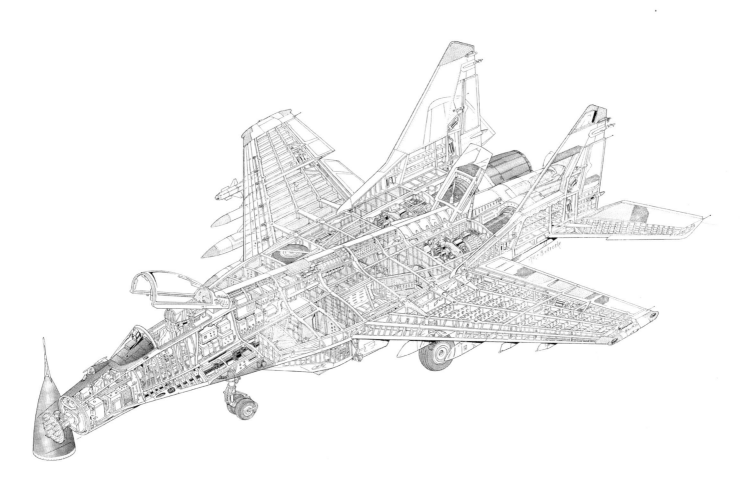

An insight into the design, construction, operation and maintenance of Russia's deadly air superiority multi-role combat jet

David Baker

Contents

OPPOSITE **Displaying a semi-conformal centreline fuel tank a MiG-29 of the Polish Air Force performs a loop.** *(Steve Rendle)*

BELOW **A MiG-29 of the Bangladeshi Air Force during a Victory Day flypast in 2016.** *(Fahad Faisal)*

Introduction

There have been many books written about the MiG-29. Several of them describe the variants and derivatives which evolved from this iconic late-Cold War combat aircraft, and there have been, and still are, a wide range of resources on web-based sites that discuss the aircraft's capabilities and purport to assess its place in the history of Russian military aircraft. This book, however, focuses on the technology of the aircraft and its systems and does not repeat the type's history, of which numerous descriptions already exist.

It has been a particular pleasure for me to write this book, revisiting Soviet-era aerospace engineering after a lapse of more than 25 years. I first encountered that world during the early 1980s when, for professional reasons, I had the privilege of visiting the Soviet Ministry of

BELOW A MiG-29KUB with wings folded of the carrier *Vikrant*. *(MiG)*

Defence and Marshal Dmitry Ustinov and having discussions with several aircraft companies, eventually visiting the closed facilities of manufacturers such as Tupolev, Ilyushin, Antonov and MiG.

I had for several years nurtured a tremendous respect for Russian aircraft design and engineering, based as they were on principles and mechanical techniques completely different to those we were schooled in in the West. It was an education in lateral thinking and the creative application of physics and chemistry.

To a youth growing up just after World War Two there was perhaps a somewhat romantic association based upon the legendary and stoic achievements of the Red Army, supported by massed concentrations of aircraft, in defeating Nazi aggression. Visits to TsAGI in Moscow to discuss advanced aerodynamic applications during the 1980s only heightened my fascination with this great country and its highly talented aeronautical engineers, whose ability to rewrite the laws of aerodynamics is equally legendary.

Sustained in my fascination by a professional involvement with the US space programme, on one memorable day in 1990 I had the unique opportunity to be inducted as a flight engineer on the world's largest aircraft, the six-engine Antonov An-225 Mriya, bigger than the Airbus A380, courtesy of the Soviet defence minister Marshal Dmitry Yazov. Designed to carry Buran, Russia's space shuttle, it epitomised the boldness of Russian aerospace design and the audacity of its flight crew to put this behemoth into the sky as we did 90° wingovers to the accompaniment of a demonic stick-shaker!

In the crew bus on the way to the Mriya I was accompanied by a man who would become a friend – test pilot John Farley OBE, AFC, CEng, famous for his development flying with the Hawker P.1127, the Kestrel and the Harrier. While I was off to share throttle levers with the hands of the two Mriya pilots, John was on his way to fly the MiG-29UB. In this book I am delighted to be able to share with you his thoughts on the capabilities and flying characteristics of this remarkable aircraft – a true icon of Soviet-era aerospace genius – in this book celebrating a unique aircraft, an epitome of Russian aeronautical design and aircraft engineering.

David Baker
East Sussex
February 2017

Chapter One

MiG – the company

The names Mikoyan and Gurevich, accomplished as aircraft designers, are famous in the lexicon of world aviation manufacturers and there can be few military aviation enthusiasts who have not acquainted themselves with the numerous products from this outstanding design bureau. For those unfamiliar with the story, a brief summary is in order.

OPPOSITE The memorial to Artyom Mikoyan in his native Sanahin, Armenia, birthplace of one of Russia's most famous aircraft designers, surmounted by a MiG-21. Some of Artyom's success may have rubbed off from his brother, Anastas Mikoyan. The longest-running member of the Soviet Politburo, serving under Lenin, Stalin, Khrushchev and Brezhnev, Anastas was a key negotiator of the Molotov–Ribbentrop pact between Stalin and Hitler in August 1939. *(David Baker)*

ABOVE Artyom Mikoyan (1905–70) (right) and Mikhail Gurevich (1893–1976) pose with a model of the MiG-3 fighter that emerged from the Polikarpov bureau after an earlier design and became the basis for a wide range of variants.
(Via David Baker)

The origin of the MiG design bureau begins in 1939 with the Polikarpov I-200 fighter, produced out of urgency when the clear superiority of German military aircraft became a potential threat to Russia's national security. The new *Luftwaffe* had been growing for several years, since Hermann Göring publicly announced in 1935 the formation of an independent air force and tore up the agreement that had constrained German military expansion since the Treaty of Versailles in 1919.

The Germans had been working with the Russians to develop military aviation since shortly after World War One, and also with the Italians since Mussolini seized power in 1925. When Adolf Hitler came to power in 1933 the days of German subservience were over and the parlous state of its military aircraft industry was brought to an abrupt end. A balance of fear emerged between Nazi Germany and the communist Soviet Union until an unholy alliance was struck during the second half of 1939. But Josef Stalin feared German hegemony and quietly began to rearm Russia for a possible confrontation.

The pact between Germany and Russia signed in August 1939 came at the end of a series of diplomatic visits by military personnel to each other's countries, where it became apparent that the USSR lagged far behind the highly mechanised and militarily superior *Wehrmacht*, one arm of which – the *Luftwaffe* – instilled grave concern in the Soviet leadership.

Long before this, in January 1939 a competition was launched to create a new generation of fighters for the Red Army Air Force, the VVS RKKA, in which several Soviet design teams would submit proposals. It was one of the first actions of the four new People's Commissariats, one each for shipbuilding, ammunition, armament and aviation. Head of the aircraft industry, A.I. Shakhoorin, visited German factories and was given a courteous display of *Luftwaffe* capabilities, returning to report that the entire Russian aviation production capacity was half that of Germany.

Responding to the competition, several leading figures in aircraft design produced a range of proposals, and agreements were reached to develop specific aircraft. Working for Polikarpov, Artyom Mikoyan and Mikhail Gurevich were instrumental in work on the I-200. I stands for *istrebitel*, or fighter, and in the factory it was given the type number (*izdeliye*) 200. Out of favour with Stalin, who was taking an intense interest in Soviet rearmament plans, Polikarpov's operation was split up and a new special design office, OKO-1, was set up under Mikoyan and Gurevich on 25 November 1939.

Polikarpov had sought to place the biggest and most powerful engine he could find and integrate it with a minimum-size airframe. Known for his love of radial engines, Polikarpov had adopted the 1,030kW (1,400hp) Mikulin AM-37 in-line engine, with which he calculated

RIGHT Artyom Mikoyan played a dominant role in the development of the MiG design, manufacturing bureau and machine-building factory, but he would not outlive his partner, who would himself only survive long enough to see the detailed design of the MiG-29 and a fourth generation of fighter.
(Via David Baker)

the new fighter could achieve 670kph (470mph). Re-designated MiG-1, the aircraft flew for the first time on 5 April 1940 but with the less powerful 883kW (1,200hp) AM-35A. As a sleek, low-wing monoplane, the aircraft was dominated by its massive engine and displayed a top speed of 640kph (397mph) with its alternative power plant.

While the aircraft had an impressive performance it was a handful to fly and a succession of improvements were made. The AM-37 was installed in the second prototype, which made its first flight on 6 January 1941 but crashed on 7 May, killing its pilot. The third prototype was employed on weapons tests with various guns being trialled on the type. Throughout the period up to the German invasion on 22 June, the MiG-1 began to enter service but less than 100 were on hand, spread across several fronts from the Baltic to the Black Sea. Almost all were swept away in the German whirlwind that was Operation Barbarossa.

Nine months before that, OKO-1 was frantically trying to solve persistent problems with the MiG-1. These changes resulted in the MiG-3, officially I-200 No 4, which took to the air for the first time on 29 October 1940 with an AM-37 engine. Faster than anything else in the sky at high altitude and only marginally slower than the Messerschmitt Bf-109F at sea level, the MiG-3 was less than desired. Nevertheless, production requirements were high, with

ABOVE Looking not dissimilar to a Curtiss Kittyhawk, a MiG-3 gets full throttle as its pilot guns his warbird across the grass on the airfield at Mochishche, Russia. Not faultless, the MiG-3 nevertheless sponsored a national reputation for its design bureau. *(Alex Polezhaev)*

BELOW A plan-view of the MiG-3, of which more than 3,000 were produced in 1940 and 1941. Extraordinarily fast for its day, the fighter carried a single wing-mounted 12.7mm machine gun and two 7.62mm machine guns above the engine and within the cowling. *(Kaboldy)*

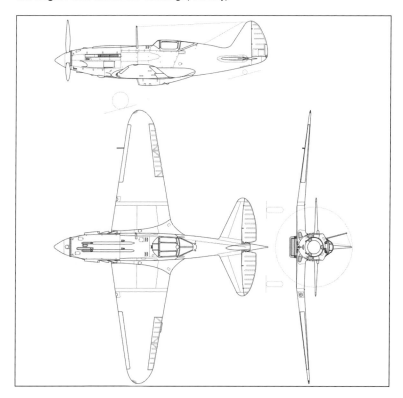

ABOVE The second aircraft to receive the MiG-9 designation, some 600 of this jet-powered fighter were produced between 1946 and 1948, with more than half this total delivered to China's People's Liberation Army, in Stalin's support for the Chinese communists. Only three survive, one of which is here seen at the VVS Museum. *(David Baker)*

BELOW The MiG-9 carried two 23mm Nudelman-Suranov cannon and a single 37mm Nudelman N-37 cannon, all mounted in the nose around the single intake for the two RD-20 axial-flow turbojet engines. *(Arz)*

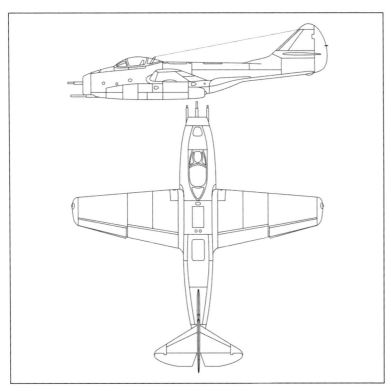

approved plans to build 3,500 in 1941 alone. After the German attack those plans evaporated, but the type remained in service, albeit through dwindling production. But mass production priorities denied it the AM-37 engine and it flew instead with the V-12 AM-35A of 993kW (1,350hp).

Throughout the war, increasingly as the balance tipped in favour of the Soviet Union, MiG produced a range of different developments of the MiG-3, including the piston-engine MiG-9 (not to be confused with the turbojet-engine aircraft of the same designation). By the beginning of 1944 word had reached the Soviet Union of developments in Germany and Britain with turbojet-powered aircraft, and this excited the various aircraft and engine design bureaux. The Russians had development work already under way on jet propulsion but it was fragmented among various groups.

On 28 February 1944 NII-1 NKAP was formed to unite all the disparate work on jet propulsion. One of the more bizarre MiG ventures along these lines was the oddly enumerated I-250, which was powered by an early form of hybrid engine. Working on the principle of air reaction engine compression, the engine was developed by Konstantin V. Kholshchevnikov, beginning in 1942, and involved a crude form of turbofan which had a compressor that fed a combustion chamber.

The compressor was driven by a piston engine to which was attached a conventional propeller.

With a maximum speed of 820kph (510mph), it went into development misidentified as the MiG-13 but only as a conversion trainer for Russia's pure jet aircraft that, by 1946, were beginning to emerge. The MiG-13 was ensnared by the bloated post-war paranoia of Josef Stalin and was swept up in accusations of sabotage and a conspiracy to delay transition from 'turner' to 'burner', all of which were entirely unfounded but which nevertheless sealed the fate of this unusual aircraft.

Russian aviation was only able to begin design work on first-generation jet aircraft after Soviet ground forces overran German facilities and sent back to the USSR examples of the Junkers Jumo 004 which, in its function as the power plant of the Messerschmitt Me-262, played an unhelpful role in pushing Russian designers toward the configuration of this German jet fighter. Sukhoi's Su-9, Lavochkin's I-211 and the MiG I-260 all fell into the same trap.

The directive for Soviet industry to develop a jet fighter was given in February 1945 and OKB-155 was charged with developing such an aircraft powered by twin BMW-003 engines and carrying 37mm or 23mm cannon. Two of these engines had been retrieved from the Basdorf-Zühlsdorf plant outside Berlin and they were installed in what became the MiG-9. A production plant to produce this engine in Russia was set up in Leningrad and designated RD-20. From this same engine design would come, in the West, the larger French Atar that powered the Dassault Ouragan, the Mirage III and several Mystère types.

With large bomber fleets available to the British and the Americans, the Russians were fearful of a massed air attack should the smouldering political difficulties break out into conflict. To deter such attacks the MiG-9 was placed in quantity production with around 610 being built, and despite it being less than ideal it provided the manufacturer with hard-won experience in designing and flying jet aircraft and gave the Air Force experience in handling and maintaining these exotic aircraft. But the MiG-9 would never be the solution sought by Russia, and for the more robust role of national border defence MiG turned to a different design.

MiG-15/17/19

One of the most iconic aircraft to come out of the early years of the Cold War was the MiG-15, a truly unique break from the inherited legacy of German debris carted off to the Soviet Union. The intense pressure to produce immediate results for defensive jet fighters, failure of which could readily result in dire life-threatening consequences for the failed designer, forced manufacturers to adapt German designs, with German engines reverse-engineered and copied in Russian factories. In parallel, considerable theoretical knowledge on jet aircraft and turbojet engines that already existed in the USSR resulted in a programme to build completely different types of aircraft. The MiG-15 was one of those.

The origin of the MiG-15 dates to March 1946 when a meeting of aircraft designers at the Kremlin was given the requirement for a highly manoeuvrable day interceptor with a maximum speed of no less than Mach 0.9 at 11,000m (36,098ft) and an endurance of at least one hour. The aircraft had to be easy to maintain, operate from rough field strips and carry heavy armament. The existing Lyulka engine was far from ideal and the German turbojets and their Russian derivatives were already obsolete. The solution became apparent when Mikoyan and Major General V. Ya. Klimov

ABOVE The German BMW-003 axial-flow engine formed the basis for several copies post-World War Two, including production of the MiG-9's RD-20, which on some jets were replaced with the Lyulka TR-1 turbojet as confidence in an indigenous Russian engine industry began to grow from the embers of a scorched country. *(MisterBee1966)*

ABOVE German aeronautical research and advanced aerodynamics worked well to equip the *Luftwaffe* with some cutting-edge technology, but futuristic projects such as the Ta-183 helped push the victorious powers into the jet age. Not least with swept-back wings. *(Via David Baker)*

BELOW Designed by Hans Multhopp, the Ta-183 was the product of the 1944 emergency fighter competition and incorporated a 40° swept-back wing, set forward to maintain the centre of pressure as close as possible to the centre of gravity. This design would be adopted by Kurt Tank when he produced the FMA IAe33 Pulqui II in Argentina, powered by a Rolls-Royce Nene turbojet. *(Via David Baker)*

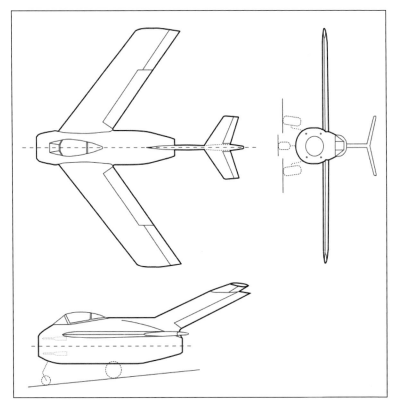

scrutinised a Rolls-Royce Nene engine at the June 1946 Farnborough air show.

At this date the Cold War had not really set in and the British Labour government was keen to sell anything that would revive the economy after six years of war. To the utter astonishment of the Russians, acting on behalf of the British government, Sir Stafford Cripps readily agreed to a request from Mikhail V. Khrunichev and Aleksandr V. Yakovlev for the direct purchase of what quickly resulted in the delivery of 30 Derwent engines and 25 Nene engines. Ironically, immediately after Klimov saw the Nene at Farnborough he set up a programme to copy it under the VP-IPO designation while Soviet intelligence set about the business of trying to obtain the drawings.

With the espionage effort now redundant, some of the Nene engines were put on test beds while four others were meticulously taken apart, the materials analysed and their parts copied for production in Klimov's Factory No 45 in Leningrad. The first copy was in Moscow by 21 September 1946 and production of the RD-45 began with the first manufacturing drawings available by 30 October. In February 1947, MiG had a full set of RD-45 drawings for deigning installation in their new jet fighter.

Benefiting from German wind tunnel research, MiG opted for swept wings to delay tip stall close to the transonic regime, while Yakovlev opted for straight wings for his Yak-23. However, Lavochkin's 35° swept-wing La-160 proved that swept wings were a winning choice when it flew for the first time on 24 June 1947, followed by the straight-wing Yak-23 on 8 July. Meanwhile, MiG was developing what was known as aircraft S around the chubby Nene and would adopt the same 35° swept wing as Lavochkin, who had very little success with the La-160. Together with swept wings, the MiG-15 had a nose air intake and jet pipe that ran all the way out to the tail. Some comparisons have been made to the German Focke-Wulf Ta-183 but the similarities were superficial, although all design engineers, East and West, were benefiting from German research plundered as spoils of war.

Another aircraft to make its first flight in 1947 was the North American F-86 Sabre, it too adopting a 35° leading-edge wing sweep,

LEFT A Rolls-Royce Nene 102 engine of the type that was fitted to the Supermarine Attacker, which made its first flight in July 1946. The basic Nene was sold to the Russians by Stafford Cripps, to the incredulity of Khrunichev and Yakovlev, who visited the 1946 Farnborough air show. *(David Baker)*

BELOW Remodelled into the Klimov VK-1, the Rolls-Royce Nene powered the MiG-15 as Russia attempted to rebuild its indigenous aircraft and aero-engine design and manufacturing base with post-war jets and improved aerodynamics for the transonic flight regime. This example is displayed at the Pacific Air Museum, Hawaii. *(David Baker)*

RIGHT Not all aircraft design teams were convinced about the swept-back wing. The Yakovlev Yak-23, this one preserved in Poland, employed a straight-wing design as required for comparative evaluation with swept-wing designs. *(David Baker)*

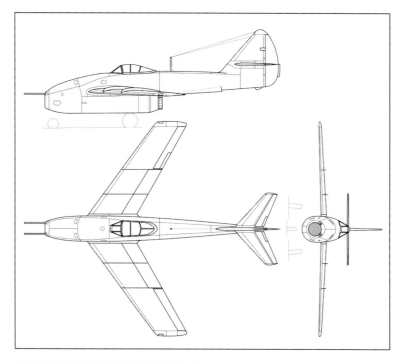

LEFT The Lavochkin La-160 flew for the first time in June 1947 and demonstrated superb handling qualities and flight characteristics from its 35° swept-back wing, clearing the way for similar designs from MiG. *(David Baker)*

quickly incorporated when German research reached the United States. This prompted North American to change the straight wings of the FJ-1 Fury, which first flew in November 1946 and from which the Air Force's version emerged as the F-86. Both Russia and America were building aircraft on stolen secrets, helped along with a massive dose of British naivety and a desire to sell engines.

Unlike the Sabre, the MiG-15 had a mid-wing planform for optimised aerodynamic reasons and innovative features were introduced that would influence later British designs. One example was the removable gun and ammunition tray winched down, serviced and refilled before hoisting up again and reconnected, the whole operation taking less

LEFT The MiG-15 was a winner from the outset. Simple in design, efficient in layout for ground crew accessibility, and with a reliable engine derived from the Rolls-Royce Nene, few would realise that within three years of its first flight on 30 December 1947 it would be tipped into a heroic struggle for air supremacy against its American lookalike, the North American F-86 Sabre. *(David Baker)*

RIGHT Like the F-86, the aft fuselage and tail section of the MiG-15 was removable to gain access to the engine and related accessories, making the aircraft easy to service, with little additional work to change engines.
(David Baker)

RIGHT The 1950–53 Korean War, still today an unresolved stand-off between North and South, pressed the MiG-15 into combat against United Nations forces, providing an opportunity for the first jet-on-jet combat. From this came many lessons that would alter the strategies for dogfighting in the jet era and also drive home the vulnerability of ageing piston-engine bombers, now prey to slash-and-dash attacks. This example is preserved in the Victorious Fatherland Liberation War Museum in Pyongyang, North Korea. *(John Pavalka)*

than three minutes. Hawker would adopt this innovation for the Sea Hawk jet fighter, which, incidentally, was powered by a Nene engine.

The MiG-15 was placed in mass production and built the company a huge reputation when Russian and Chinese pilots flew the type against F-86 Sabres during the Korean War of 1950–53. The equal of the best the US could put into the sky, F-86E and F variants of the Sabre were rushed into theatre to counter these fast and nimble Russian jets. Soon export orders began to flood in from countries in political sympathy with the Soviet Union. MiG had become well known in the USSR for its World War Two fighters, whereas in the West it was just another Russian design bureau; the MiG-15 brought it worldwide renown, its name becoming synonymous with Soviet technical and military prowess.

In all, more than 18,000 were produced, including about 6,000 built under licence in foreign countries. Some 43 nations either produced or operated the MiG-15 and several are still flying them today, in military service or as restored warbird display aircraft. Before the Korean War was over, however, the signs of a new 'MiG' appeared, distinctively identified by its 45° wing sweep. Ironically, following close on the heels of the MiG-15, the -17 was held up by accelerated production of its predecessor and the first flight did not take place before 14 January 1950.

But the new wing and the adoption of the VK-1F, the first Russian aircraft engine with afterburner, gave the type a distinctive edge and freed it from the Mach 0.92 limiter set on the MiG-15, allowing it to enter the transonic zone

in level flight. Delivering a thrust of 33,800N (7,423lb) with afterburner, the type was rated at Mach 0.968 at 3,000m (9,843ft). The MiG-17 saw service in Vietnam, downing types such as the F-105 Thunderchief, F-4 Phantom II, A-1E Skyraider and A-4 Skyhawk. Several variants and adaptations – including one with two engines – followed, and the MiG-17 would see service with 42 air forces supported by a total production of approximately 11,000 aircraft.

Tests with twin turbojet engines on a variant of the MiG-17 became standard specification for the MiG-19, the precursor prototype of which made its first flight on 24 May 1952 as the world's first truly supersonic combat aircraft to fly, beating the North American F-100 which

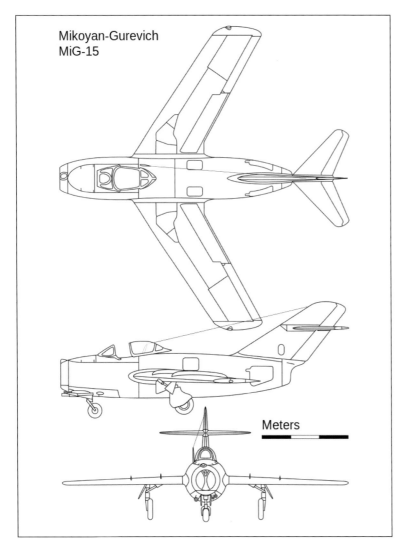

Mikoyan-Gurevich
MiG-15

Meters

LEFT A mid-wing monoplane, the MiG-15 inherited several distinct features from German legacy designs. A few German technicians and design engineers were employed in the USSR to improve extant knowledge about high-performance aircraft but the essence of the design emerged from a very Russian approach to engineering and aircraft design. With emphasis on rugged operation and high survivability, the design had inherent growth potential. *(David Baker)*

took to the air for the first time almost exactly one year later. Repeatedly, sources continue to claim the F-100 as the world's first supersonic combat aircraft to fly, and one website even claims a first flight for the MiG-19 prototype as late as September 1953, but that is not so.

The type evolved under the guiding leadership of Mikoyan, Gurevich suffering ill health and essentially playing a passive role. On 17 February 1954 the Council of Ministers ordered the type into quantity production, by which date the F-100A was entering operational service. Powered by two Tumansky RD-9B turbojet engines with an afterburner thrust of 25,500N (5,730lb), the MiG-19 had a rated top speed of 1,452kph (902mph). Derivatives improved on that, the SM-70 flying with two RD-9BM engines with an afterburner thrust of 32,369N (7,275lb) reaching Mach 1.8 in 1959.

RIGHT UN forces sought access to details of the MiG-15 from the moment it first appeared over Korea. Slightly smaller than the F-86, it could climb faster, had better turn characteristics and more effective armament. It first saw combat in the Chinese civil war and made its first kill over Korea on 28 April 1951. To get their hands on a MiG-15, UN forces dropped leaflets like this offering a $100,000 dollar reward for a defection with aircraft intact. *(Via David Baker)*

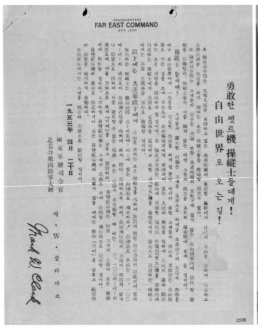

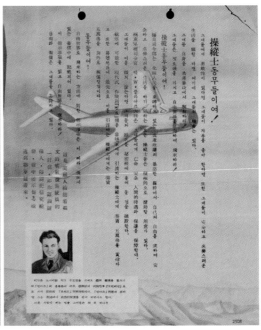

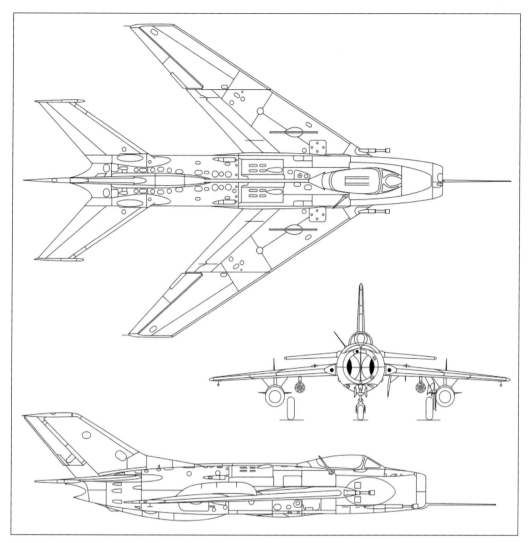

LEFT With a first flight on 24 May 1952, powered by a Tumansky RD-9B turbojet, the MiG-19 had a wing sweep of 55°. It was the world's first truly supersonic combat aircraft and would see widespread service in the Middle East and over Vietnam. *(David Baker)*

LEFT A MiG-17 takes to the skies at an air show at Durant, Oklahoma. The type appeared in 1950 with a 45° wing sweep and an improved engine carrying an afterburner, a first for Russia. *(David Baker)*

States, and MiG was tasked by the Kremlin with responding to problems encountered during the Korean War. It was acknowledged (on both sides) that the MiG-15 could out-fly anything in the sky, US pilots with very high levels of training and experience being the only deciding advantage. Further development of the essential principles embodied in the MiG-15 was expressed through the transonic MiG-17 and the supersonic MiG-19, but by the early 1950s it was already apparent to MiG that a leap forward was necessary to take the challenge to the opposition.

MiG-21

ABOVE A MiG-19 with four Kaliningrad RS-2-U air-to-air missiles, epitomising the rapid growth of the original MiG-15 in just five short years of development. *(Via David Baker)*

The aircraft brought a formidable improvement in performance, with a 55° wing sweep, a very high-aspect ratio which, with 25% chord imposing huge aeroelastic problems, challenged the designers to produce what became a remarkable fighting machine. About 6,500 were built, of which fewer than 2,200 were manufactured in Russia, the rest being produced under licence in China as the Shenyang J-6. The MiG-19 saw combat action in Vietnam and the Middle East, performing well despite its increasing obsolescence. In one instance an F-100 'straying' into Soviet airspace was brought down by a MiG-19.

During the 1950s the Russians were to a large extent reacting to prolific expansion of combat aircraft capabilities in the United

Competition among aircraft design bureaux in the USSR was strongly encouraged by the government – developments tried unsuccessfully, sometimes in desperation, by one manufacturer could be adapted and made to work by another. To break free of the 'legacy' evolution from the MiG-15 and try new and ambitious design possibilities, several prototypes of a next-generation fighter were developed and test-flown by MiG, as they were by other design bureaux.

Through a series of experimental design alternatives, where delta-wings, delta-tails and various lift aids were tried, work that began in 1953 on a lightweight fighter matured into the swept-wing Ye-2, which took to the air on 14 February 1955. The Ye-2 prototype was

RIGHT Through a series of experimental prototypes and various design changes, the MiG-21 emerged in 1955 with a delta-wing configuration and a leading-edge sweep of 57°. *(David Baker)*

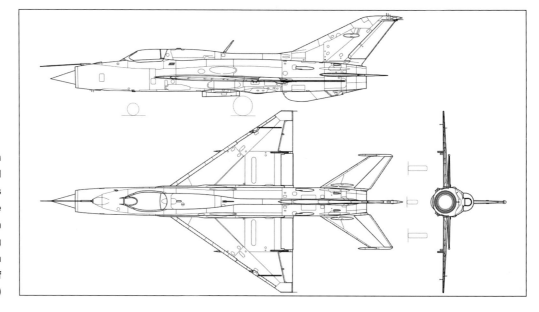

modified to the Ye-2A engined by the powerful RD-11 that had an afterburner thrust of 59,000N (8,380lb). But from the Ye-2 emerged the Ye-4, and this made its first flight on 16 June 1955.

In August 1953, shortly after Stalin's death, the Kremlin had decided that both MiG and Sukhoi would be involved in each designing, building and testing of new tactical fighters featuring thin swept wings and delta wings. MiG would build the delta design and Sukhoi would go on to produce the swept-wing Su-7. The legacy of this decision was that MiG would focus on the delta configuration and select a wing with a thickness/chord ratio of 4.2% at the roots, 5% at the tips and a leading-edge sweep of 57°. The tapered ailerons were aerodynamically balanced and the slotted flaps had constant chord. The vertical tail had a sweep of 60°.

The definitive Ye-5 took to the air for the first time on 9 January 1956. Test pilots praised it for its improved view from the cockpit compared to the MiG-19, and in 98 flights it demonstrated stable and effective handling out to Mach 1.8 and altitudes up to 18,000m (59,056ft). It had met the requirement set three years earlier and was the first Russian aircraft to combine the roles of fighter (the MiG-21F) and interceptor (the MiG-21PF). The initial volume production version was the MiG-21F with the 37,274/56,267N (8,380/12,650lb) thrust R11F-300 engine. Range was very poor, less than 1,000km (1,600 miles), but the maximum speed was 2,175kph (1,350mph) with a service ceiling of 19,000m (62,335ft).

Not uncommon on Soviet fighters, but little used in the West, the shock cone and front intake limited the front-end radar antenna, but the Mach 2 combat aircraft was at least the equal of emerging fighters such as the Lockheed F-104, the Northrop F-5 (arguably in some respects America's lightweight export hope) and the Dassault Mirage III. But in the hands of skilled pilots, capable of avoiding its idiosyncrasies, the MiG-21 proved the perfect choice for low-priced visual air defence and was sought and used by almost 60 air forces on that basis.

With 10,645 produced from Russian factories and a total of 851 built in India and Czechoslovakia, the type still flies today with

the air forces of 19 countries. Progressive improvements, upgrades and modifications increased engine power and overall performance but the MiG-21 could never get over its limitations on avionics, fire-control systems, radar and somewhat limited firepower. It did operate in the ground-attack role and has seen combat in every theatre of war since it formally entered service in 1960 at Kubinka air base.

Tactical reconnaissance and two-seat trainer variants were developed and several were employed as test beds for avionics and systems development. Mid-life upgrade programmes were launched by Romania in the early 1990s, their Lancer III version evolving as a multi-role fighter with dorsal spine and additional fuel capacity. Several experimental versions were flown and various paper studies were made

ABOVE The MiG-21 had a significantly modified cockpit and, while the aircraft itself bore several legacy design aspects going right back to the first Russian jet fighters, the type had distinctively new features of which one was the enhanced use of fire control systems, albeit in their infancy.
(Via David Baker)

ABOVE This Romanian
Air Force MiG-21
Lancer shows off the
type's clean lines and
distinctive features,
with in-flight refuelling
capability and an
expanded weapons
load. (Via David Baker)

promising a complete revitalisation of the aircraft's role, with canard foreplanes, STOL capability and as engineering support and test vehicle and technology development aircraft for the Tupolev Tu-144 SST, in which application, as the MiG-211, it was fitted with a double-delta wing and no horizontal tailplanes.

Obsessed with producing aircraft capable of operation from rough fields and temporary bases with few maintenance facilities, existing Soviet jet fighters required long runways that obviated the opportunities afforded by designing rugged aircraft with few frills. In fact the frills were so spartan that no Russian fighter had BVR (beyond visual range) engagement capabilities in either radar or weapons. A major breakthrough in designing for long-range engagement came in 1958, when the Russians got their hands on an infrared AIM-9 Sidewinder during the Quemoy crisis over Taiwan. MiG was given the task of integrating Soviet copies of the missile, designated the K-13, into the MiG-21.

Soon the Soviet top brass had convinced themselves that the indigenous cannons were no longer necessary and that air-to-air missiles could do the job for which guns had been essential in the past. So the cannons were taken out and replaced with two K-13 missiles. That philosophy held sway, despite opposition from some Red Air Force pilots, and only after hard-won lessons from Vietnam were fed back into the design considerations for future fighters did guns make a comeback. The wars of the

1960s, in South-East Asia and the Middle East, rewrote a lot of textbooks about fighter design and combat choices, and with new and more powerful engines the possibilities for a new generation of fighters and interceptors resulted in the next major development from the MiG design bureau.

MiG-23/27

Pressure to increase the size, weight and load-carrying capacity of the fighter/ interceptor category stemmed from a major surge in the development of weapons for air-to-air combat as well as offensive air-to-ground applications. Uniquely, and for the first time, Soviet planners began to merge the requirements and specifications for the new generation of fighters with the development of weapons that were being designed for specific aircraft. The variable-geometry (VG) MiG-23 was one of the first Russian combat aircraft to have a weapon suite pencilled in for it before the design had begun. This was the R-23 AAM, which was required to have very long-range, high-agility and all-aspect engagement capability.

Increasingly, as nuclear weapons became smaller and expanded in application into the tactical role delivered by fast fighter-bombers, the need to disperse fighters quickly to obscure and remote operating stations where runways were relatively short dominated thinking. It was received wisdom that early in a major conflict nuclear weapons would be used to take out the known airfields and operating bases, denying aircraft safe operating havens in time of war. The Air Force sought solutions from MiG that focused on STOL capability and variable geometry: high-aspect ratio/high-lift wings for short take-off subsonic flight and swept-back delta planform for high-speed, supersonic flight. Low-level speed and manoeuvrability was also to be improved.

The swept-wing concept had been around for decades and TsAGI had conducted much research on this, carrying out its own wind tunnel tests. The reports that came back were discouraging, revealing a loss of stability and control, reduced lift and a lack of aerodynamic efficiency. Mikoyan favoured VG but decided to hedge his bets and examine STOL with supplementary lift engines.

Almost universally, in the mid-1960s the US and countries across Europe recognised the problem of sustained operations from remote fields, which resulted in a plethora of STOL, VSTOL and VTOL proposals. The most obvious was the development of the Hawker P.1127,

first into the Kestrel and then the Harrier, but plans for a supersonic P.1154 were shelved when government cutbacks cancelled further development. The French were experimenting with their Dassault Mirage IIIV VTOL fighter, and the Americans were struggling to find a solution to the TFX requirement in the swing-wing General Dynamics F-111 for the Navy and the Air Force.

The short, rough-field performance coupled to long range, Mach 2 performance and advanced avionics and weapon systems defined by the TFX requirement was almost exactly the same requirement issued by Russian defence officials when Mikoyan set about the MiG-23 programme. The designation had been applied a couple of times before, first for the Ye-2A, but now it would define a very different combat aircraft. The STOL capability was provided by dual Kolesov RD36-35 lift engines aligned almost vertically in the centre fuselage with intake doors on the top.

The profile of the aircraft was a delta planform with a long extended dorsal fin from the vertical tail to the top of the fuselage and two horizontal tailplanes. Both the STOL and the variable

BELOW The variable-geometry MiG-23 was the third wing-form applied by this design team, producing a heavy fighter and ground-attack aircraft, superficially similar to the General Dynamics F-111. Development dragged on from the early 1960s, when the type was designed. In service until 1990, it was manoeuvrable and had a top speed of Mach 2.35. This example is at the National Museum of the US Air Force. *(David Baker)*

RIGHT The geometric lines of the MiG-23/27 carried the extended vertical stabiliser that emerged on earlier MiG fighters and was favoured as an aid to roll stability. *(David Baker)*

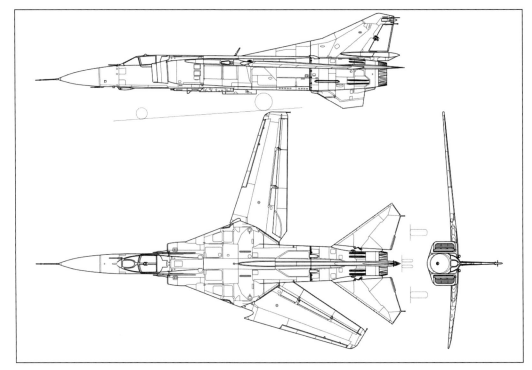

BELOW The cockpit of the MiG-23, displayed in an example in the Museum of the Great Patriotic War in Kiev, Ukraine. *(David Baker)*

LEFT The wing sweep mechanism was problematic for MiG until they saw how General Dynamics had solved the problem on the F-111. Denied the design-sharing opportunities in the West, Russian aircraft designers were unapologetic about studying contemporary design trends outside the USSR, but with a view to improving ideas originating elsewhere. In that they did achieve some success. *(David Baker)*

geometry (VG) versions had the Khachaturov R37-300 engine for primary power. Several flight trials with the STOL version took place, dramatically when the 23-01 took part in the Moscow-Domodedovo air show on 9 July 1967, a modest public relations exercise to show the Americans that they were not alone in demonstrating innovative concepts. But the STOL prototype failed to match the performance of the VG concept and eroded confidence; moreover, the consequences of the loss of a lift engine on landing could be disastrous.

Former test pilot Grigoriy A. Sedov had been appointed to head the VG design team, but the challenges with this unusual configuration prompted the Ministry of Defence to request assistance from other manufacturers. But help came from the Americans too when publicity and coverage in the specialist aeronautical press of the first flight of the F-111A on 21 December 1964 provided confirmation of the wing pivot location and mechanism. There had been much discussion about this within MiG and at other facilities and determination of the wing-root position from which the mean aerodynamic chord could be calculated cleared the way for designing the wing-root glove and the mechanics of the hinge mechanism.

Almost by coincidence, both the F-111A and the MiG-23 used the same sweep values: 16°

for take-off and landing, 45° for cruise, and 72° for supersonic dash. TsAGI provided the wing geometry, set into the top of the fuselage with a thickness/chord ratio of 5.5% to 6.5%, with four-section slotted trailing-edge flaps operating in concert with the leading-edge droop flaps. Two-section spoilers were set on the upper surface that operated differentially in conjunction with the horizontal stabilisers. In other respects the fuselage was similar to the STOL prototype.

A major engineering development for MiG was to incorporate rectangular intakes with large boundary layer splitter plates set 5.5cm (2.16in) from the fuselage. A ram inlet was positioned in the gap for the cockpit environmental control system and for cooling the avionics. The primary function of this gap, however, was to allow the splitter plates to bleed off boundary layer air above Mach 1.15, and this was a technology developed jointly between MiG and TsAGI. The splitter plate had a piano hinge on the aft edge connected to two hinged panels attached in tandem to vary the throat area and the wall angle. This allowed the shock waves to be controlled and provided a path for the boundary air to escape through perforations in the wall.

The aero-engineering design of the MiG-23 foreshadowed the work that would define the MiG-29 and the design and aerodynamic interactions were reaching new levels of sophistication. Addressing the issue of range, which had been far lower than desirable on all previous MiG fighters, three fuel tanks were located in the fuselage and six in the wings for a total internal load of 4,250 litres (935 gallons).

The first flight took place on 26 May 1967, but this was only the beginning of a development programme that went on long after the type had become operational. As was characteristic among many Russian aircraft, it was an incomplete type when cleared for operations, bringing several performance restrictions until certain developments had cleared it for full-spectrum duties. Several rolling improvements were made which gave it superior performance to Western types such as the F-4 Phantom II, the F-16A Fighting Falcon and the F-15 Eagle.

The initial production version cleared for service was the MiG-23M, but with the MiG-23ML in 1976 the g-limit was raised to 8.5 at subsonic speeds and 7.5 above Mach 1. With the MiG-23MLA came better radar, it being equipped with the new R-24 AAM and eventually the R-73A which was nimble, highly effective and deadly. The final variant, the MiG-23MLD, had greatly improved transonic and supersonic acceleration, and even after the introduction of the MiG-29 it was preferred by some pilots flying intercept sorties. As a dogfighter, however, the MiG-29 was far superior.

The MiG-23MLD remained in front-line service into the 1990s, a highly capable Mach 2.35 fighter/interceptor but with a range on internal fuel of only 1,210km (752 miles) and a ferry range of 1,550km (963 miles) utilising a centreline tank. An evolved version for ground attack was beefed up with a more powerful engine and designated MiG-27, but the type gained strong respect from NATO pilots who flew the MiG-23 when certain foreign governments gave the United States aircraft of this type in exchange for weapons deals.

Most believed the MiG-23 to be superior to the F-16 in the climb, about equal to it in the horizontal and definitely superior in BVR engagements. Some Israeli pilots who have flown the type believe it to have better targeting HUD capabilities, enabling it to double as a radarscope. But American pilots claim they dislike its effect. Just over 6,000 MiG-23/27s were built.

MiG-25

The late 1950s and early 1960s saw a major spurt in overall performance capabilities in the raw but not in the round: development of very powerful turbojet engines and the airframes in which to fly them were not uncommon, but the attempt to combine the two and create an effective airframe for front-line service was more protracted an evolution. For MiG, this eventually produced what NATO codenamed 'Foxbat' – the MiG-25 – the development path for which began in the search for a heavily armed and powerful straight-line interceptor.

The spur to this phase of development was the appearance of very large and fast tactical nuclear strike aircraft such as the shipborne North American A-5 Vigilante, which first flew in August 1958 and put in an appearance at the 1959 Paris air show. Strategic bombers too were in the offing, with the WS-110A requirement being met with the XB-70, a Mach 3 behemoth with a range of 6,900km (4,288 miles) and capable of attacking Soviet targets from an altitude of 23,500m (77,350ft).

Already the US Air Force was about to take delivery of its first Convair B-58 Hustler, a Mach 2 bomber with a combat radius of 3,220km (1,740 miles) and a service ceiling of 19,300m (63,400ft). The fact that none of these types would fulfil the aspirations of their designers was unknown to anyone, not least the Russians, at the end of the 1950s.

Responding to the requirement for a truly heavy interceptor that the Russians had been seeking since the early 1950s, the opportunity for a very fast and heavy solution appeared nearer with the development of the Tumansky R15B-300. Designed for the Tupolev Tu-121 cruise missile, the R15B had a five-stage compressor, single-stage turbine and a maximum thrust of 73,500N (16,523lb). The Tu-121 was cancelled in February 1960 when it proved technically difficult to achieve and Premier Khrushchev favoured ballistic missiles, believing that in the face of Western early warning defence nets and the NORAD system, the long-range strike role should focus on ballistic missiles.

Tupolev responded to a requirement dated 16 August 1960 for an unmanned supersonic

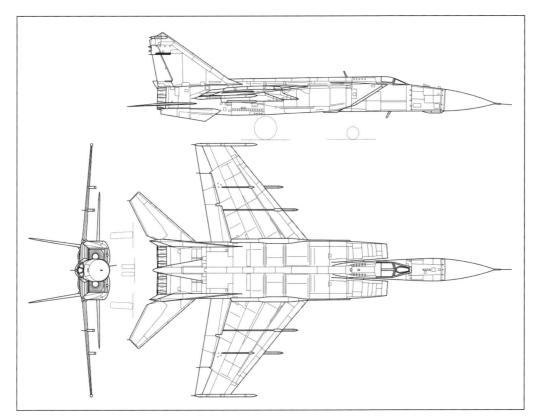

LEFT The MiG-25 was a complete departure yet bore some of the inherited trends of the later MiG-21 variants, if not altogether apparent. The wing planform actually evolved from internally proposed modifications to the MiG-21, but the fuselage and fuel tankage would pioneer the approach used in development of the MiG-29. *(David Baker)*

photo-reconnaissance system with the Tu-123, powered by the R15B-300. With a cruising speed of 2,700kph (1,680mph) it had a range of 3,200km (1,990 miles) and would return after a high-speed photo run to deploy its payload by parachute close to base. The system was developed and deployed in limited numbers until 1979. Long before then the RB15B-300 had found another application with the MiG family of very high-speed interceptors.

As said, since the early 1950s MiG had sought to provide the Air Force with its much sought-after heavy interceptor, and a series of experimental projects had been developed to prototype stage, several of which (such as the I-3 and the I-3P) were built but never flown. Completed in July 1956, the I-7U interceptor was similar in appearance to the MiG-21 and was at first to have been powered by an AL-7F axial flow turbojet claimed to have an afterburner thrust of 98,056N (22,045lb) – which was discovered on flight trials not to be the case, providing the I-7U with a top speed of only 1,420kph (882mph)!

In parallel development, the Uragan-5B automated on-board/ground-control guided and intercept system was to give the I-7U the ability to attack supersonic bombers at very high altitude and at least 100km (62 miles) from their targets. MiG began work on a range of aircraft to fly with Uragan-5, Russia's first integrated monobloc radar, and retained the R15B-300 turbojet engine. In the Ye-152 the airframe proved a match for the powerful engine and after a series of changes to the requirement the prototype flew on 10 July 1959 with twin interim R11F-300 engines, eventually achieving a top speed of 2,135kph (1,326mph). The type was displayed at the 1961 Tushino air show, much to the surprise of Western observers.

The first flight of the Ye-152 with the R15B-300 took place on 21 April 1961, the type eventually showing a top speed, with missiles, of 2,650kph (1,646mph). In the latter part of 1961 the Ye-152-1 set several world records and a year later grabbed the absolute world speed record at 2,681kph (1,665mph) over a set course. When on display the aircraft was given the bogus designation Ye-166, in which guise it was reported in the Western media, which at the time was not particularly reliable. Even the specialist aviation press thought the Ye-150 was the MiG-23 and that the real MiG-23 was built by Sukhoi, according to

ABOVE The MiG-25 cockpit with Smerch-A radar and a Smerch-AV computer. The aircraft also carries the Polyot-1I navigation system.
(Via David Baker)

PVO (Air Defence Forces) as well as the Soviet Air Force, which still sought a very high-speed reconnaissance platform.

The OKB received formal approval from the Central Committee in February 1961 and the project got the designation Ye-155 in a formal start on 10 March. Mikhail Gurevich would be responsible for the airframe with Matyuk in charge of the overall project, which would incorporate advanced manufacturing techniques utilising some exotic materials and radical approaches to aerodynamic problems.

The Ye-155R-1 was rolled out in December 1963 and bore only marginal differences from the aircraft which would go into production. The R15B-300 engines had been uprated to deliver an afterburner thrust of 109,825N (24,691lb), although production engines would be less powerful. The separate interceptor and reconnaissance versions of the aircraft required dedicated prototypes and pre-production was halted temporarily while manufacturing switched from the Moscow factory, now busy gearing up for MiG-23 production, to the one at Gorki, from where MiG-25s began rolling out by the end of 1965. But, conforming to the tendency for aircraft to be rushed into production without smoothing all the wrinkles, serious control problems near Mach 3 imposed a limit of Mach 2.83, above which loss of control could prove fatal.

Of stainless steel construction and nickel-steel in high temperature areas but with 8% titanium alloys and 11% of heat-resistant Duralumin in non-stressed sections of the airframe, the MiG-25 was in a class of its own. Presenting a very large wing with an area of 61.4m² (660.93ft²), Western observers at first believed it indicated a highly manoeuvrable aircraft until Victor Beleneko defected with one in 1976 and it was seen to be necessary to compensate for the high gross weight of 36,720kg (80,952lb).

Deeply flawed as an interceptor, it had a g-limit of 2.2 and was impossible to manoeuvre quickly. The interceptor had a range of only 399km (186 miles) but the reconnaissance version could carry a massive 5,280 litres (1,161 gallons) external fuel tank on the centreline under-fuselage position. It employed avionics using thermionic tubes although this had great advantage in that it was not prey to an electromagnetic pulse in nuclear

Jane's All the World's Aircraft 1960/61. The Soviet obfuscation and disinformation machine was at full throttle.

With the B-58 Hustler supersonic bomber in service, in 1960 the Soviets got word of the development of the highly classified single-seat YF-12A, which would fly as the A-12 in April 1962 and as the two-seat SR-71A in December 1964. By this time MiG was working on what would emerge as the MiG-25, design activity having begun in mid-1959 when Rostislav A. Belyakov (head of the preliminary design section), Niklolay Z. Matyuk and Mikoyan conferred over a radical design concept only very loosely based on the Ye-152, which had already served its purpose of trying out the new R15B-300 engine. Support came from the warfare, as solid-state electronics in Western aircraft would be. Moreover, it produced an enormous 600W of power from the radar, and because of their tolerance to heat the vacuum tubes had no need of cooling in the avionics bay. What was considered very old technology in the West, was, to the Russians, strong, robust, practical and survivable, enduring where solid-state electronics in other aircraft would have succumbed.

A replacement for the MiG-25 began when the Ye-155MP began to emerge in the early 1970s, this materialising as the two-seat MiG-31 that made its first flight on 16 September 1975. Several improvements and upgrades were made to the basic aircraft and two Soloviev D-30F6 turbojets with an afterburner thrust of 152,000N (34,172lb) each were employed. When the type entered service in 1980 it was the first Russian aircraft capable of countering high-performance US aircraft and of deterring the SR-71A, which made frequent passes over areas of potential interest in the Far East.

To deter these intrusions a unit of four

MiG-31s was deployed to Sokol air base on Sakhalin Island in September 1983, a week after the shooting down of a Korean Air Lines Boeing 747 after it strayed into prohibited Soviet airspace. The direct response to the deployment of these aircraft, and to others based at Monchegorsk in the far north, brought a decline in intrusions and alerts.

Almost 1,200 MiG-25 and nearly 600 MiG-31 aircraft were produced between 1964 and 1994 and, despite rumours to the contrary, the latter is expected to remain in service with the Russian Air Force until at least 2030. Despite severe limitations the type evolved into an operationally efficient high-altitude/high-speed interceptor with capabilities and performance respected by foreign air forces, and it represents the culmination of a generic line of jet fighters that goes right back to the MiG-15.

BELOW Developed into the MiG-31, the type has seen modest success both in Russian deployment and in being considered by several foreign air forces, but the aircraft is expected to remain in service until 2030. *(David Baker)*

Chapter Two

The MiG-29 story

━━━⬤━━━

Designed to out-perform Western combat aircraft, blending aerodynamics with a wing-body planform new to Soviet military types, Russia's fourth-generation fighter excelled in high-g manoeuvring. With inherent growth capability and an adaptable mission role, the MiG-29 has found application across a range of duties with many air forces around the world carrying a wide range of munitions.

OPPOSITE The ultimate derivative of the MiG-29, this is the MiG-35 displaying its four stores points on each wing that carry a variety of AAM and ASM weapons, providing a multi-role capability. *(MiG)*

ABOVE The MiG-29 marked a decisive turning point in Russian aircraft design, which along with the Sukhoi Su-27 displayed a blended wing/body design where a considerable percentage of lift came from the underbody of the fuselage. Note the eight underwing stores points. *(David Baker)*

Developed during the 1970s, the MiG-29 was designed as one of two solutions to the imminent operational deployment of the McDonnell Douglas F-15 advanced tactical air superiority fighter and the General Dynamics F-16 lightweight fighter. The parallel solution was perceived to be the Sukhoi Su-27, the MiG-29 being developed as a fourth-generation lightweight fighter while the Sukhoi played the heavy role, aiming to counter the F-15 and the Grumman F-14 Tomcat shipboard fighter and long-range interceptor. Both Russian fighters would make their first flights in 1977, the Su-27 on 20 May and the MiG-29 on 6 October. But the MiG-29 would enter service in July 1982, three years ahead of the Su-27.

The challenge to Russian fighters and interceptors of the 1960s came about as a result of lessons learned by the United States in its wars across South-East Asia, particularly in the skies of Vietnam. To their surprise, US types such as the Republic F-105 Thunderchief became vulnerable to older, ostensibly less capable aircraft such as the first-generation Russian MiG-17, challenging the air superiority role the US Air Force had acquired during the Korean War of 1950–53.

In the United States, the rethink on aircraft roles and requirements stimulated by these developments promoted the F-X programme for a new air-superiority fighter that resulted in the F-15, the first in a new generation of heavy fighters, theoretically aiming to gain an advantage over the emerging Soviet combat aircraft. Second-generation fighters such as the MiG-21 and the F-4 Phantom II were stretched with upgrades but each was seriously challenged by avionics and weapon systems that were getting ahead of the capabilities inherent in the airframes in which they were carried.

Both Russia and America were developing new aircraft designs based on an evolving series of technical and theoretical capabilities fuelled by air-combat experience to which they had both been exposed. Airframe and engine technology was stimulated by new developments in materials and in the advanced aerodynamics of aircraft design teams. Moreover, there was a new realisation on both sides of the need to blend airframe, engine and weapons into a single homologated design concept and it was that which would characterise the new fourth-generation combat aircraft.

Toward the end of the 1960s several leading aeronautical engineering and machine-building factories began to study the requirement, with Artyom Ivanovich Mikoyan's OKB-155, Pavel Osipovich Sukhoi's OKB-51 and Aleksandr

Sergeyevich Yakovlev's OKB-115, seeking to present what each hoped would be the definitive solution to an evolving requirement. A division of the Soviet Ministry of Defence, the Central Research Institute No 30, distributed its general operational requirement which defined a fourth-generation fighter in the PFI (*Perspectivniyy Frontovoy Istrebetal*). The acronym was for a design requirement defined by the decision to opt for an aircraft capable of close-in combat with air-to-air missiles or cannons and providing long-range interception with either by internal radar or by ground-controlled interception. It was also required to give top cover for ground forces and point defence of vital tactical and strategic assets.

The PFI also required the aircraft to carry out ground attacks with bombs and unguided rockets and it specifically defined its principal adversaries as the F-15 and the anticipated F-17, while its ability to down F-4E Phantom IIs, F-111As, Tornadoes and Jaguars was specifically quoted. But the F-17, one of two contenders for the US Air Force lightweight-fighter contest, never made it, losing out to the General Dynamics F-16.

Across the spectrum, however, agility, high levels of manoeuvrability and advanced avionics would be coupled to a new aerodynamic layout calling for high lift/drag ratio aerofoils with highly efficient engines producing a thrust-to-weight ratio greater than unity. Digital computers, infrared sensors for search and track and solid state electronics with semiconductors instead of vacuum tubes would be the hallmark of the fourth generation.

Work started at Mikoyan in early 1970 and the aircraft was given the designation MiG-29. Programme management was given to Gleb Ye. Lozino-Lozinskiy while general layout and configuration of the aircraft was the responsibility of Aleksey A. Choomanchenko, a highly respected aerodynamicist. And it was in this latter sector that the primary shaping of the future fighter was guided, mindful as the design team were that they would have to completely re-scope their thinking on what constituted a combat fighter.

Key to the entire project was the early involvement of TsAGI, the Moscow-based Central Aerodynamics and Hydrodynamics Institute. Only the Russians would blend air and

BELOW The prototype McDonnell Douglas F-15A (71-280) on its first flight, 27 July 1972, gave cause for concern to the Russians, who lacked anything capable of countering this air superiority threat. This stimulated concern at the Ministry of Defence that led to the Su-27 and the MiG-29. *(USAF)*

water in legitimate coupling of two fluids, the physical study and mathematical definition of which were in reality inseparable. To help with merging all the disparate design requirements of the PFI, GosNII AS (the State Research Institute of Aircraft Systems) would focus on connecting the several discrete operating requirements with an advanced avionics suite.

A great deal of agonising and deliberation surrounded the aircraft during the preliminary design phase, where a wide range of disparate ideas and proposals were mooted by the engineering teams and the theoretical design scientists at TsAGI and GosNII: the former wanted to break the mould on conventional fighter design by exploiting radical new ways of achieving a quantum leap in performance; the latter sought an integrated design to accommodate and improve the latest developments in electronics and avionics – still the poor cousins of the Russian aviation industry.

A key feature of the discussion was a revolutionary idea that followed a trend towards functional homologation of fuselage, wings and tailplane in an integrated design set defined by equations based on aerodynamic

solutions rather than specific performance needs. It had been common – as it had in Western aircraft design teams – for separate individuals or groups to be assigned specific elements of the aircraft. The variable-geometry MiG-23/27 series had gone some way towards countering that and the MiG-25 had displayed strong leanings towards an integrated solution. But the fresh approach would present a completely new way of solving demanding performance requirements.

Conventional design layouts were compared with a radical blended wing/body concept where aerodynamic performance hinged on the distribution of lift across a substantial portion of the airframe as a whole and not merely the wings. Some engineers wanted a single, powerful engine that would have required a single nose inlet but this was rapidly replaced by a decision to incorporate two powerful engines for a very high thrust/weight ratio exceeding unity. That decision necessitated integrating specialists from the engine bureau in with the airframe design people, and it had a practical value as well: two engines significantly enhanced reliability, survivability and durability,

BELOW An F-15C of the 71st Fighter Squadron typifies the threat that prompted a fighter requirement in some way paralleling the division in the West between light and heavy fighters for specific and defined requirements. *(USAF)*

to losses in battle-damage encounters and to accidents in peacetime flying.

The initial design configuration after the two-engine selection had a trapezoidal wing with a low-mounted horizontal tailplane, and a single fin and rudder similar to the MiG-23/27. It incorporated span-wise leading-edge slats with the sharply raked box air intakes of the MiG-25. It also featured leading-edge root extensions for added control at high angle of attack. The MiG-25 had first flown in 1964 and possessed a theoretical top speed in excess of Mach 3 and was just about to enter service when the early design iterations on the MiG-29 were getting under way. This initial MiG-29 configuration bore all the hallmarks of a hastily selective application of separate successful design features of contemporary Russian aircraft and was consequently less appealing.

Nevertheless, there were some modest improvements, including a more sophisticated airflow control system employing ramps and hydraulic jacks, and flow management that had been a feature on the MiG-25 began to get

greater attention with the new fighter. Attention was also paid to the dual role of the aircraft, required as it was to perform modest ground-attack functions as well as perform as a highly manoeuvrable dogfighter. The initial concept had six underwing stores points for a mix of air-to-air weapons for medium-range and short-range engagement. But the entire programme still required formal authority.

The central research and development institute – TsNII-30 – formally issued a general operational requirement in 1971 for a fourth-generation fighter, a year after work began on the MiG-29. Converging design layouts for the MiG-31 with the new fourth-generation fighter resulted in some commonality, not least the boxy, rectangular intakes and the high wing setting on a slab fuselage. Arguably the MiG-25 had launched the wing/body blend concept, here to stay for all fast jets both East and West. But the design that was emerging was much lighter than the one which would be built, maxing out at 13.5 tonnes.

As well as preparing for a fourth-generation fighter, production and deployment were

ABOVE The cockpit of this F-15 displays a legacy of the second and third generation of fighters that only gradually began to take on solid state electronics and the glass displays replacing dials and barber-pole indicators. The US would begin to outpace the USSR with cockpit design and systems integration with this generation. *(USAF)*

ABOVE Despite preference for air-to-air missiles, feedback from front-line fighter pilots and their units suggested a reluctance to give up the gun, the F-15 being equipped with an M61 Vulcan. The Russians never challenged the need to carry out dogfights and always equipped their fighters with a gun. *(USAF)*

survivable and simple and quick to maintain. The pilots wanted performance. The MiG-29 programme, therefore, had three customers and had to satisfy each without compromising the basic requirement. A contrasting, and potentially disruptive, philosophy had been the decision to go for a twin-track solution – a lightweight fighter and a heavyweight interceptor, and for a little while that muddied the development schedule for both the MiG-29 and the Su-27.

This research was completed in 1973, when the T-10 and the MiG-29 were selected to go forward in development. MiG began *izdeliye* (type) 9.11, which stipulated requirements from the Air Force for radar working in multiple wavebands, semiconductors in the avionics, photo-electric targeting systems, infrared search and track and a Gyazev/Shipoonov GSh-23 or -30 gun. As the design appeared to have so many unique features MiG proposed an interim version that would adopt the avionics and electronics of the MiG-23 as type 9.11A (MiG-29A). The Air Force was not interested at all in the aerodynamic shape of the aircraft, only in its ability to meet requirements, and most of the detailed definition was in the operating systems, avionics and weapon systems.

evolving too. Being a mass-production aircraft builder, the MiG production side wanted to keep the aircraft as simple as possible in the way the assemblies would break down. The Air Force wanted an aircraft that was both

RIGHT Another exponent of variable geometry for carrier-based aviation was the Grumman F-14A Tomcat, evolving out of the failed TFX solution which found the US Navy without a long-range fighter when the F-111B failed to provide the successor to the F-4 Phantom II as intended. This long-range challenge to Russia would tip the USSR towards a carrier-based fleet and turn it to the MiG-29, as well as the Su-27, for a solution. *(US Navy)*

The key to the latter was power and the Klimov RD-33 power plant for the MiG-29 was selected in 1974, an engine that had a 20% less specific fuel consumption than the R25-300 fitted to the MiG-21 and the R-29-300 in the MiG-23, with thrust-to-weight ratios better by 26% and 11% respectively, while weighing 15% less.

The highest level of authority in the Soviet government formally approved the MiG-29 on 26 June 1974 and the two-tier approach proceeded. The only difference between the two was in the lower-grade electronics and avionics. But two-tier processes were not at all uncommon in both East and West. On 19 January 1976 the Council of Ministers again proclaimed on the type, ordering full-scale development of the MiG-29 and the Su-27. It was only at this point that MiG could be assured that the aircraft would go ahead to service introduction, hopefully later that decade. But the appearance of the F-15 and F-16 and knowledge of their advanced avionics and weapons systems changed the course of the programme.

With a none-too-delicate degree of shock at the advanced level of the weapons control system employed by these new US fighters, the Kremlin ordered a massive and highly intensive development effort to close the gap that had been widening over the last two decades. Fire control, radar and avionics were the key to combat equivalence of type, air superiority and control of the skies. Engagement beyond-visual-range was the key feature in air combat. Contested by infinitely superior systems carried on fourth-generation platforms negated the aerodynamic superiority of the Russian aircraft designs.

Out went the two-tier approach and great progress was now made with prioritising a new range of digital computers, where once there had been an emphasis on electro-mechanical systems, and a new level of development coursed through the Russian aerospace industry. It was quite universal and reverberations were felt in both aircraft design and in the systems approach for the Buran space shuttle, which was to have a level of electronic sophistication at least the equal of the NASA shuttle, a fact that still surprises many outside Russia.

The MiG-29 and the Su-27 were the first Russian fighters with digital avionics and, through the integration of those systems, fully exploited for the first time the advanced aerodynamics from TsAGI and the manufacturers. With a need for multiple functions and high processing speed, MiG set in motion the Feniks avionics programme involving 29 other research and development organisations working on the BTsK-29, the largest Soviet development programme of the 1970s, led by Yuriy A. Yanyshev. Incorporating fibre optics, the NIITsVERT was developed for the MiG-29 while the TsVM-80 was produced for the Su-27.

The detailed design of the MiG-29 was frozen in 1977 with the 9.12 configuration and the drawings were signed off on 17 July that year by the general designer, Rostislav A. Belyakov. There were changes to the configuration, wing area was increased to 38m^2 (408.6ft^2) with a span of 10.8m (35.43ft), a length of 15m (49.21ft) and a height of 4.56m (14.96ft). Empty

ABOVE The dorsal speed brake sported by this F-15E would see an equivalent solution to slowing down adopted by the MiG-29. *(USAF)*

weight was 9,670kg (21,320lb) and the normal take-off weight was 13,570kg (29,920lb) with an internal fuel load of 3,650kg (8,050lb). The take-off thrust ratio was 1.23:1 at a specific wing loading of 350kg/m² (71.75lb/ft²).

Due to the sophistication and complexity of this aircraft, MiG wanted to build 25 prototypes (901–925) to test all the many new features designed into it. Belenko's defection to the West with his MiG-25 compromised the Yantar radar and the Phazotron S-25 had to be produced for the MiG-29. Due to these expensive changes 11 prototypes were cancelled, leaving 14 to fully evaluate the aircraft and carry it through acceptance trials. But never having built an aircraft with an integrated layout, for safety MiG over-engineered the initial prototypes, and the weight they hoped to remove as the learning curve developed was never fully realised.

The first flight took place on 6 October 1977. Piloted by Aleksandr V. Fedotov, it was the first in a protracted series of test flights that went on for more than three years. The 14 pre-production prototypes had ventral fins and 901 was retired after 230 flights. After a succession of modifications, changes to the exact location

of the landing gear to avoid foreign-object damage, improvements to the avionics and some changes to the engines, the 14th and final prototype took off on 30 December 1982 for its first flight as the standard production template for the initial tranche off the line.

ABOVE Bulgarian MiG-29 Fulcrum-A fighters give a visual display that presents key aspects of the aircraft's design, including the unique wing for this design bureau, different from earlier MiG-designs, and the outwardly canted vertical stabilisers. *(Bulgarian Air Force)*

Design outline

The MiG-29 is a lightweight high-performance interceptor available either in single- or two-seat variants with a mission capability that includes air defence using radar and infrared-guided missiles as well as a 30mm gun.

Its outstanding and visually distinguishing feature compared to earlier MiG designs is the conformality of the blended wing/body structure, which has been designed to provide an overall aerofoil. As reported elsewhere in this book, this is a now familiar feature of many current aircraft but for different reasons to that which controlled the shape and design layout of the MiG-29.

Emphasis on high performance, combat turn radius and high alpha-change rate dictated that the fuselage and wing became a merged

wetted area so that the entire undersurface of the aircraft was available for aerodynamic performance. Aerodynamic considerations drove a cantilever wing design with leading-edge flaps and a trailing edge equipped with slotted flaps and ailerons.

The aft cantilever structure supports two vertical stabilisers each fitted with small rudders and two tailerons. The control surfaces are positioned with the aid of irreversible hydraulic actuators.

The overall design incorporates fuel tanks in the fuselage and wings fed from a single fill point and vent system for simplicity and ruggedising the maintenance and servicing in the field. This is characteristic of Russian aircraft and is somewhat at variance with Western types of the period. Provision is also made for a single ventral centreline tank and two underwing drop tanks as necessary.

Hydraulic power is provided through two independent systems feeding the main and boost systems with an emergency pump in the event of a failure to the primary. This also controls the landing gear. Pneumatic pressure delivery consists of a main and an emergency system for control and pressurisation of aircraft systems. It supports brakes, anti-skid wheels and nose steering.

Supplementary systems include a main drag parachute installed in the aft fuselage for reducing rollout distance and bringing the aircraft's operating capabilities within the support services of small airfields. The zero-altitude ejection seat is available at low speeds and is fully automated throughout the sequence of events to return the pilot safely to the ground after an emergency.

Pilot provisions include a dual redundant oxygen system with main and emergency supplies. The primary system supplies the pilot with oxygen and is fed to the auxiliary power unit for start-up and engine relight. A separate emergency system provides the pilot with oxygen during and after ejection. A rocket-assisted ejection seat is designed to provide safe escape under minimum speed/zero altitude conditions, fully automatic throughout the ejection sequence.

Flight control provisions include main and emergency pitot tubes, electrically heated, with angle of attack limiter sensors and an associated automatic flight control system, which also incorporates automatic pitch control.

The fire control system includes a Doppler radar suite, infrared search and track system (IRSTS) and a weapon computer, supporting missile launchers and the 30mm gun. Two digital computers are provided for data to support armament control and for displays of navigation, steering information and for weapons-aiming data fed to the head-up displays (HUD) and the head-down display HDD).

In addition, there are also provisions for a helmet-mounted sight (HMS), which is used to assign visually designated targets to the radar, to the IRSTS and to the missile infrared seekers. Designated target information is fed to an integrated laser rangefinder for operation in conjunction with the infrared search and track system.

The aircraft navigation equipment includes TACAN with electronic protection measures (EPM) equipment and a radar homing and warning receiver (RHAW) as standard. Appropriate to the specific variant, flare dispensers are usually provided for protection against infrared homing missiles from air or ground launch.

The MiG-29 introduced to Russian military aircraft a fault-identification and isolation concept in systems design and engineering and this was a notable improvement for operational military aircraft of the period. Voice and visual cues were provided through a telelight panel, from the voice information and warning system (VIWAS) and AEKRAN (acronym for a horribly long and convoluted Russian phrase), a fault identification and readout display. This information also feeds to the flight data recorder, which is analysed after the flight. Supporting that, a HUD camera is installed on most variants for displaying visually identified targets.

Variations exist for the MiG-29 trainer versions, which are usually missing the radar although they can carry missiles and the 30mm gun. However, a panel simulating the position of the radar is installed in the rear cockpit to project the simulated targets on to the HUD and the HDD, but the emergency panels are deactivated. A periscope ensures a clear view forward from the rear cockpit.

Design layout

Due to the blended wing/body shape, the fuselage and wing-root extensions provide 40% of the lift in horizontal flight and greatly increase lift over drag at angles of attack in excess of 17°. From the outset the engineering plan sought a robust and solid structure designed for rough field use and relatively high stress levels through the airframe. To accommodate that, large extruded panels cut down the number and distribution frequency of stress points across the fuselage and wing structure. In areas where high stress and thermal loads are unavoidable the aircraft has titanium, most commonly found in the wing spars and aft fuselage where thermal loads from the two powerful engines can be high.

Rather surprisingly for its late 1960s origin, the airframe incorporates about 7% in composite materials, but it is in the ruggedness of the construction that the aircraft gains advantages infrequently found in Western land-based aircraft of the period. To emphasise that, the main fuselage comprises three sub-assemblies with three frames in the forward section, three in the centre-section and four in the aft section with frames 3 and 7 providing sectional interfaces and load transfer paths between the three sub-assemblies.

The cockpit is structurally located within frames 1 and 2, which also include the hinged canopy and activation mechanism. The

electrically de-iced Triplex cockpit canopy has a magnesium alloy frame and three rear-view mirrors and the aft section hinge mechanism is attached to frame 3 with four locks. Forward of the cockpit, the equipment bay contains radar and combined infrared search and track/laser rangefinder (IRST/LR) with the dorsal transparent ball sensor offset to the starboard side of the nose.

The lower section of the forward equipment bay contains the identification-friend-or-foe (IFF)

RIGHT The physical dimensions of the MiG-29A adopted by the German Air Force after the collapse of the Warsaw Pact alliance in 1989 and the reunification of Germany in October 1990. Under Soviet control, East Germany had received 20 MiG-29A and four two-seat MiG-29UB types. In comparative fly-offs, US pilots judged the aircraft to be at least equal to the F-15C and in some situations superior. *(Via David Baker)*

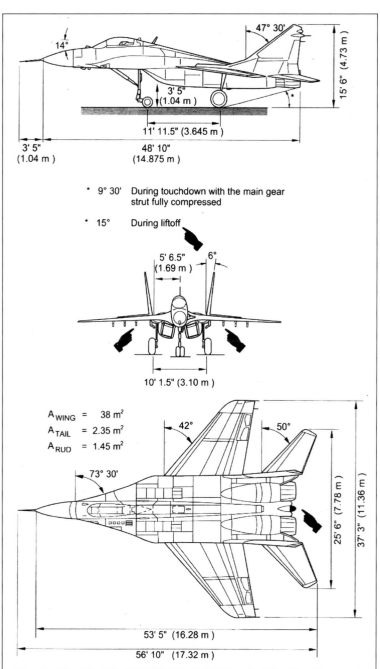

* 9° 30'   During touchdown with the main gear strut fully compressed

* 15°   During liftoff

A_{WING} = 38 m²
A_{TAIL} = 2.35 m²
A_{RUD} = 1.45 m²

transponder, air-traffic control, short-range air navigation (SHORAN) and the radio altimeter plus the yaw vane for the air data system. For the MiG-29K and MiG-29M a third, backup pitot tube is installed on the starboard side of the forward equipment bay beneath the cockpit. The K also features a retractable refuelling probe offset to the port side.

The pilot has a Zvezda K-36DM zero-zero ejection seat canted at a 16° pitch-back angle, with guide rails attached to the cockpit

bulkhead at frame 2 providing a downward view over the nose of 14°. A second equipment bay is located between frames 2 and 3 but access can only be gained when the canopy is fully open. A further bay, aft and between frames 3 and 3D, contains the ARK-19 automatic direction finder. The frame sequence along this part of the forward fuselage is defined as 3, 3A, 3B, 3V, 3G and 3D, and ADF aerials are attached in the dorsal position with a loop antenna beneath a dielectric panel between frames 5 and 6. The nose gear well is set between frames 2 and 4, with the hydraulic actuator attached to the bottom of frame 2 and the gear itself attached to frame 3.

The twin rectangular air intakes are supported between frames 3 and 4. Early aircraft have rounded leading edges with auxiliary dorsal air intakes between frames 3D and 4 (see later), but the MiG-25K and M have no dorsal intakes.

The two-seat MiG-29UB training variant is different in design, frame 1 being moved forward by 90cm (35.3in), which increases the length of the pressurised cockpit to 3m (9.8ft) within a common hinged canopy, a retractable periscope being incorporated for the instructor improving the view on take-off and landing. The only other major change in the trainer variant is the metal nosecone – as the aircraft carries no radar – with a small dielectric panel for the marker beacon receiver. The forward equipment also contains the IRST/LR components, which allows the fuselage aft of the cockpit to remain completely unchanged.

The centre fuselage contains the five body-mounted fuel tanks, and frames 7 to 8 delimit the engine bays while frame 6 provides the attachment point for the centreline fuel tank. Details of these tanks can be found in the technical section, but suffice to state here that the paired No 3 tank is the main load-bearing unit in the aircraft, taking stresses from the wings, the engines and the main landing gear. The aft fuselage assembly houses the common engine accessory gearbox, the auxiliary power unit, hydraulic pumps for fuel and oil and the aft fitting for the centreline fuel tank at frame 8.

Frame 9 carries the attachment points for the main braking parachute container and for the hydraulically actuated split airbrakes. The

BELOW The physical dimensions of the two-seat MiG-29UB.
(Via David Baker)

47° 30'
14°
15' 6" (4.73 m)
3' 5" (1.04 m)
11' 11.5" (3.645 m)
3' 5" (1.04 m)
49' 1.6" (14.972 m)

* 9° 30'   During touchdown with the main gear strut fully compressed

* 15°   During liftoff

5' 6.5" (1.69 m)   6°
10' 1.5" (3.10 m)

A_{WING} = 38 m²
A_{TAIL} = 2.35 m²
A_{RUD} = 1.45 m²

42°   50°
73° 30'
25' 6" (7.78 m)   37' 3" (11.36 m)
53' 9" (16.38 m)
57' 2" (17.42 m)

upper brake has a deflection of 56° and an area of 0.75m² (8.06ft²) and the lower brake a deflection angle of 60° and an area of 0.55m² (5.91ft²). The K and M variants differ in that they have a single large airbrake located between frames 8 and 9. The strap-on fuel tank 3B is attached between frames 7 and 8, while the K variant also incorporates an arrester hook attached to frame 8.

The leading-edge root extensions (LERXs) occupy an area of 4.71m² (50.64ft²) with a sweep of 73.5° and are built integrally with frame 1. Located between frames 1 and 3 on the port side is the internal gun, its ammunition box and the gun-blast panel, fabricated from heat-resistant steel with cooling vents, the upper skin spanning from frames 2 to 3. The starboard LERX houses the air-conditioning equipment and both LERXs have cover panels for a number of aerials according to the specific variant.

The cantilever all-metal wings have an area, excluding LERXs, of 38.056m² (409.2ft²), a root chord of 5.6m (18.37ft) and a tip chord of 1.27m (4.16ft). The trapezoidal planform has a leading-edge sweep angle of 42° with a 3.5:1 aspect ratio. The wings are built around a three-spar structure with two false spars ahead of the torsion box and another false spar aft. The 16 ribs are reinforced by stringers, as are the upper and lower skins. Five fittings attach the wing spars to the fuselage at each of three frames – 6, 6-V and 7 – and the wing torsion box itself serves as an integral fuel tank.

Three-section trailing-edge flaps (two on the MiG-29M) and ailerons are complemented by leading-edge flaps, each of which are deflected 20° by six hydraulic actuators. Total area of the leading-edge flaps is 2.35m² (25.26ft²) and the area of the trailing-edge flaps is 2.84m² (30.53ft²). The ailerons have an area of 1.45m² (15.59ft²). The MiG-29K has a different TsAGI P-177M wing aerofoil design with two-section leading-edge flaps and double-slotted inboard flaps with ailerons of slightly greater area situated outboard, the whole made of steel rather than 01420 Al-Li alloy. RP-280A hydraulic actuators drive the ailerons, which have a deflection capability of +15°/-25° and a surface area of 1.45m² (15.59ft²). The wings fold upward for stowage in the limited space aboard the carrier.

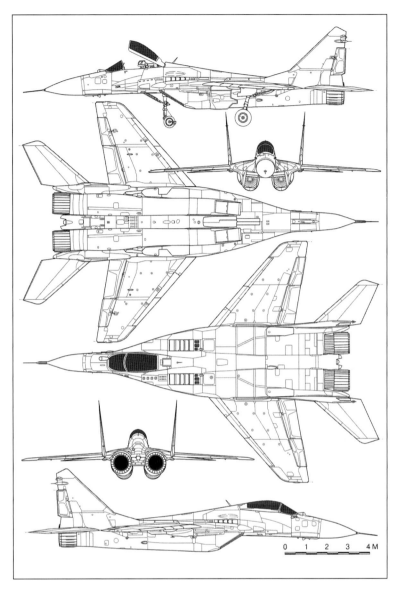

The tail unit includes two vertical fin/rudder assemblies with two horizontal stabilisers moveable independently for roll or in unison to operate as tailerons for pitch control, to which they are referred in this book. With a leading-edge sweep of 50°, and an anhedral of 3.5°, they are fabricated in a single-spar structure with a false spar, 16 ribs and upper and lower skin incorporating a composite trailing-edge with honeycomb core. The horizontal stabilisers adopt the TsAGI S-11S symmetrical aerofoil section with a leading-edge dogtooth and have a surface area of 7.05m² (75.8ft²); the total span of both stabilisers is 7.78m (25.53ft), although the K and M variants have a slightly greater area. RP-180A hydraulic actuators are attached to frame 10 and have a deflection capability

ABOVE Structural layout of the MiG-29 Fulcrum-A showing the break lines and control surface areas plus flaps, tailerons and leading-edge flaps. *(Via David Baker)*

ABOVE A revealing overhead shot of the MiG-29 displays the general layout and balance between the twin engines and the blended wing/body airframe with raised air brake. *(MiG)*

BELOW Another view of the same aircraft showing the nose area and retractable refuelling probe. *(MiG)*

of +15°/-25° on take-off and landing, or +45.75°/-17.75° during cruise.

With a leading-edge sweep of 47.83°, the twin fins are canted outboard 6° with a total area of 10.1m² (108.6ft²), attached to the aft fuselage with rectangular root section fillets which have a leading-edge sweep of 75°. The fins are each fabricated from reinforced carbon-fibre plastic with false spars fore and aft and are attached by three brackets. They have a honeycomb trailing edge which, on aircraft built since 1984, have a 21% longer chord on the rudder. Each rudder has an area of 1.25m² (13.44ft²) and has a fibreglass tip which contains various aerials and GCI (ground control intercept) links and is operated via RP-270 hydraulic rams with a ±25° radius of travel. Early MiG-29s had a ventral fin outboard of each engine nacelle, but these were removed on subsequent aircraft. Later aircraft have chaff and flare dispensers attached to strake-like fillets ahead of the fins.

The hydraulically retracted landing gear has a track of 3.09m (10.138ft) and a wheelbase of 3.645m (11.96ft), with all three legs incorporating oleo shock absorbers. Each main gear leg has a single 84 x 29cm (33 x

11.4in) KT-150 wheel (or KT-209 on the MiG-29M) that retracts forward, rotating 90° as it does so to assume the horizontal plane within the wing centre-section bay. Due to its more severe operating environment, the MiG-29K has a longer leg stroke, shortened by links during retraction.

The nose leg supports twin 57 x 14cm (22.4 x 5.5in) KT-100 wheels that retract aft into the tunnel between the two engine intakes. The nose wheels can turn ±31° for taxiing and ±8° for an emergency during take-off or landing. The landing gear has received some modifications during the life of the aircraft, originally carrying a much longer nose leg attached to frame 2 with semi-enclosed nose wheel units similar to those on the MiG-23.

Production variations

The following list of variants is not intended to be a complete and comprehensive inventory of all the different aircraft produced under this type number, but it does carry information on the variants incorporating changes that distinguish major engineering differences. The NATO codename 'Fulcrum' is used as a universal identification for those significant differences in type variant. Most of the changes applied to the two-seat MiG-29UB or

UBT are identified and explained in the technical section that follows in the next chapter.

The MiG-29 Fulcrum-A entered production in 1982 with the lot 9.12 contract for 250 aircraft, incorporating anti-spin ventral fins that were later removed, as was the *babochka* gravel deflector in front of the nose wheels. The first 30 aircraft had composite inlet ducts, cowlings, leading-edge flap control surfaces, spines and tailfins. D19 aluminium was introduced on the intake ducts and flaps after the 30th aircraft off the line, albeit with a weight penalty of 20kg (44lb), and the composite cowlings were also deleted slightly later along the production line. The ventral fins were removed with BVP-30M chaff and flare dispensers added. The A-312 Radikal NP SHORAN was replaced by the A-323.

In 1984 changes were introduced whereby the control surface deflection range was increased and the rudder chord was enlarged by 21%, which improved control at extreme angles of attack. Spin characteristics were improved by setting the ailerons at 5° up in the neutral position with the dorsal fins extended forward to accommodate chaff and flare dispensers. This had the effect of increasing the area of the keel without compromising flight stability. The Air Force base-lined the weapons load at 2,000kg (4,409lb) and a reinforced port inner pylon allowed the 30KT RN-40 nuclear

LEFT The first prototype MiG-29 (01 Blue), preserved at the Central Air Force Museum, Monino, about 40km (25 miles) east of Moscow at the Gagarin Military Academy, shows the engine air inlets situated above the leading-edge extensions.
(David Baker)

bomb to be carried. Approximately 840 were built in lot 9.12 by 1991.

Production lot 9.12A was specifically produced for Bulgaria, Czechoslovakia, East Germany, Poland and Romania and consisted of downgraded IFF and the OEPrNK-29E electro-optical system and lacked the capacity to carry nuclear weapons. Most were modified to the 9.12B configuration and Warsaw Pact aircraft carried the RLPK-29E Rubin radar with only three of the original five radar modes. The production lot ran from 1988 to 1991 and after the break-up of the USSR in 1991 the IFF and datalink capability was removed.

Beginning in 1986, production of the 9.12B factory lot was for non-Warsaw Pact and export countries, and all lacked the Laszlo datalink but had avionics including the N-019EB radar, the OEPrNK-29E2 electro-optical system and the L006LM/101 radar homing and warning system. It also had downgraded electronic countermeasures and IFF capability. Aircraft from this lot were modified for NATO use by those countries that retained production MiG-29s when the Warsaw Pact was dissolved. It also saw service with Hungary, Iraq, Syria, and a few other countries.

From 27 July 1993, Daimler-Benz Aerospace and MAPO MIG cooperated on D-level maintenance and the modernisation of German

ABOVE A German MiG-29 GT, a Fulcrum-B, prepares to take-off from Ramstein air base, Germany, piloted by *Luftwaffe* Major Gassner and CINC-USAFE General Robert C. Oaks. *(USAF)*

BELOW In the knowledge that the type would see service among Third World states friendly to the USSR, and also that the skills of servicing technicians may be less than those in the Warsaw Pact countries, rapid turnaround and ease of maintenance were crucial elements within its design and manufacture. This Polish Air Force MiG-29 remembers the life of Merian C. Cooper (1893–1973), a pilot with the US Air Force, the Polish Air Force and founder of the Ko ciuszko squadron during the Polish–Soviet War of 1919–21. *(Via David Baker)*

MiG-29s, equipping them with Western IFF systems, VHF/UHF radio, TACAN systems and later with GPS. It also carried out ICAO I and II Level One changes and a similar rework of other MiG-29s across Europe followed. In parallel, various upgrades were introduced including the Honeywell KLU-709 TACAN or, in some cases, the German AN/ARN-118 and the Trimble 2101 GPS systems. Some Polish MiG-29s acquired the SB-14 IFF automatic direction finder as installed on the then contemporary F-16A aircraft.

A succession of changes and modifications, upgrades and improvements tracked other non-Russian-operated Fulcrums, with Bulgarian and Romanian aircraft receiving life-extension programmes while Slovakia came close to a major datalink upgrade with the MIL-STD-1553B data bus. In the general melee after the collapse of the USSR, Western companies offered a wide range of systems to replace Russian and East European equipment with which the aircraft had originally been equipped. Aircraft were 'donated' by former Warsaw Pact countries to be demonstration models of what was on offer with the Paris air show, ILA and Farnborough International events hosting discussions and demonstrations of performance improvements and upgrades.

Initially flown on 4 May 1984, the first of a modified aircraft design change introduced a deeply curved top deck to the aft fuselage to provide additional volume for extra avionics equipment. Known as the Fulcrum-C, this design emerged as factory lot 9.13 with production from 1986 to 1991. The new avionics included the L-203BE Gardeniva 1 FU active jammer, internal fuel capacity increased by 240 litres (52 gallons), a 1,500-litre (329-gallon) centreline under-fuselage drop tank and an increase in weapons load to 3,200kg (7,055lb). The 9.13 could carry a much wider range of weapons too, and six FAB-500M54 high-drag bombs could be lifted instead of four by utilising a special tandem carriage adapter.

Several small modifications were necessary, such as the modified shell case disposal chute to avoid conflict with the new drop tank, and RWR/ECM antennas were added to the wing tips. The numbers 1, 2 and 3 fuel tanks were modified and the upper cover of the engine accessory gear box was redesigned. All the hydraulic and pneumatic systems were improved and the oxygen feed system changed. Three prototype aircraft were adapted from production-line aircraft and some 207 were manufactured. None were exported but some East European air forces acquired a few after the collapse of the Soviet Union.

Also known as Fulcrum-C, factory production version 9.13S first flew on 23 December 1990, although it carried forward several of the basic changes from the 9.13 production version. It appeared with East German units just before the collapse of the Soviet system and had a significant increase in weapons load to 4,000kg

ABOVE Note the periscope sight for the rear-seat pilot/instructor position on this Bulgarian Air Force MiG-29 performing at the Thracian Star exercise at Graf Ignatievo. *(USAF)*

ABOVE Royal
Malaysian Air Force
MiG-29 aircraft from
No 17 Squadron, which
is now disbanded,
operating out of
Kuantan air base. The
type was introduced
to the country in 1995
and has continued in
service as decisions
over a replacement
stagnate. Note the
refuelling probes in the
stowed position.
(RSC MiG)

(8,818lb) with provision for two drop tanks, features retrofitted to Russian 9.12 and 9.13 aircraft. The additional fuel capacity increased the range to 2,900km (1,802 miles) and in several respects introduced elements of what would characterise the MiG-29SD, the NE and the N series.

A major improvement was in the application of the RLPK-29M N019M radar, which had a detection range of 100km (62 miles) and was able to track ten targets simultaneously and engage two simultaneously. This BVR (beyond visual range) interception capability, matched with an enhanced alpha operating angle of 28°, gave the type a distinct advantage over the General Dynamics (Lockheed Martin) F-16 dogfighter. Advanced air-to-air weapons capability made great use of the additional combat-load mass and provided a greatly expanded ground-attack capability while raising all-up weight to 19,700kg (43,430lb).

The primary export version of the 9.12S appeared as the MiG-29SD, where 'D' stands for *dozaprahvka* – orbital refuelling – internally known as lot 9.12SD. This carried the same radar targeting system as the 9.13S but differed from the existing version (9.12B) in having a semi-retractable in-flight refuelling probe that had been tested on a standard 9.12 airframe as a removable device. The elongated fairing was located on the port side of the fuselage and this, plus associated support hardware, increased the weight of the aircraft by 95kg (209lb). Nevertheless, the refuelling probe allowed all integral and external tanks to be filled at the same time.

The launch contract for the MiG-29SD was signed with Malaysia on 7 June 1994 with the refuelling probes retrofitted to 14 of the 16 on

RIGHT A German
MiG-29 with S-31E2
KOLS infrared search
and rescue sensor.
(David Baker)

order. Development of this probe relied heavily on experience with similar retrofits to variants of the thirsty MiG-25 Foxbat and this would be fitted to later versions of the MiG-31 Foxhound. The problem with fitting it to the smaller MiG-29 was finding the amount of space required and it had to be placed lower down on the fuselage than initially proposed, with a fairing added to the external surface of the nose area to accommodate the fuel-delivery plumbing.

But the design was adaptive, the entire system being installed, or removed, within one hour. Added to which it could be retrofitted to any MiG-29. Refuelling trials were completed with an Ilyushin Il-78 in January 1996, demonstrating no adverse effects while flying and handling the refuelling process. The tests also simulated tanking off a Lockheed C-130, since the Malaysian Air Force had acquired six for this specific purpose. Concern about the less than sparkling range of the basic MiG-29 had spurred adoption of underwing drop tanks and this latest development made the aircraft attractive for its export potential.

Like so many Russian combat aircraft, most of which were designed for export at some stage in their life, the MiG-29 found itself working alongside, or being retro-equipped with, Western kit in the form of upgrades to avionics, radar or sensor packages. And so it was with the Malaysian MiG-29SD, even down to the flight instruments marked in Imperial units. But the ability to integrate with some of the more advanced ancillary equipment designed and built in the West added value to the superior aerodynamics and performance characteristics

of the MiG-29. Navstar GPS receivers, TACAN and SHORAN short-range radar (highly effective in air-to-air refuelling operations) provided the aircraft with new capabilities.

As the expert version was swept up in the changes brought about by the end of the Soviet Union, NATO-standard equipment was readily incorporated. Upgrading to NATO/ICAO standard was a big step toward smooth integration into Western air forces. Additional data processing suites were incorporated, with new LCD screens in the cockpit; NATO IFF equipment and integration with commercial air traffic control was an essential prerequisite for effective operation among Western military and commercial air lanes.

As a further offering to the export market, the MiG-29SE (9.13SE) was a downgraded version of the 'fat back' 9.13 incorporating additional fuel in the dorsal fuselage hump. The weapon control system was identical to the MiG-29SD and there was provision for installing the export version of the active jammer. The maximum take-off weight was the same as the 9.13, but beginning in the mid-1990s Russia began to export it with a larger internal fuel capacity, an improved weapons suite including semi-active radar-homing air-to-air missiles, and an active radar-homing AAM. In this version the maximum weapons load was increased to 4,500kg (9,920lb).

Long before the appearance of these export versions, a new experimental development began under the factory number 9.14, a variant of the 9.13 that would evolve via a circuitous route into the MiG-29S. The prototype took to the air for the first time on 13 February 1985

ABOVE A Serbian Air Force MiG-29 with two Aphid missiles. Originally developed for the MiG-23, the short-range AA-8 Aphid appeared in the mid-1970s and was the missile type used by an Su-15 to shoot down the Boeing 707 of Korean Air Lines Flight 902 on 20 April 1978. *(Kasimir Grozev)*

ABOVE A MiG-29 of
the Russian Air Force
at Abbotsford air
display showing the
position of landing-
gear lights and a good
view of the slab-sided
fuselage section in the
cockpit area.
(Via David Baker)

as a platform specifically developed to carry
the Ryabina low-light level TV/laser designator,
which at the time of this flight was not available
for installation. It was an attempt to significantly
improve the aircraft for iron-bomb roles and
for pinpoint strikes and it was to have carried
the AS-10 Karen and As-14 Kedge TV-guided
or laser-guided bombs and the KA-500 smart
bomb. Although it was displayed at several
internal air shows in 1990–91, it never entered
production. The requirement had been met by
another variant, the MiG-29M, a much more
effective platform.

Nevertheless, the 9.14 contributed to
a variant that evolved more directly from
the 9.13S (described earlier), which was
used as the basis for a new tactical fighter
version designed to adapt the R-77 active-
homing radar capable of guiding two missiles
simultaneously. Despite great expectations and
a recommendation in 1993 approving major
production for the Russian Air Force only 16
were produced, but the modifications were later
retrofitted to existing MiG-29 aircraft. Not to be
confused with the MiG-29S based on the 9.13,
another MiG-29A evolved from the preceding
9.12S, with the original low-profile spine and
lacking the improved jammer. It too appeared at
several air shows, and four aircraft were used
by MiG as display aircraft, sporting different
colour schemes.

MiG-29M

The first major development of the MiG-29
into its inherent potential had been under
way since the late 1970s when the company
sought to integrate new advances in aircraft
systems technologies and to combine those
with new and improved engines and a superior
and much more advanced avionics suite. Lack
of adequate range had always been a problem
for the MiG-29, and added to that was the less
than optimum combat capability. Impressive
as it was, there was greater potential within
the aerodynamic design that required better
systems, subsystems and engine. Moreover,
new and more capable weapons were
beginning to appear for which the basic aircraft
lacked support infrastructure from radar, fire
control systems and avionics.

An evolution bearing the factory designation
9.15, the MiG-29M Fulcrum-E was the first
new-generation MiG-29 and would incorporate
redesigned air intakes and significant changes
to the airframe, replacing riveted sections with
welded ones. With new alloys possessing a
lower specific gravity the airframe would be
lighter and allow more fuel to be carried due
to the increased sealing. Composites were
introduced for the airbrakes and a strengthened
landing gear with KT-209 main wheels, engine
cowlings and inlet ducts. In addition radar-

RIGHT A MiG-29 wrecked in a Coalition air strike on Iraq during Operation Desert Storm in 1991. At the start of the campaign to expel Iraqi forces from Kuwait, the Iraqi Air Force had 929 combat aircraft of which 29 were MiG-29 Fulcrum-As and four were two-seat MiG-29UBs. Only 13 Fulcrum-As and three MiG-29UBs survived. *(USAF)*

absorbent materials (RAM) reduced the frontal radar cross-section (RCS) of the aircraft tenfold.

Changes were made to the cockpit area, the pilot adopting a slightly higher position with a new 15° downward field of view, the canopy became more convex and higher by 4cm (1.5in), the wing leading-edge extensions had a sharper edge which would generate more powerful vortices at high angles of attack, enhancing slow-speed handling, the area of the tailerons was increased with leading-edge extensions which also helped handling, and the fin chord was increased below the rudders.

The fuselage was reshaped in a subtle manner, making a flatter line between the concave dorsal shape of the initial MiG-29 Fulcrum-A and the convex shape of the modified Fulcrum-C. A new bonded 01420 aluminium-lithium front fuselage section was attached to the welded steel structure aft and the nose lengthened by 20cm (7.5in). The APU (auxiliary power unit) was relocated to the starboard side of the fuselage and the split airbrake of the original design was replaced with one similar to that of the Sukhoi Su-27, a one-piece honeycomb composite structure mounted in the dorsal position on top of the fuselage between the fins and extending beyond the exhaust nozzles. Modifications to the control system ensured full aerodynamic control when the airbrake was deployed.

A major change effected by removing the auxiliary air intake louvres in the dorsal position,

RIGHT Launched on the cusp of dramatic political changes about to overwhelm the Soviet Union, MiG saw in its M variant of the MiG-29 an upgrade and capability enhancement that could have significant appeal on international arms markets, setting up a vigorous set of appearances at air shows and trade fairs. *(David Baker)*

with retractable downward-hinging intake grids, allowed redesign of the internal ducting and the incorporation of a lightweight aluminium-lithium alloy centre-section. This permitted more fuel to be carried, raising capacity by 1,000 litres (220 gallons), increasing the internal quantity to 5,720 litres (1,258 gallons). With a total fuel load of 4,460kg (9,832lb), the range of the 9.15 increased by 30–40% and with three drop tanks the total capacity increased to 9,200 litres (2,024 gallons).

Major changes beefed up the landing gear, and the single braking parachute of 17m² (182.79ft²) was replaced with a twin unit of 13m² (139.78ft²). More powerful brakes were also fitted to ensure short-field performance and better braking on rollout.

Klimov produced an improved version of their standard engine, the RD-33K, which had been under evaluation for the MiG-29 carrier version and which included modifications to the engine core, the turbine first-stage cooling, increased thrust to 53,932N (12,125lb) in military power and 86,290N (19,400lb) in afterburner. A 6–7% lower specific fuel consumption brought potentially higher reliability since it lacked the emergency power rating of 92,162N (20,720lb) that was considered prudent for carrier take-off. The engine had a duplex full authority digital control unit replacing the old analogue unit, a duplex automatic fuel flow management system and a KSA-3 engine accessory gearbox.

Also introduced on the MiG-29M was the unusual quadruplex analogue fly-by-wire pitch control channel but no mechanical backup. The triplex fly-by-wire roll and yaw control channels did have mechanical backup with 50% control surface deflection. Making the aircraft statically unstable in pitch reduced the drag that was otherwise caused by pitch trim in cruise mode, and that improved fuel efficiency which fed into greater range.

The MiG-29M would carry the Phazotron NIIR N010 Zhuk (RLPK-29M) terrain-following and ground-mapping radar with a 680mm (26.77in) dish antenna in the radome, which had a larger diameter as an element in the S-29M weapons control system. This had the more efficient Ts101 digital processors and the Ts100 series processors were supplemented with new and improved software. The N010 pulse-Doppler radar was capable of tracking ten targets and simultaneously guiding four air-to-air weapons. The detection range for a target with a frontal RCS of 3m² (32.25ft²) in a head-on attack was 80km (49.6 miles) compared to 70km (43.4 miles) for the N019. The radar had a flat-plate slotted array with mechanical scanning in azimuth and electronic scanning in elevation.

The N010 also operated in ground mapping with low, medium or high resolution from the standard beam with Doppler beam compression and synthetic aperture radar modes respectively. It could measure the aircraft's ground speed for navigation purposes and it could make corrections during the missile-firing phase and allow the aircraft to perform automatic terrain following. The N010 weighed 220kg (485lb), considerably less than the 350kg (771lb) N019. The new radar allowed the radome to be shaped to a simple curvature versus the double curvature needed for the N019, which had a bulky structure.

Considerable capability expansion in operational combat roles was achieved primarily through the incorporation of the OEPrNK-29M optoelectronic combined infrared/TV search and track laser ranging unit coupled to a helmet-mounted sight. It had increased detection range, detecting and measuring the coordinates of aerial targets and designated ground targets for laser-guided and TV-guided weapons, tracking them in real time. This system replaced

BELOW Although a view of the MiG-29SMT, this shows the M2 variant as developed from the 'M' series of upgrades and modifications. Note the raised turtle deck-shaped upper fuselage, characteristic of this evolution. *(MiG)*

the infrared search and track system on previous aircraft, which had an eyeball mounted to an elongated fairing.

This system alone considerably increased the target detection, tracking and intercept capability, shifting it from a very 1970s capability to match the performance exhibited, for instance, by the Northrop AN/ASX-1 electro-optical target identification system fitted to the McDonnell Douglas F-4E, significantly increasing the guidance of on-board missiles.

The 9.15 incorporated a completely different electronic flight instrumentation system with an improved head-up display, two multi-function CRT (cathode ray tube) displays for flight and weapons targeting with growth potential to colour CRTs as an optional development. Backup electro-mechanical instruments were still presented in the centre of the main display console but incorporated the hands-on-throttle and-stick (HOTAS) approach, also carrying a new inertial navigation system, a new datalink for interrogating ground control interception stations and new IFF transponders.

The driving imperative behind 9.15 was the need to provide a carriage and launch platform for a new generation of weaponry, and the enhanced load-carrying capacity (4.5 tonnes) served that purpose well. The most sought-after application originated in the Vympel factory as the R-77 AAM which had been evolving since first designed in 1982, the first Russian missile of its type with active radar homing, utilising inertial guidance after launch

with mid-course corrections picking up from the MiG-29M radar and switching to active homing for terminal guidance.

With a projected range of 90km (55 miles) the R-77 was the Soviet equivalent to the Hughes AIM-120A AMRAAM, a major step up from the Sparrow. The R-77 was slated for future employment on a wide range of tactical and strategic aircraft and would continue to be carried by many to the present day. While the design and test of the R-77 was not the sole reason for development of the 9.15, the new generation of weapons represented by this missile was a fundamental match with the new fire control and radar systems carried on the MiG-29M. The design demand on the R-77 was high, with the capability for the missile to make aggressive and violent manoeuvres of up to 12g to maintain lock on an out-manoeuvring target.

The 9.15 was designed to carry up to eight R-77s of the short-range R-73 infrared homing variety with a wide assortment of existing stores and missiles. It was also capable of carrying TV-guided bombs, unguided rocket pods and a variety of gravity bombs. The GSh-301 internal cannon was downgraded in importance, with only 100 rounds provided. But the Soviet Air Force was reluctant to disregard the value of close-in dogfighting and this belief in direct combat using guns prevailed, and would inspire several further proposed generations of MiG-29, as well as other Russian combat aircraft. It was a view not altogether accepted in Western air forces.

ABOVE In contrast to the evolving series of Fulcrum types, a USAF F-16C and a MiG-29 Fulcrum-A fly formation over Krzesiny air base, Poland. *(USAF)*

53

RIGHT Displaying a much modified airframe, this evocative shot of the MiG-29M Fulcrum-E climbing away on a turn reveals the modified nose section, absence of LERX engine air intakes – replaced with sieve-like screens in the modified intakes – and less convex curvature on the upper fuselage deck. *(Alex Beltyukov)*

With a normal take-off weight of 15,800kg (34,830lb) and a maximum take-off weight of 18,000kg (39,680lb), the MiG-29M compared very favourably with competitors in the same category and improvements in serviceability followed the Soviet practice of building robust aircraft for rugged performance in rough-field conditions with rapid turnaround. The revised serviceability programme required seven technicians 30 minutes to carry out pre-flight checks and no longer than 25 minutes to carry out post-flight checks. Service life on the airframe was increased to 2,500 hours and there were improvements that could raise this to 4,000 hours. The MTBF (mean time between failures) was no less than eight hours with maintenance conducted every 200 hours.

Initial flight trials incorporated the original RD-33, and six aircraft were assigned to carry out tests. The first 9.15 prototype made its initial flight on 25 April 1986 as 151 Blue, piloted by Valeriy Ye. Menitskiy and bearing distinctive black-and-white calibration markings on the tail for the phototheodolites. While carrying full fly-by-wire, it was assigned to verifying structural modifications and control and handling characteristics. The first flight with the RD-33K took place on 26 September 1987, having been first flight-tested on aircraft 921. Designated 152 Blue, the second prototype flew with the standard RD-33 engine but this received the new RD-33K engine in 1989. It was also the first to be fitted with the N010 radar, the HUD and the two CRT displays, becoming essentially the full MiG-29 prototype.

The formal display of the MiG-29 to senior Air Force and defence ministry officials took place at Kubinka air base with the third

prototype, 153 Blue, on 23 June 1989 and this was followed by the other three aircraft for specific test programmes leading up to full acceptance trials, which were completed in September 1991. Flight tests and performance trials uncovered several necessary changes and each prototype introduced an evolving series of minor modifications. These were addressed by senior design engineers, who were allocated specific prototypes for the duration of the test phase to focus on particular aspects of the redesigned aircraft and supervise changes or recommendations.

In general test pilots were impressed by the improved handling and flight characteristics of the aircraft and it was shown to have a true maximum air speed of 2,450kph (1,451mph), or Mach 2.3, and a rate of climb of 310m/sec (61,000ft/min) at 1,000m (3,280ft). The service ceiling was 17,000m (55,770ft) and the maximum ferry range with three external fuel tanks was 3,200km (1,987 miles). Equipped with 3,500kg (7,720lb) of ordnance it had a loiter time of 20 minutes at a range of 520km (323 miles). The effective combat radius was 1,250km (776 miles) or 1,440km (894 miles) in the subsonic intercept role with all three jettisonable tanks and with AAMs and two air-to-ground missiles.

During the development phase the normal take-off weight increased to 16,800kg (37,040lb) with maximum TOW up at 22,300kg (49,160lb) and very little difference in field performance, the take-off run being 250–300m (820–1,640ft) depending on weight, and landing distance of 500–600m (1,640–1,970ft). In other respects the performance of the aircraft was similar to the standard MiG-29, although there were great improvements in the angle of attack capabilities which pushed the airframe to 9g under high accelerations with a full warload. Set initially at 30°, the alpha limiter was said by project engineer Mikhail R. Val'denberg to be increased when the aircraft entered service.

One of the design changes got an unexpectedly realistic test when a duck was sucked into one of the engine intakes, the new retractable grille screen effectively stopping it entering the engine with only a minor dent in the mesh. There was high acclaim for the aircraft's stall and spin recovery, confirming the claims of the original design team that the basic aerodynamic shape was capable of much more than the initial variants could demonstrate and that in critical handling and manoeuvrability it could out-fly any other combat aircraft.

After many years of development work which involved engine, airframe and systems manufacturers, the MiG-29M was scheduled to gradually replace the Fulcrum-A and Fulcrum-C types, with talk of an initial order for 60 joining the existing production line in 1989. Thereafter, during the 1990s MiG expected production to run to up to 400 more MiG-29M types, gradually replacing the Fulcrum-A/C types. But there were still impediments to a smooth transition, not least the relatively slow pace of acceptance trials and resolution of a range of minor problems with the avionics, the radar and the weapon systems. But there were strong expectations that, with these corrected, final approval for full-scale production would be forthcoming in 1990.

The dawn of a new decade sustained an inherited shortfall in development funding, with little money now coming from the State for essential trials work and certification tests. When the USSR fell apart all MiG-29 production stopped in 1991 and undelivered aircraft stood idle on the MiG airfield at Lookhovitsy while the government regrouped for a new national democratic structure. Everything went on hold and the Russian government was unable to find the money to continue development work. The MiG-29M was 'shelved' as a possibility until resurrected several years later.

But MiG never lost faith in the improvements and the company carried out design work at its own expense to prevent the development under

9.15, carried out since the early 1980s, from falling into obsolescence. Under the factory designation 9.25, the advanced development of the MiG-29M would present to the Air Force the prospect of a completely new fighter aircraft only superficially similar to the original design. MiG had engines uprated to 98,56N (22,045lb), moved them 910mm (35.83in) to make room for an additional fuel tank, added foreplanes to the fuselage, increased wing area to further improve the performance and introduced a completely new fire control system. Weapons load was increased to 5,000kg (11,020lb).

In rearranging the internal structure, engineers enlarged tank No 1, added a new tank No 4 and increased fuel volume by 20%. The company proposed a three-phase introduction programme sequentially bringing on board the basic change in the shape of the aircraft's fuselage, the canards and the increased wing area in the second stage, and finally the new engine which would be combined with a yet further increase in fuel capacity. A new tank No 5 would raise fuel quantity to 8,000 litres (1,760 gallons), representing a 90% increase over the original Fulcrum-A. Presented as the first of a fifth-generation fighter programme, the Air Force

BELOW The cockpit of the MiG-29M with glass screens, replacements for the general layout of earlier variants, and with a new optoelectronic infrared/TV search and track laser ranging equipment with a helmet-mounted sight.
(David Baker)

ABOVE One of the 35 Sudanese Air Force MiG-29SEs, of which many are unserviceable or non-operational. With a capacity for carrying three external tanks and greater range, the type was the first step toward the new M-series generation leading to the SMT. *(Sudanese Air Force)*

was interested but there was no money and the 9.25 too was shelved.

During the second half of the 1990s MiG proposed a new multi-role fighter development spinning off from the 9.15 and 9.25. The 9.35 was a complete redesign and incorporated a stretched fuselage, with more fuel tanks placed in ahead of the engines and in the fin roots, two drop tanks under the fuselage and two wing-mounted drop tanks plus in-flight refuelling. To accommodate the growth in weight the wing area was to have been increased and changed in planform to more closely resemble that of the MiG-25 Foxbat, with square-cut wing tips and straight trailing edge. Supported on a newly

designed and stronger landing gear, the structure employed D16 Duralumin to replace the 01420 aluminium-lithium alloy, aspects which in effect completely transformed the original MiG-29, in design, layout, function and performance.

MiG-29K

Russia's desire for an aircraft carrier emerged during the late 1940s but was unrealised due to the almost complete lack of experience in building this class of warship. After the Cuba missile crisis of October 1962, Admiral Gorshkov received high praise for his determined resolve to never again allow Russian

RIGHT A MiG-29KUB operated by India shows the modified wing with folding outer sections inboard of the ailerons. The type developed as a carrier-based variant for the Russian Navy, at a time when investment in naval forces was slowing as the USSR neared collapse. *(MiG)*

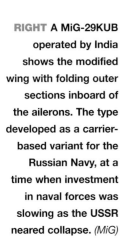

RIGHT A close-in view of the wing fold mechanism shows the roller hinges and hydraulic pistons, together with hydraulic and electrical lines between inner and outer wing sections. *(MiG)*

naval forces to be humiliated on the world stage. Lacking the strike power to confront the Americans at sea, at first the Russians turned to a vigorous anti-submarine warfare capability, looking again in the 1970s to producing a carrier strike force that could counter US pre-eminence on the high seas.

Encouraged by the successful Kiev-class cruisers with angled flight decks for Yak-38 and Yak-41 V/STOL fighters, the MiG-23ML was modified for carrier use along with the Sukhoi Su-25. As naval plans evolved the Soviet Union planned a series of carriers, the first being the *Kuznetsov* launched in December 1985 with a maximum displacement of 61,390 tons. Development of navalised versions of the MiG-29 and the Sukhoi Su-27 had been endorsed by the Ministry of Defence in 1981 with the design of the new carriers adopting a ski-jump bow.

The MiG-29M was the template basis from which the navalised MiG-29K would emerge, with the welded aluminium-lithium only part of a complete re-examination of materials employed in the aircraft's assembly – including those for seals, gaskets, coatings and finishes – to ensure corrosion protection. Additional loads experienced by the navalised version during heavy or non-arrested landings would be accommodated in part by strengthening the main fuselage fuel tank, but in several respects the aircraft would be very different to the M variant.

Designed by a team under Mikhail R. Val'denberg, the K was powered by two RD-33K engines with a dry thrust of 53,932N (12,125lb) and an afterburner output of 86,290N (19,400lb). To provide a further contingency on take-off the engines had an additional rating of 92,160N (20,720lb), which certified the aircraft to take off from either of the two bow launch positions

BELOW India operates the MiG-29K from the carrier INS *Vikramaditya*, much modified from its original configuration as the *Admiral Gorshkov*, sold to India in a deal which included 12 single-seat MiG-29Ks, and commissioned into the Navy in 2013. *(MiG)*

RIGHT An impressive view of the INS *Vikramaditya* during trials in 2014. The post-Cold War era has seen a gradual shift back to naval aviation and the ability of land-based aircraft to find a new home at sea, especially ruggedly built aircraft such as the MiG-29, despite their abysmally poor range, supplemented by drop tanks which limit the weapons-load carried. *(Indian Navy)*

at a weight of 17,700kg (39,021lb) or from the third launch position further back at a weight of 22,400kg (49,382lb). In other respects the engine installation was the same as that for the MiG-29M, down to the FOD screens in the intakes.

To allow a reduced approach speed, the wing space was increased to 12m (39.37ft), increasing wing area to 43m² (462ft²) with a modified TsAGI P-177m aerofoil shape. It also incorporated double-slotted flaps inboard and flaperons outboard. The aft fuselage deck housed chaff dispensers and the stabiliser

chord was increased to enhance low-speed pitch control, displaying a more characteristic dogtooth as a result. The outer wings were folded hydraulically to present a reduced span of 7.8m (25.59ft), with a folded radome reducing overall length to 15.1m (49.54ft) and for greater resistance to fatigue the wings were fabricated from welded steel.

Additionally, the landing legs were lengthened and fitted with heavy-duty shock absorbers with links to reduce the stroke length on retraction. The wheels had higher-pressure tyres inflated to

BELOW A MiG-29K of the Indian Navy displaying the stowed arrester gear at the rear fuselage between the twin engine exhausts. *(MiG)*

1,965kPa (285lb/in^2) and the nose gear had a modified steering unit giving the wheels a ±90° turn capability for deck handling. An arrester hook was provided.

By removing the dorsal auxiliary intakes additional fuel could be carried in the leading-edge extensions, increasing capacity to 5,720 litres (1,258 gallons) with a total load including three external tanks of more than 6,500kg (14,329lb). For extended-range operations, the K had a refuelling probe offset to port. The braking parachute was eliminated but the dorsal airbrake of the M was retained. Eight underwing stores points and a centreline pylon were available with a total external load capability of 4,500kg (9,920lb), with eight combinations of AAMs and 24 air-to-surface missile options.

ABOVE A close-up of the Indian Air Force MiG-29K displays the recessed air-refuelling probe securely inset to the port side of the forward fuselage, essential for providing the aircraft with the greater range it requires for the naval force protection mission. *(MiG)*

RIGHT The deployed refuelling probe of MiG-29 357 Blue showing the telescoping probe extension piston and brace, automatically extended and retracted with deployment. *(MiG)*

BELOW It was always the intention of the Russian Navy to supplement the MiG-29 with the Su-27 Flanker, this latter type representing the heavier and longer-range response to the emergence of US fighters in the early 1990s. This Su-27K is seen aboard the *Kuznetsov*. *(Via David Baker)*

The weapon control system was virtually the same as that carried by the MiG-29M but the cockpit had a major upgrade, with a single multi-mission control panel for designating air-to-air missile types and the SOI-29K data system, which included a collimator HUD and two CRTs on the instrument panel. To assist with navalised operations, the K had the SN-K navigation set which incorporated an INS-84 inertial navigation system with satellite receiver, an air-data system and a digital processor.

The first flight of the MiG-29K took place on 23 July 1988 but on 1 November 1989 it fell to a Sukhoi T10K2 to be the first Russian aircraft to make a conventional landing on a Russian aircraft carrier. Less than 90 minutes later the MiG-29K Fulcrum-D followed. The imminent demise of the Soviet Union brought change to the plans for an ocean-going carrier force and the second carrier in the class, the *Varyag*, was launched in December 1988 but sold to China in 1998 and renamed *Liaoning*. MiG eventually equipped the *Kuznetsov* with the MiG-29K and sold 45 to the Indian Navy, with 41 delivered by the end of 2016. The Russian Navy ordered 20 MiG-29Ks and 4 two-seat MiG-29KUBs.

MiG-29SMT

During the first half of the 1990s the frustration ran deep that MiG engineers and managers were unable to gain production orders from the cash-strapped government as it reinvented itself in a new political order. While many 'experts' in the West were reluctant to accept the general consensus that the Mig-29 was superior to aircraft such as the F-16, F/A-18 and the Mirage 2000, pilots from outside the Soviet or Warsaw Pact blocs who had the opportunity to fly the aircraft became convinced that it was an exceptionally lethal opponent unlikely to succumb in combat. But lack of range was the one flaw in its performance.

With experience from the 9.15/MiG-29M development, proven in several years of flight tests that scoured out imperfections in the detail, the company re-scoped the basic aircraft, rejecting the 9.35 as too hybrid a step, and worked on an upgrade in direct and linear evolution from the 'M'. The alternative to an outright 'next-generation' leap was a step up through an extensive upgrade and this approach was favoured by Mikhail V. Korzhooyev, who had replaced the sagely Rostislav A. Belyakov who had been the brains and the energy behind the MiG-29.

Work on the new upgrade commenced in an authorisation dated 2 December 1997 and took the essential characteristics of the 9.12S/9.13S as the baseline and opened up a new programme designated 9.17, based on the fat-back version plus the N019MP Topaze multi-mode radar. In essence, what evolved into the SMT took selective aspects of the MiG-29M and applied them to the new variant but without the lightweight aluminium-lithium airframe. MiG aimed

BELOW A derivative of the M variant, the MiG-29SMT was a major upgrade from the 9.12/9.13 type and incorporated a new forward fuselage, cockpit, flight refuelling probe and new humpback profile, visible here during a quiet time at MAKS-2009. *(Via David Baker)*

to make it compatible with the existing production jigs but to install fifth-generation avionics.

The new aircraft would incorporate a revised forward fuselage with a raised cockpit and retractable flight refuelling probe and the intakes and ducting would be a direct transfer from the MiG-29M, including the protective intake grilles. The humpback was increased in convex profile, enlarging the avionics bay with the 'stinger' tail extension and accommodating additional fuel in the leading edges. The new dorsal airbrake was adopted, with the actuating hydraulic rams attached between frames 8 and 9, while a modified ventral airbrake was refined in design. The new wings were of the same area but with four hard-points instead of three and an additional 390 litres (85.8 gallons) each side. The tailerons also had increased area with the leading-edge dogtooth of the MiG-29M.

The Topaz radar could lock on to both air and ground targets and the synthetic aperture radar provided ground mapping with a resolution of 15m (49ft), but as installed for the SMT it was upgraded with cost-saving advantages. All-weather capability was acquired with the N019MP, a centimetre-band radar capable of operating under any weather conditions. The radar was very effective in the

ground operating mode and provided an added role as an effective reconnaissance platform, scanning in three increasing surface areas but with proportionately degraded resolution: 15 x 15km (9.3 x 9.3 miles); 50 x 50km (31 x 31 miles); and 77 x 77km (48 x 48 miles). This information could be datalinked either to a ground control centre or to aircraft such as the A-50 Mainstay AWACS.

A highly useful application allowed the pilot, or a ground controller, to paint a specific target with a marker, which would then provide a much higher resolution of that specific area for targeting a precision-guided munition. The fifth-generation avionics system was built around compatibility with the MIL-STD-1553B datalink bus that had been developed in pursuit of orders from the West.

The cockpit featured an electronic flight instrumentation system (EFIS) which supported four rectangular-shaped multi-function MFI-68 displays. Two of these were 13 x 18cm (5.1 x 8.1in) with full colour LCDs and they were located on the main instrument panel. Additionally, two 7.5 x 7.5cm (2.95 x 2.95in) monochrome LCD displays were on the side consoles. The MiG-29M HOTAS system was installed which integrated flight control and

ABOVE Very much a product of the 'new' Russia, the SMT variant aimed to counter upgrades to the F-16 and the F/A-18 Hornet. It featured an expanded space within the fuselage for a larger and more comprehensive avionics package together with fifth-generation systems. *(MiG)*

weapons selection, designation and firing in a fully hands-on activity.

The new fuel capacity provided a mission radius of 1,550km (963 miles) for the air superiority role and 1,100km (683 miles) for air-to-ground operations as a tactical strike and ground-attack aircraft. Ferry range grew to 3,500km (2,714 miles) or 6,700km (4,163 miles) with one mid-air refuelling. MiG marketing people boasted of the definitive upgrade for the SMT which with integral outboard wing tanks, tanks in the leading-edge extensions and tailboom tanks would increase capacity by 3,170 litres (697 gallons), or by a further 1,800 litres (396 gallons) with underwing drop tanks. The maximum take-off weight had grown to 21,000kg (46,297lb) and the service life had been stretched by 50%, to 6,000 hours.

But all the optimism of the early stages in the evolution of the 9.17 were dashed when serious objections were raised by the MiG production factory which saw all the many structural changes as working against the efficiency of the facilities and creating an aircraft so over-modified that performance would be compromised.

Out went the complicated new air intakes and new wings and tailplane and the changes refocused entirely on the revised avionics and electronics, upon which the enhanced performance of the SMT would rest, further testimony to the outstanding performance growth inherent in the aerodynamic design of the first MiG-29. Fuel capacity would increase by only 1,880 litres (413.6 gallons), with the forward strap-on tank holding 1,400 litres (308 gallons) set between frames 3B and 7 shaped so as to contour around the existing equipment access hatch. The aft strap-on tank would hold 408 litres (105.6 gallons) and would be located between frames 7 and 8. These tanks could be removed to afford access to various components and elements of the aircraft requiring attention for maintenance.

The MiG-29M dorsal airbrake would be incorporated and the actuators situated between frames 8 and 9. The KT-209 main landing gear wheels would also be adopted from the MiG-29M. The aircraft would retain the six underwing store points and have the capacity to carry the same weapons and bomb options designed into the M variant.

In all, cutting back reduced maximum take-off weight to 16,850kg (37,150lb) undoubtedly played an important part in retaining the outstanding handling and manoeuvrability of the type. As the factory had surmised, the added weight of the 'desired' version would have seriously compromised performance. With a maximum load of 4,000kg (8,820lb), the SMT now had a range of 2,100km (1,304 miles) on internal fuel. With a single centreline fuel tank this increased to 2,700km (1,677 miles).

The last pre-production Fulcrum-A (925) was rebuilt to have the new cockpit and refreshed avionics and was displayed at the 1997 Moscow air show in August 1997, and the MiG-29SD 05533 was brought up to the same standard and made the type's first flight on 29 November. Redesignated, and as Blue 405, it carried the aerodynamic mock-up with the revised fuselage spine and made its first flight in that form on 22 April 1998.

This aircraft appeared at the ILA '98 air show at Berlin-Schönefeld with the Thomson-CSF laser designator pod under the fuselage and sporting the semi-retractable refuelling probe. The first fully equipped 9.17 configuration was the MiG-29S demonstrator 35400 Blue 917, with a fully equipped revised fuselage and the new fuel tanks. It made its inaugural flight on 14 July 1998. The first MiG-29SMT (01) was completed on 29 December 1998 and made a demonstration flight for potential customers at Zhukovsky airfield on 12 January 1999.

OPPOSITE **The increased area of the tailerons can be seen in this overhead shot of a MiG-29SMT variant, with the bulging upper fuselage decking enlarged in breadth as well as length.** (MiG)

BELOW **A MiG-29 of the Serbian Air Force carrying AA-8 Aphid missiles under each wing. Note the close clearance for the rearward retracting nose gear.** (via David Baker)

ABOVE Equipped with
the Phazotron Zhuk-
ME all-weather radar,
raising its potential
for seeing-off Western
fighters with new
navigation systems
– a true reflection of
what its designers had
hoped for with the
MiG-29M. *(MiG)*

With Russia now in a very different political
environment to that which prevailed when the
MiG-29 was conceived, marketing against
Western fighters was a vital part of engaging
with capitalist opportunities for export sales to
a much wider and potentially more lucrative
market. Inevitably, comparisons were made
with the new generation of fighters such as the
Dassault Rafale, the Eurofighter Typhoon and
the Boeing F/A-18E/F Super Hornet, and MiG
believed they were at least equal among peers.
Some felt the MiG-29SMT to be superior. But
while range, always the Achilles heel of the type,
was being largely solved, engine performance
was still an anchor on possibilities.

The new and improved RD-33 engines were
now marketed with a 2,000-hour life, which was
an inconceivable accomplishment for a Russian
high-performance engine yet one which brought
the MiG-29SMT fully up to date with Western
standards of reliability and durability. Another
first for the Russian aviation industry. But this
was not the end of the story and changes in
the leadership at MiG brought in the former
head of the design team on the Sukhoi Su27M,
Nikolay F. Nikitin, who forced changes and a
new approach that resulted in such convulsions
that he and the aircraft fell victims to hubris. He
was sacked and the original MiG-29SMT was
abandoned also.

But this was not the end of the SMT.
The designation was reapplied to another
development, arising from the 9.18 design
iteration specification which sought to adapt
the original SMT to the somewhat changed
requirements of the new century. Instead

RIGHT MiG-29SMT
RF-92934 provides
a good view of the
retracted in-flight
refuelling probe
and the reworked
geometry of the engine
intakes. *(Alex Beltyukov)*

of specifying upgrades and improvements originating at the design bureau and offered to customers by the production and sales executives, the new approach provided a menu of possibilities selectively chosen by the customers themselves. In this way the technical package is defined by the buyer and not the producer – a sure sign that capitalism has displaced communism!

The basic premise underpinning the design iterations was to respond to potential customer requirements (including the Russian Air Force) by providing a multi-role fighter out of what had begun life as an air superiority fighter. An idiosyncratic aspect of the evolution on MiG variants and proposed upgrades was the way each change tracked the appearance and disappearance of different design managers or executives. The 9.17 had secured avionics equipment from the Roosskaya Avionika company and it was over this work that Nikolay Nikitin had changed the suite to favour the one developed for the 9.15 iteration. The latest derivation, known as the MiG-29SMT2, emerged through factory project 9.18.

The 9.18 would utilise the Zhuk-ME from Phazotron-NIIR that had been developed as a pulse-Doppler radar incorporating a mechanically scanned slotted array that was intended from the outset for medium and heavy fighters. Developed in part on earlier versions of the MiG-29, the radar operates well in all-weather conditions and produces a 50% better acquisition range than the N019 was capable of, the air-to-ground mode offering a resolution

of 5 x 5m (16.5 x 16.5ft) and with a projected improvement to a resolution of 3 x 3m (10 x 10ft). Development of this particular radar proved a winner for Phazotron-NIIR, this aircraft application beating some of the company's more exotic products in its mission-fit.

A further advantage with this selection of weapon control system opened a broader range of air-to-air and unguided weapons than carried by earlier variants. In adapting the aircraft to the multi-role application, the MiG-29 was truly equitable with comparative

BELOW The Vympel R-77 is a fire-and-forget AAM with a range of up to 110km (68 miles), developed during the 1980s and now equipping MiG-29 and MiG-35 units of the Russian Air Force, with the first export country being India, for its MiG-29K. (Vympel)

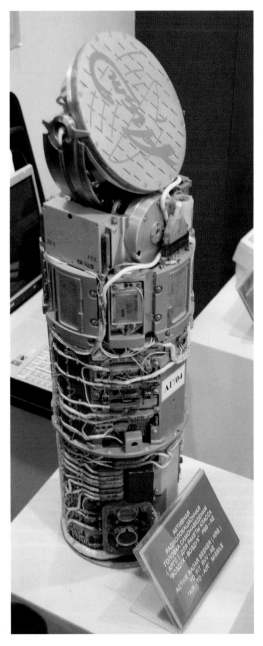

RIGHT The sensor package and head of the R-77, marketed as a synergistic weapon system both with the MiG-29SMT and the MiG-35. *(David Baker)*

BELOW Selected for the MiG-29K and the MiG-35, the TMC KH-31 is an air-to-surface missile with a range of 25–103km (15.5–64 miles), incorporating an L112E seeker in the head as displayed here. *(TMC)*

Western aircraft and this was supplemented with increased internal and external fuel capacity. In-flight refuelling was also designed for compatibility with both Russian and non-Russian tanker aircraft. Fully compatible with NATO-standard requirements, the new avionics were compliant with ICAO standards that opened the aircraft to a wider range of potential customers and to long-range applications.

The 9.18 SMT incorporated the integrated weapon control system and the navigation system combined with the OPrNK-29SM. The SAU-451-05SMT automatic flight control system (AFCS) was produced by Elara Joint-Stock Company and MNPK Avionika. With these integrated into the SMT it truly becomes a Generation 4+ fighter and is close to the original requirement that produced the MiG-29M. An adaptation to make the aircraft even more customer-friendly was an invitation to customers to prepare the upgrades not only to the requirements of the client but to carry them out at the customer's own facilities.

The new MiG-29SMT has benefited from the demands of the customer base and several upgrades selected for export versions have found a home within Russia as the Air Force adopts systems and subsystems requested from the buyer and incorporates them in the domestic production line.

MiG-29M OVT

Six pre-production MiG-29M types that had been manufactured prior to 1991 and the collapse of the Soviet Union received full thrust-vectoring control (TVC) engine nozzles and a fly-by-wire control system to create the first fully vectored combat fighter. The Lockheed Martin F-22 has 2D vectoring and not the full 360° vectoring of the OVT.

For more than a decade MiG had recognised that the aerodynamic flexibility and high manoeuvrability of the basic aircraft could be extended still further by nozzle vectoring, changing the direction of the exhaust and incurring a reaction which would take the aircraft to a new level of slow-speed control. The principal advantage of the 360° rotating nozzle allowed the aircraft to conduct control changes impossible with aerodynamic controls

ABOVE The MiG-29 had demonstrated its ability to out-fly several front-line Western fighters, and sometimes to the embarrassment of pilots in other countries, but the performance of the aircraft was enhanced further with the application of a swivelling nozzle to each engine giving a completely new meaning to thrust-vectoring – hitherto the province of V/STOL types: the MiG-29M OVT. *(MiG)*

RIGHT Unlike the 2D thrust vectoring nozzle of the Lockheed Martin F-22 Raptor, the OVT nozzle was developed after many years of research using the MiG-29M prototype 301 Blue combined with a new engine with greater power and a higher thrust-to-weight ratio. *(Via David Baker)*

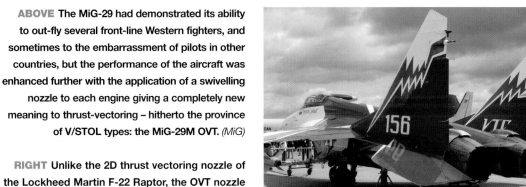

LEFT In almost every other respect, the OVT is a MiG-29M, a type that evolved to the SMT and the OVT, an aircraft which has revitalised interest in the type at home and abroad through spectacular performances at air shows around the world. *(David Baker)*

and to perform highly variable pointing angles for close-in combat.

Research at MiG began in the mid-1990s after Klimov started development work on its own answer to the Lyul'ka-Saturn TVC engine for the Su-27, the AL-31P axisymmetrical nozzle. MiG wanted a more flexible system and instead of a nozzle that could flex in fixed axes built a variable petal element into the nozzle proper, giving it 3D properties. The additional stresses these imposed on the afterburner required reinforcing of the casing, however. Other changes were made to the power output, thrust being increased to 54,900N (12,345lb) at military power and 88,248N (26,455lb) in full afterburner.

Fabrication of the first nozzle assembly, known as KLIVT (*Klimovskiy vektor tyagi*), was completed in 1997 and 50 hours of bench testing prompted almost a thousand modifications. The petal leaves of the terminal exhaust outlet were able to vector the thrust 15° in any direction, initially at a rate of 30°/sec and later 60°/sec. But engineering development outran resources and work was terminated when the Air Force ran out of money for this innovation. Finally, it was resurrected in 2001 and placed on display at the MAKS international air show that year.

Reactivated after a hiatus of eight years, MiG-29M 301 Blue was assigned to test the new engines and their petal exhausts. In August 2003 test pilot Pavel N. Vlasov took it into the air for the first time, and just days later gave a stunning display at the MAKS show. Three years later Vlasov brought the aircraft to the Royal International Air Tattoo and received awards for his aerobatic display, emphasising that it was not about aerodynamics at all but about thrust dynamics! Holding the aircraft almost motionless in the air he demonstrated a 360° backward loop and performed manoeuvres no other aircraft in the world is able to achieve.

Interest in utilising the research and development phase provided opportunities to market the modified MiG-29M to foreign air forces and India expressed an interest in acquiring the type, entering it into its wish-list but without success for the Russian builder. MiG also looked at exporting the KLIVT technology for adaptation to Western fighters, which the company says can be easily

achieved. Outside the traditional customers such as India there are few takers of Russian equipment due largely to the worsening political situation, where there is much encouragement from alpha-countries in the West not to do business with Moscow. Nevertheless, several prominent European aerospace companies are providing Western equipment to foreign air forces flying the MiG-29.

Armchair critics, amateur pundits, even journalists from the so-called 'technical press' leapt to dismiss the MiG-29M OVT as a stunt, as they had when the MiG-29's remarkable aerodynamic handling was seen more than 35 years earlier. But the ability to carry out such extraordinary omnidirectional pointing angles irrespective of the flight path would give the pilot an enduring advantage denied to the opponent. Even the Lockheed Martin F-22 Raptor is no match in such close-quarter combat. Very few defence analysts in the West believe such possibilities would ever exist in future air fighting, believing instead that highly advanced electronic equipment would prevent an enemy aircraft ever getting that close. Suffice to say that it is 60 years since many 'experts' believed that in the age of the missile the day of the manned fighter had gone.

MiG-35

When MiG sought to upgrade the existing aircraft with new fifth-generation data acquisition and targeting systems, equipping it with the capacity to carry the latest weapons from Russian and from non-Russian manufacturers, it issued type number 9.61 and redesignated it the MiG-35. In effect, the aircraft is a consequence of the collapse of the Soviet Union and the rigorous export and sales trade now open worldwide to Russian manufacturers and dealers. It integrates the type with a truly international marketplace and takes the best of the MiG-29M and M2 variants and progresses them further.

One of the most obvious changes is the adoption of the greatly improved RD-33MK engine delivering a dry thrust of 53,000N (11,915lb) and a thrust of 88,300N (19,850lb) with afterburner. This engine addresses several issues with the earlier versions, including a clean

LEFT The Dubai air show 2006 and MiG push out their OVT and the much refined ultimate derivation, the MiG-35. *(David Baker)*

and smokeless exhaust, considered a very great improvement in that it greatly reduces infrared and visual signature, and the use of more exotic materials in the cooled turbine blades.

Perhaps of greater significance is the adoption of the Phazotron Zhuk-AE (export) active electronically scanned array (AESA) radar, which is the first time this type of equipment has been installed in a Russian fighter. The FGA-29 has a 57.5cm (22.6in) antenna and was claimed to have a detection range of 120–130km (74.5–80.8 miles) and to be

BELOW The considerably revamped cockpit and instrument displays with glass displays and a new generation of electronics commensurate with the fourth-generation MiG-29M series and its derivatives. *(MiG)*

ABOVE With fifth-generation avionics and fire-control systems, the MiG-35 has the new and greatly improved RD-33MK engine, providing a clean and virtually smokeless signature, and a new AESA radar, the Zhuk-AE. *(MiG)*

capable of tracking 30 targets of which 6 could be engaged simultaneously. With a weight of 220kg (485lb) the performance was said to have increased, providing a detection range of 148km (92 miles).

This capability was developed further when the designation was changed to FGA-35, carrying a 68.8cm (27in) antenna and providing a detection range of 220km (137 miles), raised later to 250km (155 miles). The manufacturer has claimed (to MiG customers) that the FGA-35 can detect 60 targets, track 6 and engage 8 simultaneously. Scaled variations tailored to specific operational requirements are marketed by Phazotron with a capability of detecting ships at a distance of 300km (186 miles).

Key to the MiG-35 is its open architecture avionics and electronics systems concept that

LEFT The MiG-35 has evolved into a multi-mission capability using a wide range of weapons developed by customers in whose air forces the aircraft can be inserted, with elements of the aircraft offered for regional assembly and updated according to customer requirements. *(MiG)*

allows it to be tailored for customers' specific requirements both in equipment and on performance of the total integrated system. The Zhuk-AE alone warranted careful and favourable comparison with other capabilities on Western-built fighters and, apart from the extended detection range, provided a high resolution in ground-mapping capability. The new optoelectronic targeting system has significantly enhanced the pursuit modes and a podded laser designator can also be carried.

The MiG-35 has nine hard points, with four under each wing and the centreline position, for a total load-carrying capacity of 7,000kg

(15,435lb), with air-to-air weapons including the AA-10, AA-8, AA-11 and AA-12, or air-to-surface weapons AS-17 and AS-14. A wide range of guided and unguided bombs can be carried for the ground-attack role and the type has, in addition, acquired a new set of self-protection jammers from the Italian company GEM-Elletronica.

The MiG-35 was 'launched' at the 2007 Aero India show in Bangalore. Two MiG-35 demonstrators included the single-seat example (961) and the two-seat MiG-35D (967), which had been converted from the MiG-29M2 demonstrator.

ABOVE A fine shot of the MiG-35 showing the remoulded top fuselage reminiscent of earlier variations. *(MiG)*

LEFT The cockpit interior of the much improved layout and systems installed in the MiG-35. *(MiG)*

Chapter Three

Anatomy of the MiG-29

In building a fourth-generation fighter, the MiG design bureau broke the mould and introduced a new blended wing-body combat aircraft unlike anything it had produced before. The challenge for MiG was to come up with a combat aircraft capable of extracting high performance from a uniquely Russian expression of aerodynamic design. At its core was the mighty Klimov RD-33 turbojet engine giving the MiG-29 excess power and operability.

OPPOSITE A forward-facing view showing the brake parachute container and aft structural frames with the engines removed and the enclosure panels constituting the aft fuselage assembly. *(MiG)*

73

ABOVE The RD-33
engine was developed
in OKB-117 during
the early 1970s with
a team led by S.P.
Izotov. As the first
afterburning turbojet
produced by Klimov,
it was selected for
the MiG-29 over the
Tumansky R-67-300.
(Via David Baker)

Engine and associated subsystems

Designed specifically for the MiG-29, the two Klimov RD-33 dual-shaft, axial-flow, turbofan engines incorporate a 13-stage compressor (four low pressure, nine high pressure) with ring combustion chambers and afterburners, located side by side in the aft section of the fuselage. The turbine is of single-stage high-pressure, single-stage low-pressure design.

Each engine has a length of 4.229m (166.5in) with a maximum diameter of 1.04m (40.9in) and a dry mass of 1,055kg (2,326lb). It has a maximum thrust of 50.0kN (11,230lb) or 81.3kN (18,285lb) with afterburner. It has a pressure ratio of 21:1 and a bypass ratio of 0.49:1 with a turbine inlet temperature of 1,407°C (2,565°F) and a thrust-to-weight ratio of 4.82:1 dry or 7.9:1 with afterburner.

Two variable intakes installed in nacelles below the wing roots ensure a coherent flow of air to the two engines; variable exhaust nozzle sections are also provided and foreign object damage (FOD) mitigation is effected through closing the air intakes after landing and for normal ground operations. When these ramps are closed, air is ingested through louvres located on the upper surface of the wing root, a characteristic feature of the aircraft.

The two engines each drive a dedicated engine gearbox which together are bifurcated to a single accessory gearbox. This is started by an auxiliary power unit (APU), which spins up the accessory box to start the main engines. Electrical power is provided by an AC and a DC generator, both driven by a gearbox, while two batteries provide emergency power for contingency situations. The design of this emergency power arrangement went through several changes and evolutions before the current configuration designed to accommodate cut-in and cut-out situations.

The APU gas turbine unit is supported by electrical power supplied from either batteries or an external power source and the entire engine start procedure is sufficiently flexible to ensure safe start and operation from poorly equipped ground units or from remote and isolated airfields, a prerequisite for much of the design and engineering philosophy stipulated at an early design phase.

As indicated above, air is provided to the two engines by dedicated intakes located beneath the wing roots and, on the ground, air ingested through louvres on the upper surface of the wing roots. In flight, the variable ramps

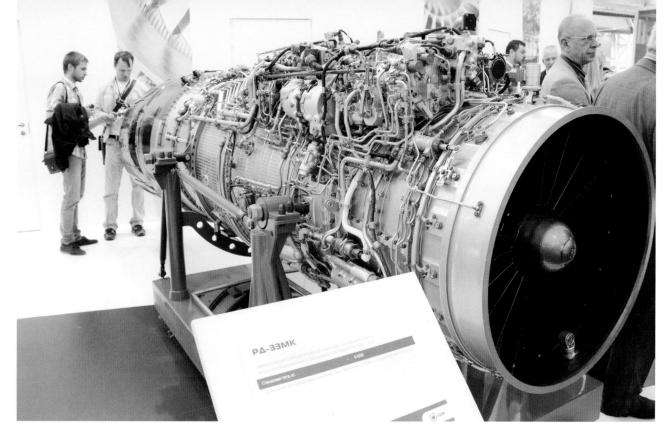

control air intake and flow and by stator vanes on the first two stages of the high-pressure compressor. This arrangement did much to improve handling under a wide range of operating conditions and situations.

From the intakes, air is routed to the four stages of the low-pressure compressor and from there to a hot main stream and a cold

ABOVE The RD-33 has been subject to several variants, upgrades, modifications and adaptation into several applications. The RSD-33N/B is the basic engine with afterburner and has been applied to aircraft such as the Ilyushin Il-102. The RD-93 powered the JF-17, while the SMR-95 has repositioned the accessory gearbox below the engine. The series 3 had a revised service life and was adopted for the MiG-29M and SMT as well as OVT applications. The RD-33MK is assigned to the MiG-29K and KUB variants. *(David Baker)*

LEFT The RD-33MK has a dry mass of 1,145kg (2,524lb) and a service life extended to 4,000 hours. The 7% additional power of the engine produces 88,000N (19,800lb) thrust, which allows the MiG-29K unassisted take-off from carrier decks or from land in hot climates. *(David Baker)*

Mikoyan MiG-29M. *(Mike Badrocke)*

1 Glass-fibre radome
2 Pitot head
3 Vortex generating strake
4 Radar scanner with IFF array
5 Radome mounting ring frame
6 Scanner tracking mechanism
7 N-010 Zhuk multi-mode pulse-Doppler radar
8 Incidence vane
9 Radar equipment racks
10 Yaw vane
11 Infra-red (IR)/laser/TV seeker head
12 Dynamic pressure probe
13 IR/laser equipment module
14 Temperature sensor
15 Command guidance antenna
16 Cockpit front pressure bulkhead
17 Forward fuselage chine fairing
18 Cannon muzzle aperture
19 Gun gas suppression duct
20 Underfloor Doppler equipment
21 Rudder pedals
22 Instrument panel, dual monochrome CRT primary displays
23 Control column, analogue fly-by-wire flight control system
24 Instrument panel shroud
25 Frameless windscreen panel
26 Head-up display
27 Canopy, open position
28 Rear view mirrors
29 Ejection seat headrest
30 Seat stabilising drogue guns
31 K-36DM ejection seat
32 Slide mounted throttle levers, HOTAS controls
33 Canopy external release
34 Side console panel
35 Cockpit section framing, spot welded structure
36 Cockpit rear pressure bulkhead
37 Ammunition magazine, 100 rounds
38 Cannon barrel mounting
39 Nosewheel retraction jack
40 Levered suspension nosewheel strut
41 Twin nosewheels with pneumatic brakes, aft retracting
42 Hydraulic steering mechanism
43 Forward and forward oblique ECM antenna fairings
44 Link collector box
45 GSh-301, 30mm cannon
46 Avionics equipment bay, communications
47 Canopy pressure seal
48 Circuit breaker control box
49 Canopy hydraulic actuator and jettison strut
50 Flush ARK Mayak radio compass antenna
51 Control rod linkages, mechanical back-up system
52 Canopy hinge point
53 Avionics equipment bay, nav/attack system
54 Fuselage chine section integral fuel tank, total internal fuel capacity 6,000–6,250 lit (1,320–1,375 Imp gal)
55 Welded aluminium/lithium tank structure
56 Intake variable front ramp hydraulic actuator
57 Port engine air intake
58 Variable capture area intake hinged lower lip
59 Intake lip hydraulic actuator
60 Hinged internal FOD screen
61 Intake rear ramp hydraulic actuator
62 Boundary layer spill duct
63 Dorsal equipment bay, flight control equipment
64 Hydraulic equipment module
65 Main hydraulic reservoir
66 ADF antenna
67 Starboard mainwheel, stowed position
68 Starboard wing leading edge flap
69 Leading edge flap actuators
70 Starboard wing weapons carriage, representative fit
71 Forward radar warning antenna
72 Starboard navigation light
73 Rear radar warning antenna
74 Starboard aileron
75 Aileron hydraulic actuator
76 Starboard plain flap
77 Starboard wing integral fuel tank
78 Fin leading edge root extension
79 Fuselage centre section integral fuel tankage
80 Chaff/flare launchers, port and starboard
81 Machined wing attachment fitting main frames

82 Engine accessory equipment gearboxes
83 Central combining gearbox
84 Airborne auxiliary power unit (APU)
85 APU air intake, ventral exhaust
86 Engine oil tanks
87 Dorsal airbrake
88 Airbrake hydraulic actuators
89 Airbrake panel honeycomb composite construction
90 Starboard tailplane pivot bearing
91 Tailplane hydraulic actuator
92 Rudder hydraulic actuator
93 Starboard composite fin
94 Fin tip communications antenna fairing
95 Tail navigation light
96 ILS antenna
97 Starboard rudder
98 Starboard all-moving tailplane
99 Radar warning antenna
100 Variable area afterburner nozzle
101 Twin brake parachutes
102 Hinged tailcone parachute door
103 Fin honeycomb composite skin panels
104 UHF/VHF antenna
105 EW antenna
106 Port ILS antenna
107 Static discharger
108 Port rudder
109 Rudder honeycomb composite construction
110 Rudder hydraulic actuator
111 Radar warning antenna
112 Port all-moving tailplane
113 Tailplane honeycomb composite trailing edge panel
114 Static discharger
115 Tailplane rib structure
116 Leading edge dog-tooth
117 Tailplane hydraulic actuator
118 Tailplane pivot fitting
119 Fin root structure
120 RD-33K afterburning engine
121 Artificial feel system (Q-feel) pressure sensors
122 Tailplane control hydraulic accumulators
123 Composite one-piece engine lower cowling
124 Port flap honeycomb composite structure
125 Aileron hydraulic actuator
126 Aileron honeycomb composite structure
127 Port aileron
128 Static discharger
129 Rear radar warning antenna
130 Port navigation light
131 Radar warning receiver
132 Forward radar warning antenna

133 Wing rib structure
134 Three-spar wing panel
135 Outer wing panel pylon hardpoints
136 Port leading edge flap
137 Outboard pylon/R-73E launch rail
138 Outer intermediate pylon/AAM-AE launch rail
139 Inboard wing panel integral fuel tank
140 Inboard pylon attachment hardpoints
141 Flap hydraulic jack
142 Main undercarriage hydraulic retraction jack
143 Wing root attachment fittings
144 Pressure refuelling connection
145 Ground power socket
146 Port mainwheel bay
147 Ground test panels
148 Mainwheel door
149 Landing lamp
150 Leading edge flap actuators
151 Inboard pylons/Kh-31P launch rails
152 Port mainwheel with pneumatic brake
153 Wing tank pylon mounting
154 1,540 lit (339 Imp gal) centreline fuel tank
155 APU exhaust duct through tank rear fairing
156 Centreline tank forward attachment and fuel transfer fittings
157 KAB-500KR, television guided 500kg (1,1021b) bomb
158 KAB-500L, laser guided bomb
159 External fuel tanks inboard pylon only, 1,150 lit (253 Imp gal) capacity
160 KMGU-2 submunition dispenser
161 Kh-31P air-to-surface missile
162 R-27 (AA-10 Alamo) air-to-air missile
163 R-73E (AA-11 Archer) air-to-air missile
164 Kh-29T (AS-12 Kedge) television-guided air-to-surface missile
165 Kh-29L (AS-12 Kedge) laser guided missile nose section
166 AAM-AE ('AMRAAMski') air-to-air missile

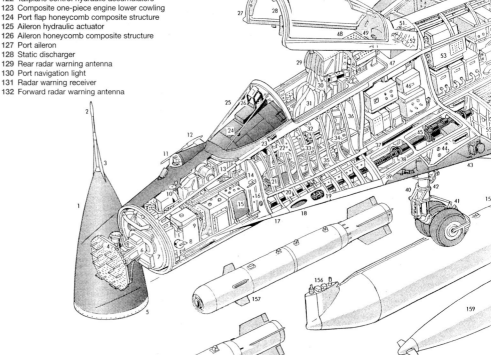

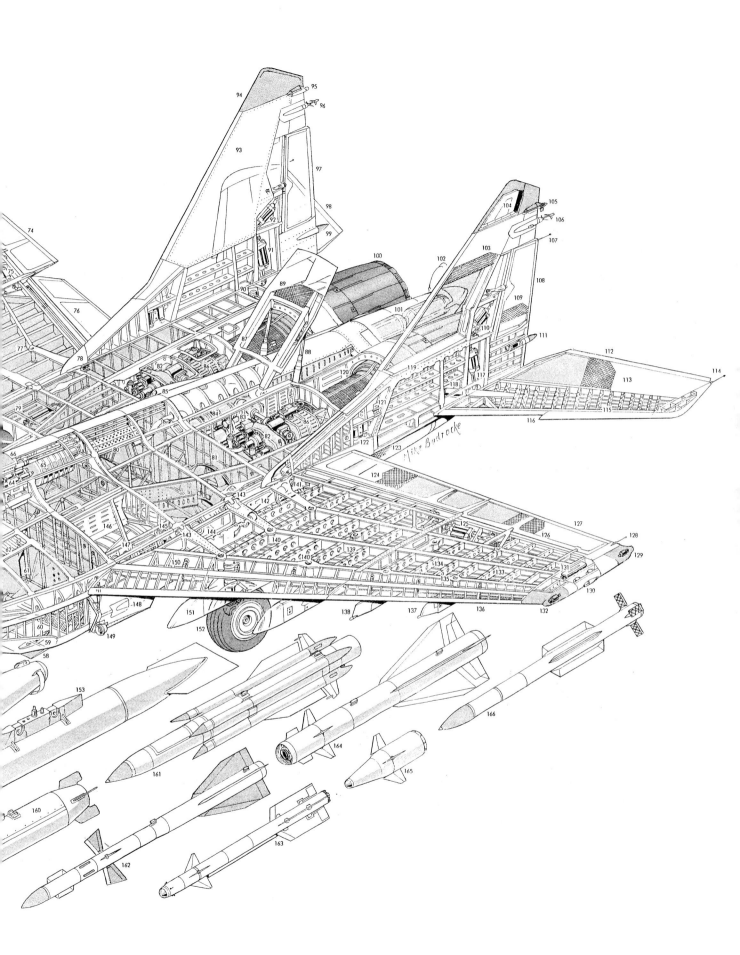

Mike Budrocke

bypass flow. The bypass air is moved to an annular duct that surrounds the high-pressure compressor, the combustion chamber and the turbine section, where it rejoins the main flow in the air mixer of the afterburner section. The main stream, meanwhile, flows through the nine-stage high-pressure compressor section to the annular combustion chamber where a controlled quantity of fuel is injected. It is ignited by igniter plugs for engine start-up.

Hot high-pressure gases from the combustion chamber expands through the turbine section and then mixes with the cold bypass air where it expands further. This proved difficult to engineer in the early stages of the engine design process and while seeming to be a simple ducting and thermal expansion issue did produce some challenges in the type of materials selected for this part of the engine.

The turbine section consists of two single-stage turbines driving the high-pressure compressor and the low-pressure compressor respectively and the two rotor speeds are mechanically independent of each other. The engine speeds are displayed through a tachometer that shows the high-pressure compressor speed of both engines as a percentage of the nominal maximum revolutions per minute (rpm). During operation of the afterburner added fuel is injected to the hot gas stream by the afterburner spray bars, which are located behind the turbine section.

The exhaust area is fully variable and is controlled automatically to obtain the desired thrust within engine operating limits. The engine control unit (ECU) controls the hydro-mechanical equipment of the engine control system and this supplies discrete fail signals to the warning system.

The engine compressor bleed air system takes air from the low-pressure (LP) compressor and the high-pressure (HP) compressor at three specific locations. The LP compressor bleeds air for the fuel accumulator tank pressurisation, for the external tank pressurisation, and for the internal tank pressurisation. Bleed air from the fifth stage of the HP compressor provides high-pressure and low-pressure turbine rotor and stator cooling while the seventh stage provides air conditioning and pressurisation as well as anti-icing for the low-pressure compressor intake.

Each engine is fitted with a self-contained dry sump full pressure oil system, which ensures oil circulation for lubrication and cooling of the engine's main bearings and of the engine gearbox. Excessive pressure build-up is averted by venting the bearings and the oil tank. Oil from the main engine bearings is returned by scavenge pumps to the oil tank by means of two separate and independent fuel-cooled oil coolers serving the engine and afterburner fuel systems. Filters are installed inside the oil return lines in front of the scavenge pumps.

The return line also contains an oil temperature sensor downstream and a magnetic chip detector that provides an indication of engine wear and a warning that components are breaking down and very likely to cause a stall or catastrophic malfunction. Two suction pipes draw return oil from the engine gearbox and feed it to the output side of the main lubrication pump. After engine shutdown, oil from the forward main bearing is drained to a separate return tank that is connected to a scavenge pump.

The three engine bearing chambers, the oil tank and the oil–air separator are vented to the engine gearbox, which in turn is vented overboard via a centrifugal breather. For accommodating negative-g flight, a pendulum-like suction pipe inside the oil supply tank ensures an adequate oil supply to the main lubrication pump irrespective of the acceleration vector.

The temperature of the engine oil is sensed by a probe installed inside the oil return line and if defined temperature boundaries are exceeded the pilot will get a warning via the fault detection unit. This will illuminate a red warning caption situated on the telelight panel in the cockpit. The upper boundary for the oil temperature limit is 195°C (383°F), above which the light will be illuminated.

Indications of a problem with the oil pressure is provided via a measurement pick-off in the port-side engine, where a low reading for 20 seconds or more initiates a red warning caption and flashing light via the engine fault detection unit. This is triggered if the actual pressure falls below 1.8(±0.18) side slip vane heater kPa/cm² at 50–89% rpm or below 2.7(±0.27) kPa/cm² at greater than 89% rpm for more than 20 seconds.

OPPOSITE The Polish Air Force put on a display of its MiG-29 Fulcrum-As at the 2015 Royal International Air Tattoo and demonstrated the excess power through a series of impressive manoeuvres that displayed the thrust band in mil-power without afterburner. *(Steve Rendle)*

Any contamination by shaved or chipped metal from the interior of the engine sensed by a detector in the oil return line illuminates a red flashing warning light and caption on the telelight panel. This too is aligned with respective engines and operates for 17 seconds when the oil pressure is low. It is assumed that abrasion will begin after 20 seconds and this usually results in an engine shutdown by the pilot.

The engine fuel system pressurises, meters, atomises and injects fuel into the high-pressure compressor discharge air stream. This system is controlled by the engine fuel control subsystem as a result of different internal operating signals. The entire system and associated subsystems consists of a low-pressure and a high-pressure system. Fuel is supplied to the low-pressure fuel pump of the low-pressure system by two fuel booster pumps situated inside the engine supply tank. The pressurised fuel then passes through a filter and from there is distributed to the engine control pump (ECP), the afterburner fuel pump and the nozzle high-pressure pump integral with the high-pressure system.

The ECP meters the fuel in response to the throttle position and to various pre-selected engine parameters. The engine fuel is routed via the drain and cut-off valve, the fuel-cooled oil coolers and the engine fuel flow divider valve to the nozzles of the first and second manifolds of the engine combustion chamber, where injection to the air stream takes place. The ECP supplies fuel to position the actuators of the variable stator vanes of the high-pressure compressor inlet, the afterburner ignition control and the automatic engine and afterburner control equipment.

The hydro-mechanical engine control system is manually controlled by throttle inputs and operated by an electronic engine control unit. It is functionally divided into four distinct subsystems: the ECU, the ECP, the afterburner and nozzle control unit and the engine starter unit. The throttle produces an engine speed demand signal which is routed mechanically to the ECP and to the afterburner and nozzle control unit. The ECU supplies electrical control signals to solenoids in the ECP, to the afterburner, and to the nozzle control unit and engine starter unit so that it can modify engine performance within the predefined safety limits for routine operation.

The performance range of the engine control system is divided into four discrete segments: idle, cruise, military-power (mil-power) and afterburner. The specific range of systems or subsystems active to control the engine depends on the place in which the throttle is positioned and is displayed on an accompanying illustration and explained in its caption.

In addition to the normal ECS modes there are several discrete functions for specific operating requirements: automatic engine start sequence both on the ground and in flight; control of the variable air intake guide vanes of the high-pressure compressor; providing a fuel pressure signal to control the afterburner ignition system through a servo unit; the supply of servo fuel to the control valve of the engine anti-icing system; and control of the air intake flow during weapon deployment so as to prevent a stall.

The ECU is designed to optimise the fuel flow for thrust demand, which is a function controlled by the throttle, by consideration of the engine's environmental factors, and by the engine-specific parameters. The parallel electronic function lanes of the ECU continuously receive speed signals from the shafts of the high-pressure and low-pressure compressors, the low-pressure compressor inlet temperature, and the low-pressure turbine outlet and exhaust gas temperature. They

BELOW The four operating settings for the throttle include idle, cruise, mil-power and afterburner. The table shows throttle position, engine control unit (ECU), engine control pump (ECP) and the afterburner and nozzle control unit. High-pressure compressor (NH) and low-pressure compressor (NL) are indicated. (MiG)

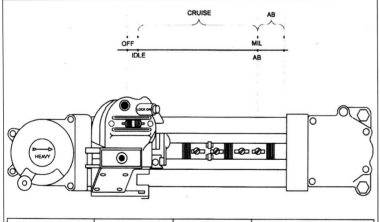

Throttle position	ECU	ECP	AB and Nozzle Control Unit
IDLE	-	NH	NL
Cruise	NL Correction depending on air mass flow	NH	NL
MIL	NH, NL, T4	-	Nozzle area
AB	T4	-	-

also receive signals from the compressor inlet temperature and from the exhaust nozzle outlet by means of sensors within the engine.

In the following discussion, the speed of the high-pressure compressor is abbreviated to NH and the speed of the low-pressure compressor to NL, with NH indicated to the pilot on the engine rpm indicator. The ECU compares these parameters against pre-set guiding schedules and limit values and responds with electrical control signals to solenoids in separate control units of the engine fuel, afterburner, ignition valve and exhaust nozzle and intake.

At engine-start the ECU, together with the hydro-mechanical control devices, provides control as a function of throttle setting, engine fuel pressure and the air pressure ratio between the compressor discharge and the ambient air. At run-up to idle, the ECU limits the exhaust gas temperature as a function of the compressor inlet temperature. During cruise operation in flight the ECU limits the NL as a function of the compressor inlet temperature and of the throttle setting. It also maintains the relationship between the NH and the NL by modulating the primary exhaust nozzle area.

During mil-power and afterburner operation the ECU inhibits the NH and the exhaust gas temperature as a function of the compressor inlet temperature by way of modulating the engine fuel flow. It also schedules the NL as a function of the compressor inlet temperature by modulating the primary exhaust nozzle area. And it limits the NL as a function of the compressor inlet temperature by modulating and controlling the engine fuel pressure. In afterburner, the ECU controls the afterburner ignition logic and operates the engine performance boundaries so as to protect against compressor surge.

The ECU has built-in test equipment designed to self-test so-called limitation lanes, defined as control paths to inhibit stress on the engine. By way of 'reversionary' lanes a failure is circumvented by controlling the NH speed controller to reduce the speed of the NH by 6–7% and transmit information to the warning system that provides an indication to the pilot on his warning display panel in the form of an instruction LEFT ENG STBY SYS.

The NH speed controller operates as an

integral functioning component of the engine control pump and adjusts the rpm of the high-speed compressor as a function of the throttle position and the compressor inlet temperature. It consists of a centrifugal governor driven at a speed that is determined to be a function of the NH and which is controlled by the throttle angle via a mechanical linkage. The set position is continuously modified by an hydraulic actuator that receives a fuel pressure signal representing the compressor inlet temperature.

The output of the NH speed controller represents corrected rpm demand and operates the fuel-metering valve to set up the required engine fuel flow. At a selected throttle setting, the engine thrust remains constant regardless of the speed or altitude of the aircraft, except when overridden by any limiters that may be set. These are adjustable and can be changed

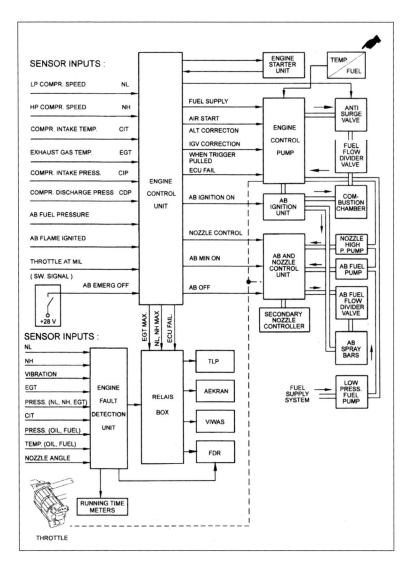

ABOVE The flow path for the engine control system (see glossary for abbreviations), which is a hydro-mechanical design allowing manual inputs via the throttle and by the engine control unit. *(MiG)*

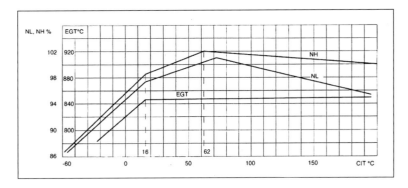

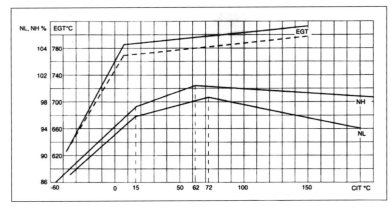

TOP The function of the engine control unit in normal power mode is illustrated, with the percentage of NL, NH indicated in the vertical column and the compressor inlet temperature in degrees centigrade along the bottom proportional to the settings. *(MiG)*

ABOVE The ECP operating in limited power mode with parameters identical to those of the normal power mode. As with the previous chart, the engine gas temperature is shown as a function of compressor intake temperature measured against high- and low-speed compressor values. *(MiG)*

BELOW The high-speed controller for the high-pressure compressor is shown for normal power mode against maximum rpm. *(MiG)*

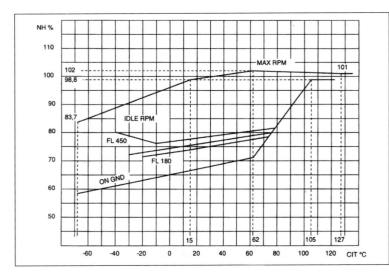

at a ground servicing level or at a strip-down inspection. The maximum speed of the engine is controlled by the scheduled limits of the engine control unit, which receives actual NH from a pulse probe. The electrical signal is converted to a positioning signal for an electrical pressure control solenoid that modifies the fuel flow.

Conflicts between the corrected rpm demand signal and the limit signal during maximum engine speed are avoided by an offset speed signal issued from the ECU so as to set the corrected rpm signal about 3% above the input signal. But should the ECU detect an NH over-speed on receiving an input from the NH pulse probe it assumes a failure has occurred in the NH speed controller. When the throttle setting is reduced the primary exhaust nozzle controller reduces the primary nozzle area, which increases the compressor discharge pressure and reduces the NL as well. When NH increases by more than 2% above the pre-set value, after two seconds the ECU issues signals to the warning system. These can also be initiated by the engine fault detection unit if the NH accelerates to 103.5% of rpm within two to three seconds. This triggers a master alarm on the cockpit display.

At idle and under cruise operation the NH is controlled only by the corrected rpm function of the NH speed controller and by the primary nozzle modulation for NL guidance. Fluctuations in compressor speed rpm are kept within ±1.5% in idle setting and within ±1.2% rpm in cruise condition. At mil-power and afterburner steady state operation the maximum speed of the engine is controlled by the patterned schedules of the ECU, by the corrected rpm function of the NH speed controller and by the afterburner nozzle control unit for thrust and NL guidance. Any rpm fluctuations of the compressor speed are maintained within ±0.6%.

The control of transients in engine acceleration and deceleration between idle and mil-power is accomplished by repositioning of the NH speed controller using appropriate throttle settings. The ECU receives values of compressor intake pressure and compressor discharge pressure and this controls the airflow through the compressor by regulating the necessary quantity of fuel. The correct fuel–air ratio is monitored by the ECU to ensure combustion. The airflow is controlled by the air inlet ramps and by the two-stage inlet guide vanes of the high-pressure compressor on demand from the ECU.

The NL speed controller works through the low-pressure compressor to provide an airflow to the high-pressure compressor and a secondary airstream to cool the hot section of the engine. Further, the low-pressure compressor provides a high increase of thrust due to the increase of airflow by mixing the cold secondary air with the hot gases from the turbine section.

The gas pressure in the air mixer must be kept lower than the turbine exhaust pressure so as to ensure that the laminar gas flows through the two turbine sections to prevent turbine stall. When the pressure in the gas mixer decreases and the difference in pressure across the turbines increases, the turbines can extract more energy from the mass flow and NH and NL values will increase. The ECU controls the increase of NH by reducing the engine fuel flow, whereas the increase of NL is controlled by increasing the mixer pressure, thereby decreasing the pressure difference across the turbine section.

The mixer pressure is controlled by modulating the primary exhaust nozzle area and the relation of the NL to NH is scheduled and limited by the engine control unit by changing the nozzle jet area at cruising, mil-power and afterburner power levels. Both parameters of NL and NH are corrected for the compressor inlet temperature. To prevent NL over-speed when the primary exhaust nozzle controller fails an NL maximum speed limiter lane within the ECU is incorporated. This prevents an NL increase of more than 2% rpm above the programmed value by reducing the engine fuel flow, also affecting the NH speed control setting. At over-speed, signals are issued by the ECU to the warning signal after a delay of two seconds. The same warnings are triggered by the engine fault detection unit if the NL accelerates to 103.5% of rated rpm within two to three seconds.

The engine fault detection unit compares actual engine parameters to pre-set schedules and generates discrete signals for the warning system if parameters exceed the limits. In addition, the unit issues a signal to engage the

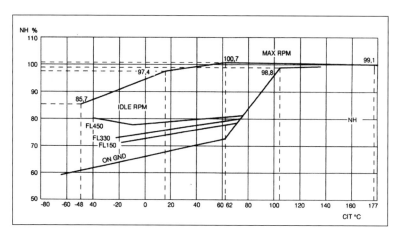

AC electrical power generator and activates the nitrogen system to pressurise the fuel system when NH exceeds 55% rpm. The fault detection unit is connected to the engine system switch on the system power control panel on the pilot's right-hand console.

Warnings for engine over-temperature conditions require the throttle to be retarded and NH and compressor discharge pressures to be decreased to normal operating values. The engine control pump limiter is activated to reduce the engine fuel flow rate and the NH and engine exhaust gas temperatures are stabilised. The master caution flashing light is illuminated on the pilot's display when the sensed engine exhaust gas temperature exceeds the design value by 40°–60°C (104°–140°F) for 0.2sec. This information, along with other sensory readings, is captured on the flight data recorder.

Special vibration sensors are installed on the engine in close proximity to vital components such as bearings and gears, which convert mechanical oscillations and vibrations into an electrical signal. The amplitude of the signal is proportional to the magnitude of the vibration. As soon as the vibration level exceeds a pre-set limit for NH greater than 35% rpm the engine fault detection unit issues a warning signal to the various warning systems, including a flashing light situated on the master caution and warning display in the cockpit. Similarly, if engine fuel pressure exceeds 7.35(±0.49)MPa for two to three seconds a master alarm light is illuminated.

The anti-surge system for the engines of the MiG-29 is selected when the pilot activates the ANTI SURGE switch on the system power panel, enabling it to automatically detect and counteract engine surge. A sensor detects fluctuations in

ABOVE Limited power mode requires lower rpm values and here the chart shows how those parameters for high- and low-speed compressor values measure off against temperature. *(MiG)*

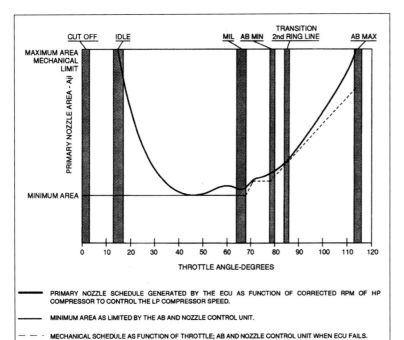

PRIMARY NOZZLE SCHEDULE GENERATED BY THE ECU AS FUNCTION OF CORRECTED RPM OF HP COMPRESSOR TO CONTROL THE LP COMPRESSOR SPEED.

MINIMUM AREA AS LIMITED BY THE AB AND NOZZLE CONTROL UNIT.

MECHANICAL SCHEDULE AS FUNCTION OF THROTTLE; AB AND NOZZLE CONTROL UNIT WHEN ECU FAILS.

ABOVE The variation of nozzle area with throttle positions at idle, mil-power and afterburner with appropriate second ring lines proportional to the area of the nozzle (Aj1). *(MiG)*

the discharge pressure of the high-pressure compressor. When fluctuations occur the ECU issues control signals and when the fluctuations cease the signals persist for a further 0.5sec but for no longer than a total of 2.4sec.

The control signals provide a variety of functions including closing the inlet guide vanes by 25°, closing the drain and shut-off valve to interrupt engine fuel flow to the combustion chamber for up to three seconds, and sending a command to the engine control pump to close the inlet guide vane of the high-pressure compressor. It also sends a signal to open the NL control lane of the ECU to shift the programme schedule for 5% NL which, as a result, opens the primary nozzle for a corrected value.

The anti-surge control also signals to close the intake ramp for an additional 10% maximum, limited by the applicable ramp travel schedule and proportionality to the duct ramp system (which see later). It also sends a start signal to the engine starter unit to actuate a preventive engine start cycle for eight seconds. This activates the green caption LH/RH ENG START light on the telelight panel.

If the discharge pressure sensor of the high-pressure compressor fails, the control signals from the ECU are automatically switched off after 2.5sec. When the anti-surge system is activated and an additional fault signal from the engine high-temperature lane is present, anti-

surge actions are operative for the duration of the high-temperature condition plus 0.5sec. The total duration of extended system operation is limited to a maximum of 8.0sec, but if the high-temperature condition persists for more than 2.4sec engine fuel flow will be alternately interrupted by the drain and shut-off valve for 2.4sec and permitted for 1.2sec.

The engine anti-surge system is deactivated at altitudes below 2,740m (9,000ft) mean sea level with air speeds below Mach 1.15, with the exception that if the 30mm gun or a missile is fired, or if an overheat condition exists, the system is activated and a preventative engine relight cycle is initiated. As with the over-speed and engine temperature warning systems, this information is preserved on the flight data recorder.

The afterburner fuel system supplies and regulates fuel flow into the engine tailpipe for combustion, the ignited fuel–air mixture increasing engine thrust. It consists of an annular casing that contains the air mixing chamber and a diffuser type of afterburner combustion chamber. The diffuser ensures reduction of airflow velocity, which results in a gain of time for hot and cold air mixing, afterburner fuel injection and ignition. The injection system consists of flame holders and three spray bars with injection nozzles for radial fuel injection.

The required fuel flow for afterburner ignition is controlled by the ECU, which also sets the exhaust nozzle to a position for minimum afterburner power while simultaneously activating the ignition unit. The system ensures ignition in the afterburner combustion chamber, stable burning at minimum afterburner thrust, modulation of afterburner fuel flow at different power settings, afterburner thrust transients control and afterburner ignition timing. Afterburner fuel mass delivered to the spray bars is controlled by the throttle and the compressed intake temperature input to the afterburner and nozzle control unit. It is constrained within safe operating limits by the ECU.

To start afterburner operation, the throttle is advanced to the afterburner range, with ignition possible at engine speeds of at least 72–76% rpm which initiates fuel flow from the low-pressure fuel pump (of the low-pressure system) to the afterburner fuel pump. When the throttle is advanced within activation range the afterburner fuel pump increases the fuel pressure and supplies it to the afterburner and nozzle control unit. The pressurised fuel is delivered via the afterburner fuel-cooled oil cooler to the afterburner pressurising valve and to the nozzles of the first of the three spray bars. A fuel-pressure sensor detects the system pressure and issues an appropriate signal to the ECU.

The required fuel flow for afterburner ignition is controlled by the ECU itself, which also sets the exhaust nozzle to a position for minimum afterburner power while simultaneously activating the ignition unit. The ignition unit controls the internal pressure and fuel flow to the ejector nozzle and spin nozzle of the afterburner torch igniter. Jet starter fuel is supplied to the ejector nozzle inside the combustion chamber and to the spin nozzle. Starter jet fuel from the ejector nozzle ignites inside the combustion chamber, and this torch also ignites the starter fuel supplied to the spin nozzle. This action extends the torch to the afterburner combustion area to ignite the limited, minimum afterburner fuel from the first spray bar.

Two flame sensors are installed behind the afterburner flame holder to detect the ignited afterburner fuel and to initialise the shut-off of the afterburner ignition process by the ECU. Simultaneously, the ECU establishes the normal fuel flow for minimum afterburner operation. When the afterburner flame sensors detect a flame, the ECU issues a status signal to the warning equipment, which responds by presenting a status indication to the telelight panel in the cockpit, which in the case of the port-side engine would read LH AB ENG.

The afterburner control system is a hydro-mechanical system using fuel as an actuating fluid. It is manually controlled by throttle inputs

RIGHT Variable throttle settings balance against aerodynamic performance in the MiG-29OVT with 3D vectored thrusting. The ability to shift between aerodynamic and thrust-vectoring and the electronic control systems that made this possible were translated across to the space shuttle Buran. In that vehicle, designed to go into orbit, aerodynamic control and thruster firings were integrated for combined use in the upper atmosphere. *(MiG)*

and is automatically operated by the ECU. The main components include the ECU itself, the afterburner and the afterburner nozzle control unit, the latter two of which regulate the fuel to spray bars at a rate proportional to the slope of the throttle setting. Because the afterburner throttle position is beyond the mil-power level the basic ECU senses a demand for 100% rpm for all afterburner throttle settings.

As soon as the afterburner is selected the ECU, the afterburner and nozzle control unit and the afterburner ignition unit control system will regulate the ignition sequence as a function of throttle setting and of compressor discharge pressure, corrected to the compressed intake temperature. It will regulate the time of torch ignition as a function of fuel pressure and it will adjust the primary exhaust nozzle setting to the minimum cross-section.

During afterburner operation the fuel is delivered to the first spray bar for ignition, with fuel to the second and third spray bars as a function of fuel pressure with afterburner acceleration according to the throttle burst, limited only by constructional drag inside the control units. When the throttle is moved from idle to maximum afterburner the system will not ignite below 72–76% rpm. When afterburner blowout occurs during operation the ECU limits the afterburner fuel flow to the quantity required for minimum afterburner operation after a delay of approximately 0.5 seconds.

In the event of a need to shut down the afterburner during an emergency, the AB EMERG OFF switch on the engine emergency panel has to be set to OFF. The ECU together with the afterburner and nozzle control unit and afterburner fuel divider valve will reduce the fuel pressure so that the spray bars close in sequence to relax the shutdown shock.

Because thrust is directly proportional to gas velocity at the exhaust, pressure and temperature in the afterburner area have to be as high as possible to obtain a high nozzle pressure ratio at the de Laval nozzle. Accordingly, two sets of cylindrical nozzles, operating together, make up the variable exhaust nozzle system. The primary, or inner, nozzle controls the convergent portion of the nozzle, while the secondary, or outer, nozzle controls the divergent portion of the assembly.

Both nozzles are mechanically linked for common operation by the synchronisation unit, using fuel as the actuating fluid. The exhaust gas leaves the primary nozzle at subsonic velocity and is accelerated to supersonic velocity by the controlled expansion of the gas. The pressure of the gas, before leaving the secondary nozzle, equals ambient air pressure.

Pressurised fuel as a control medium is supplied from the high-pressure nozzle pump to the nozzle control section of the afterburner and nozzle control unit. Depending on the inputs, the afterburner nozzle control unit modifies fuel pressure to the synchronisation unit for nozzle area adjustment. Throttle setting and corrected NL as a function of corrected NH are utilised to schedule the correct primary nozzle area. During engine operation below mil-power the nozzle is scheduled to open fully at idle and the area is decreased as the throttle is advanced toward the mil-power position.

For afterburner ignition the area is closed to minimum afterburner operation. During engine operation in the mil-power and afterburner range the nozzle control system modulates the primary nozzle area to maintain NL according to the pre-set schedule of the ECU. The secondary nozzle area is adjusted synchronously to achieve a complete pressure drop within the de Laval nozzle to ambient atmospheric pressure. When the control lane of the ECU fails, the primary nozzle area is modulated by the afterburner and nozzle control unit as a function of throttle setting and the compressed intake temperature. Should a failure occur to the port engine afterburner a status indicator in the cockpit illuminates LEFT ENG STDBY SYS. This information is also preserved on the flight data recorder.

The two independent air intakes are located beneath the wing root, standing 6.3cm (2.5in) proud of the lower surface. This separation allows the boundary layer from the wing root and the inlet duct to pass outside the bellmouth. The components consist of a variable duct ramp system and an air inlet louvre system at the upper wing root surface. The inlet louvre system is interconnected to the forward ramp system by an internal upper air intake duct as indicated in adjacent illustrations. The ramps are closed during take-off and

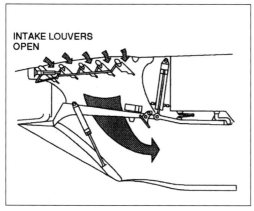

INTAKE LOUVERS OPEN

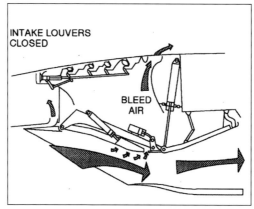

INTAKE LOUVERS CLOSED

BLEED AIR

NO.	CONDITION	DESCRIPTION	FWD RAMP POSITION	WEDGE EXTENSION	PRO-GRAM	MECHANICAL CONDITION	INDICA-TION
1	ON GND	ENG SHUT-DOWN NO HYDRAULIC PRESSURE AVAILABLE	FWD PART OF WEDGE	MINIMUM 0 %	-	WEDGE / DUCT	0 %
2	ON GND	ENG RUNNING HYDRAULIC PRESSURE AVAILABLE	SEPARATES FROM WEDGE AND CLOSES DUCT	AFT RAMP MINIMUM	-		B II
3	TAKEOFF	SPEED ABOVE 108 KIAS	FWD PART OF WEDGE	MINIMUM 0 %	-		0 %
4	IN FLIGHT	GEAR RETRACTED PROGRAM RANGE: BELOW 10 000 ft ABOVE M 1.15 OR ABOVE 10 000 ft BELOW M 1.15	FWD PART OF WEDGE	0 TO 35 %	3		0 % 35 %
5	IN FLIGHT	ABOVE 10 000 ft M 1.15 TO M 1.5	FWD PART OF WEDGE	0 TO 60 %	2		0 % 60 %
6	IN FLIGHT	ABOVE M 1.5	FWD PART OF WEDGE	0 TO 100 %	1		0 % 100 %
7	LANDING	GEAR EXTENDED	FWD PART OF WEDGE	MINIMUM 0 %	-		0 %
8	AFTER LANDING	SPEED BELOW 108 KIAS	SEPARATES FROM WEDGE AND CLOSES DUCT	AFT RAMP MINIMUM	-		B II
9	ON GND	ENG SHUT-DOWN NO HYDRAULIC PRESSURE AVAILABLE	FWD PART OF WEDGE	MINIMUM 0 %	-		0 %

FAR LEFT The variable duct ramp system for take-off and landing on earlier models of the MiG-29 used intake louvres at the top of the leading-edge extension, feeding air directly down into the engine while the intake doors were closed to avoid ingestion of foreign objects. *(MiG)*

ABOVE RIGHT For flight modes the upper intake louvres were closed and the ramp lowered to allow direct airflow into the engines. The lower ramp narrows the inlet area. Bleed air is adjusted in flow by the upper duct intake lip. *(MiG)*

LEFT The engine air intake system was more sophisticated than earlier MiG lightweight fighters and much of the technology as well as the engineering design was developed through the MiG-23 programme. This chart shows the position and mechanical condition of the air intake ramp system according to specific conditions of the aircraft's flight. The wedge extension within a specific programme is a function of the corrected low-pressure compressor speed. A high NL corresponds to a minimum extension. *(MiG)*

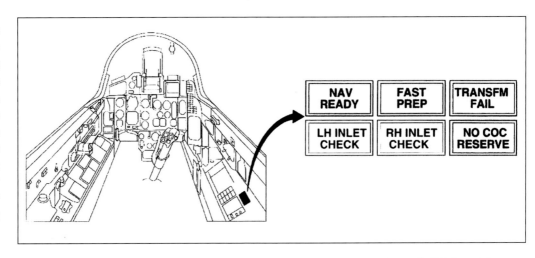

landing to prevent ingestion of foreign objects, air being supplied through the open louvres.

The variable forward ramp system provides engine air at optimum subsonic airflow to the low-pressure compressor face throughout a wide range of speeds. The ramp assembly consists of a variable forward ramp, a variable aft ramp, a bleed-off valve and a ramp control unit. The bleed-off valve and perforated sections of the ramps allow boundary layer air from the forward ramp to be bled off and exhausted overboard. In flight the forward and aft ramps are variable to modify the intake airstream to the engine.

The supplementary air intake duct at each upper wing root surface is equipped with five narrow hinged shutters, air intake louvres, which allow the duct to be open or closed. The louvres are designed so that they are spring-loaded to the closed position. During take-off and landing roll the louvres are opened by vacuum generated at the engine compressor, since the forward ramp is closed. When the forward ramp is retracted at about 180KIAS (knots indicated air speed) the louvres close. During flight, however, depending on engine rpm, they may open intermittently at Mach numbers 0.3 in idle and 0.6 in mil-power. During engine shutdown the louvres are locked in the closed position when the main hydraulic system pressure subsides.

During supersonic flight the intake airstream has to be decelerated to subsonic speed and this is accomplished by four slanting and one straight shock wave. The number of slanting shock waves, their slope angles and the position of the final straight shock wave depend on air speed, angle of attack (AOA) and the inclination of the ramps. The forward and aft ramps are controlled separately by a control unit and hydraulically positioned. The three control schedules are functions of corrected NL, altitude and Mach number.

On the ground with engines shut down, no hydraulic pressure is available and the forward and aft ramps move to maximum duct opening to provide free access for interior inspection. During engine start the forward ramp is moved to maximum extended position closing the intake duct. Depending on the setting of the ramp control unit, either both ramps close as soon as hydraulic pressure is available, or the ramp of the starting engine closes when 35% rpm is reached.

During take-off at about 108KIAS, the forward ramp is retracted to fully open. In flight, with the landing gear retracted, the third travel schedule controls the wedge angle between 0% and 35% extension. The second travel schedule controls the wedge angle between 0% and 60% extension and the first travel schedule controls this angle to between 0% and 100% extension. During landing, with the gear fully extended, the wedge is completely retracted for full duct opening. After landing, when the speed is reduced below 108KIAS, the forward ramp is extended to close the air intake completely.

After both engines start the two ramp control systems are tested automatically when engine rpm is increased to 80%–90%. At this point the pilot checks for two green captions indicated as LH INLET CHECK or RH INLET CHECK on the control and test panel at the aft section of the right-hand console. There should be no warning issued by the caution and warning system. The ramp control unit consists of two control lanes and in the case of a malfunction the built-in test equipment automatically selects the second lane.

When the ECU receives a signal from the anti-surge system (the surge detection lane of the ECU), an additional 10% extension demand signal is issued by the ramp control unit. The additional extension is limited by the maximum extension value of the actual variable duct travel schedule.

Indications and warning will be received in the cockpit if the gear is retracted and the forward ramp is not retracted to full duct opening, indicating the air intake louvres are still open. There will also be a warning if after take-off the ramp control is inoperative with main hydraulic system pressure available, in which case the wedge may extend only to 55%, which would result in a significant loss of power. If the main hydraulic pressure is not available and the ramp control system fails, the wedge will remain in the last position prior to the malfunction.

In the event of an intake ramp controller malfunction or a main hydraulic system failure, the wedges are locked in the position at the time of failure. To retract the wedges during flight or before landing, thereby fully opening the air intake duct, the spring-loaded and guarded RAMP EMERG RETRACTION LH or RH switch

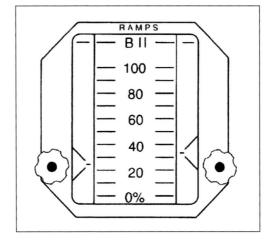

at the engine emergency panel has to be held to RETRACTION to get the wedge to move.

If the malfunction is a faulty intake ramps controller, an emergency hydraulic unit powered by the main hydraulic system will retract the wedge on switch operation. If the main hydraulic system also fails, both wedges will be retracted by the engine intake ram air upon actuation of one or both switches. After emergency wedge retraction the wedge can extend to the 8% position when the switch is released.

The ramp position indicator shows the position of both wedge and ramp positions on each air intake system as a percentage of nominal maximum extension, where the 0% mark indicates minimum extension corresponding to a fully open air intake duct.

LEFT The ramp position indicator gives the position proportional as a percentage of maximum extension. The zero position indicates minimum extension, which denotes a fully open air intake duct. When the ramp is closed for take-off or landing the indicator will be at the top of the scale, as shown by BII. *(MiG)*

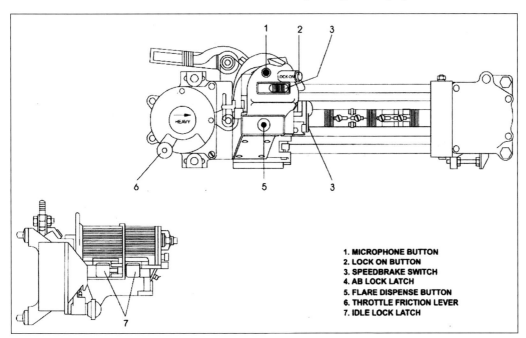

1. MICROPHONE BUTTON
2. LOCK ON BUTTON
3. SPEEDBRAKE SWITCH
4. AB LOCK LATCH
5. FLARE DISPENSE BUTTON
6. THROTTLE FRICTION LEVER
7. IDLE LOCK LATCH

LEFT The two throttle assemblies incorporate communication button, speed brake switch and relevant controls. They are situated on the left-hand side-wall of the cockpit. *(MiG)*

RIGHT The engine
start panel contains
controls for energising
the APU, the start
mode circuit and
switching to the
ground start sequence.
(MiG)

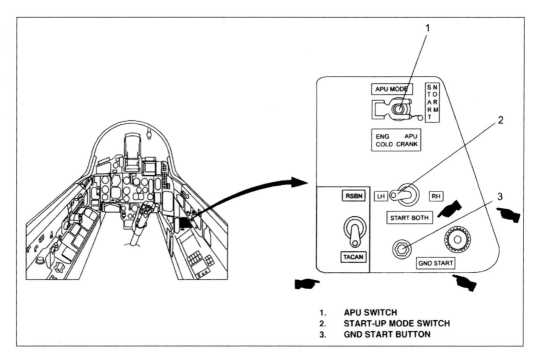

1. APU SWITCH
2. START-UP MODE SWITCH
3. GND START BUTTON

For take-off and landing, when the forward ramp closes the intake duct, the indication will be at the take-off and landing position.

The variable stator system consists of intake guide vanes and stator vanes of the first three stages of the high-pressure compressor, its function being to prevent compressor surge by limiting the intake airflow angle. When the pilot squeezes either the gun or missile trigger the engine anti-surge cycle is activated, closing the vanes by 25°. This minimises the adverse effect on the engine caused by ingesting the gun or missile exhaust gas, and upon signals from the ECU the system employs fuel from the engine control pump as the actuating medium.

The engine ignition system initiates ignition of the fuel in the combustion chamber during the starting cycle, providing an automatic engine ignition source when the weapon release trigger is pressed. The starter unit provides power to each igniter plug and controls the ignition sequence, which is initiated by pressing the GND START button. When 35% rpm is reached the ignition system is automatically switched off.

For air relight the ignition system is activated for 20 seconds for automatic and semi-automatic relight. The ignition system can also be activated manually by operating the AIR RELIGHT LH/RH switch, in which case the ignition system will be active as long as the switch is held in the ON position but should not

exceed 100 seconds, to prevent damage to the ignition coils. When either trigger is squeezed the preventative air relight mode activates the ignition system for eight seconds. For air relight, electrical power is supplied to the igniter plugs and at the same time oxygen is guided to the ignition area. During the time of the ignition cycle, the engine fault detection unit issues a signal to the warning system.

Starting the engines on the ground is accomplished through use of the auxiliary power unit (APU) and the engine gearbox, with electrical power supplied by an external unit or by two internal batteries. The high-pressure compressor shafts of the left and right engines are connected to the individual engine gearboxes, which are linked to a common gearbox by two angular drives. An APU is flanged to the gearbox and drives it through a gas-coupled turbine. The two engine gearboxes can be interconnected by friction clutches within the gearbox, this allowing each engine gearbox to be driven by the APU.

For engine start a friction clutch is installed in the gearbox. Selecting the appropriate engine with the APU running will cause the clutch controller to pressurise the appropriate clutch section with hydraulic oil and the selected engine to rotate. At the same time engine ignition will be initiated and as soon as 35% rpm is reached the APU and its associated starting system will automatically shut down under the control of the engine fault detection unit. At this juncture the engine winds up to idle by itself.

The second engine is started in the same way but if it fails to light up, or if an rpm hang-up occurs, this engine can be cold-cranked by the APU itself. If 50% rpm is not reached within 50 seconds, or if the throttle is retarded to the stop position within this period, the engine starter unit will automatically shut down. The engine start system is flexible and allows two ground start and four relight modes as follows: automatic start; manual start of each engine in any order; automatic relight; semi-automatic relight; manual relight; and preventive relight.

The automatic start procedure for both engines is provided when the start-up mode switch is set to START BOTH. The pilot must verify that the APU is in the guarded position of START NORM. He must then set both throttles to the idle position and then depress the GND START button. On receiving this command the APU will drive the right-hand engine first and when the shut-off speed is reached the APU shuts off and restart for the left-hand engine begins after a lapse of ten seconds. This provides speed synchronisation between the APU, the gearbox and the mechanical drives.

During a manual start, the left engine is started first. After checking that the APU switch on the engine start panel is in the guarded position of START NORM, the pilot moves the left-hand engine start-up mode switch to LH and the LH throttle to the idle position. Depressing the GND START button activates the APU system, the engine ignition system and the friction clutch control unit. The right-hand engine is started not less than 40 seconds after the left-hand engine by selecting start-up mode switch to RH and the RH throttle to idle. The GND START button is depressed, activating the APU and the clutch systems to start the right-hand engine, but this button must not be pressed during engine run-up or during running.

In the event of an impending failure, counteractive measures are taken automatically by the engine starting system. However, depending on the circumstances, use of the semi-automatic or manual relight may be required, and during all relight modes pure oxygen is injected into the combustion chamber of the engine. The relight controller of the engine control pump receives an altitude correction signal when above 5,490m (18,000ft) mean sea level to lean the mixture, and the controller is shut off when 85% rpm or more is sensed.

At altitudes below 12,200m (40,000ft) the air speed required for engine relight is 220–540KIAS with a minimum windmilling rpm of 12%. At altitudes between 12,200m and 17,000m (56,000ft) a successful relight may be expected between 300KIAS and Mach 1.8 if relight is initiated during engine wind-down. However, a minimum windmilling rpm of 50% may be required. At altitudes above 17,000m a normal relight and acceleration is virtually impossible. To assure a reliable air start the upper limits of the speed range is the preferred option. If the engine is not controllable over the entire rpm range, the pilot is recommended to retard the throttle to the off position and repeat the engine relight procedure at a higher speed.

1. YELLOW MARKER
2. RED SECTOR

FAR LEFT The exhaust gas temperature indicator provides a rotary display, with red and yellow markers being adjustable for left and right engines, where the engine gas temperature is displayed. (MiG)

LEFT The engine rpm indicator incorporates a dual pointer providing 0%–110% indications for left and right engines. (MiG)

Automatic relight will occur in the event that rpm drops below 50% and the throttle setting is between idle and mil-power, at which point the engine starter unit will activate the ignition system while the oxygen system will inject oxygen into the combustion chamber. Oxygen is supplied until 75% rpm is reached, but the duration of the injection is limited to 20 seconds. The warning system illuminates the green captions LH or RH ENG START on the telelight panel.

If the automatic relight fails, or an engine rpm hang-up above 50% occurs, a semi-automatic relight has to be initiated. This is achieved by first retarding the throttle of the failed engine to off for two or three seconds and then by advancing the throttle to the idle position. As soon as the throttle is advanced out of the off position, ignition takes place and oxygen is injected into the combustion chamber until an rpm of 75% is attained, but this is limited to a duration of 20 seconds, as with the automatic relight procedure. At this point the warning system illuminates the appropriate ENG START caption on the telelight panel.

If the semi-automatic relight is unsuccessful a manual air relight is possible, initiated by retarding the throttle of the failed engine to the fully off position. The pilot must then position the safety-wired LH or RH AIR RELIGHT switch, which illuminates the relevant ENG START caption. By advancing the throttle to between idle and mil-power positions the engine ignition system should start with a run-up time of up to 70 seconds. Oxygen is injected directly into the combustion chamber as long as the AIR RELIGHT switch is activated. When the engine reaches 50% rpm, the pilot moves the LH or RH AIR RELIGHT switch to the off position, but to prevent damage to the ignition coils it must be switched off after a maximum of 100 seconds. There is sufficient oxygen within the system for up to five air relight cycles.

The preventive relight mode is activated automatically for eight seconds when either trigger is squeezed, an overheat condition is sensed or a surge is encountered. As with all other relight modes, oxygen is supplied to the engines and the ignition system is activated.

Engine operation and thrust levels are controlled by the two throttles situated on the left-hand side-wall of the cockpit. A throttle lever controls each engine from off to afterburner, passing though idle and mil-power graduations. The throttles are mechanically locked when in the off position, and to progress from this position to idle or from idle to off the locks must be disengaged by squeezing latches integrated at the back of the throttle grips.

When advancing the throttles from idle into afterburner range or vice versa, locks engage at the mil-power position, but these can be disengaged by further squeezing separate latches integrated at the front side of the throttle grips. They will lock again in the maximum afterburner position, and to move throttles out of this range, or from afterburner to mil-power, the front latches must be disengaged. Positioning a throttle from the off position to afterburner actuates two different micro switches in the ECU. The first is actuated in idle to enable the starter unit, the second switch is actuated at mil-power to select the appropriate ECU schedules for mil-power and afterburner.

The throttles are not interconnected and a friction adjustment lever is attached aft of the throttles to permit adjustment of throttle friction to suit the individual preference of the pilot. For the two-seat MiG-29 versions, two interconnected throttle control levers are located in each cockpit. Full throttle control from the off position to maximum afterburner is selectable in either cockpit by a throttle stroke lever on the left cockpit side-wall behind the throttles. This allows the authority to be switched from front to back cockpit or vice versa but is exclusively available in only one cockpit at a time. With the lever in the front cockpit position the squeeze-latches on the rear cockpit throttles are disabled.

Engine controls and indicators in the cockpit include the engine system switch, the APU switch, the start-up mode switch, the ground start button, the anti-surge switch, the exhaust gas temperature indicator and the engine rpm indicator. Engaging the engine system switch located on the electric power panel supplies energy to the ECU and to the APU.

The APU switch is located at the engine start panel and controls the gearbox clutch controller and the engine starter unit. It has a switch to select either left or right engine and in APU

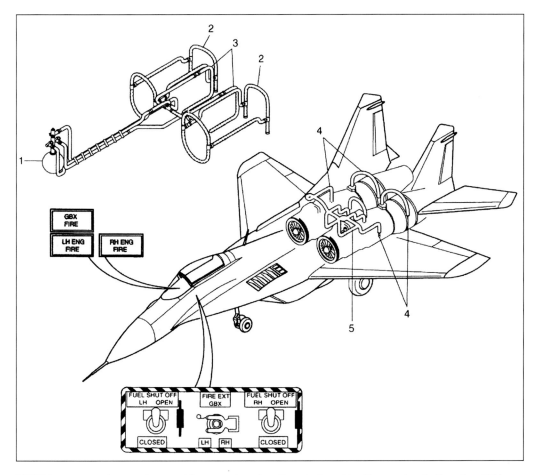

LEFT Located adjacent to the engine accessory gearbox between both engines, the fire-detection system is a heat-resistant conductor loop attached to the airframe. Key: (1) fire extinguisher pressurant bottle; (2) spray manifolds for fire extinguisher fluid at the main engine compartments; (3) spray manifolds for the engine gearbox compartments; (4) fire warning sensors in the engine compartments; (5) second fire warning sensor ring in the engine compartments. Related controls and associated cockpit displays are also shown in the box below the diagram. *(MiG)*

MODE connects the gearbox and its associated equipment. The START NORM position activates the standard engine start procedure and the ENG COLD CRANK position connects the engines, but with the ignition deactivated fuel and oxygen is not supplied. The APU COLD CRANK position cranks the APU through the electro-starter, fuel and oxygen is not supplied and ignition is deactivated. In APU MODE the various clutches will be engaged and disengaged in such a way that the engines are not connected with the gearbox, whereas the APU and all the accessories are. Since this mode is used for maintenance purposes it is not selected by the pilot and the START NORM mode is guarded and safety-wired.

The start-up mode switch is located on the engine start panel in the cockpit and allows selection of individual engine start or automatic sequence start, with selectable options for single or sequential start of both engines. The normal position is START BOTH.

The ground start button is also located at the engine start panel and pressing it initiates the start and ignition cycle of either the APU and the engines or the APU only, depending on the setting of the APU switch and the start-up mode switch.

The anti-surge switch is located on the electrical power panel and triggers activation of the anti-surge system if necessary.

The two exhaust gas temperature indicators each provide a rotary pointer display of the exhaust gas temperature from 200–1,000°C (392–1,832°F) in increments of 20°C (68°F) from 300°C (572°F) to 1,000°C and 50°C (122°F) below these values. The exhaust gas temperature sensors driving the instruments are located behind the low-pressure turbine outlets. Each dial indicator has yellow and red sector-adjustable pegs for pre-setting.

Engine rpm is indicated by a dual pointer display for both engines. The scale of the instrument runs from 0 to 110% at increments of 1%. Markings on the pointers make reference to the corresponding engine. Metering accuracy is ±1% below 60% rpm and above 100% rpm, and ±0.5% between 60% rpm and 100% rpm.

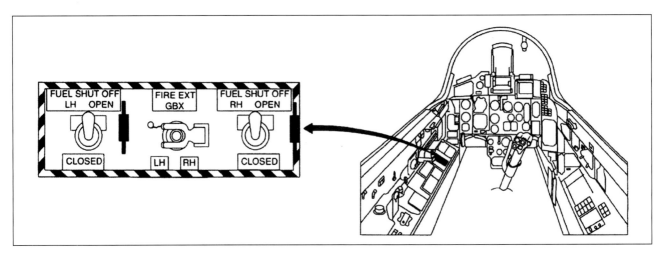

ABOVE Located on
the left side-panel in
the cockpit, the engine
emergency panel
provides fuel shut-off
switches and switches
for controlling engine
boost fuel lines, all
electrically controlled
and pneumatically
actuated. (MiG)

An engine fire detection system is installed near the gearbox and the left-hand and right-hand engines, its function based on the electrical conductivity of flames. A heat-resistant conductor loop is routed through these areas, the distance to the airframe being fixed by high-voltage stand-off isolators. In the event of a fire, the high voltage on this conductor loop discharges to the airframe, which is electronically detected and initiates a warning signal.

The fire detection system is completely insensitive to high temperatures and will not be triggered by a break in the insulation as a result of humidity or other electrical shorts. The fire detection system will be activated within three seconds of the appearance of flames. The extinguisher system consists of a spherical pressure bottle containing an extinguishing foam, three pyrotechnic charge-operated valves and the extinguisher manifolds toward the accessory gearbox and the engines.

Individual fuel shut-off switches, one per engine, are provided for the pilot to open and close the fuel shut-off valves in the engine boost fuel lines in case of fire. The fuel shut-off valves are electrically controlled and pneumatically actuated by the pneumatic power supply system. A fire extinguisher selection switch in the cockpit activates the required spray manifolds of the extinguisher system to fight the fire.

Red warning captions on the telelight panel will illuminate during the fire and extinguish if the fire suppression equipment has been successful. The extinguisher system can be activated only once and all foam will be consumed entirely. The pilot must exercise

extreme caution selecting the correct position of the guarded fire extinguisher selection switch.

The operation of the engine is controlled hydro-mechanically and the ECU governs this electrically under various flight conditions and in three different modes: normal power, combat mode, and limited power mode. These modes are pre-set by ground crew prior to take-off. The pilot has the authority to control engine bursts within one to two seconds between idle position and maximum afterburner and the time of afterburner ignition is 2–3sec.

During flight, the time for engine acceleration from idle to maximum afterburner is 3–7sec. At altitudes above 9,100m (30,000ft) and air speeds below 300KIAS during acceleration from idle to mil-power, rpm hang-up is possible momentarily. Also, g-forces can cause rpm changes up to 7%, but the rpm must not exceed 103%. A change in exhaust gas temperature is also possible but this must not exceed the maximum value for mil-power operation.

Selecting afterburner from the mil-power position is assured in the entire range of altitude and velocity, but, during throttle bursts from idle to afterburner at altitudes above 13,100m (43,000ft) and close to minimum speed, afterburner ignition may not be available. If the afterburner does light up under these conditions the pilot would retard the throttle to the mil-power position, and after the engine has stabilised the afterburner position may be selected.

Afterburner ignition can be verified by the pilot observing the green caption LH/RH ENG AB, but if the afterburner fails to shut down when deselected it can be shut down by use of the safety-wired AB EMERG OFF switch, which is located on the engine emergency panel. This switch shuts down both afterburners of both engines simultaneously.

The general performance of the aircraft and the table listing capabilities and parameters can vary in different documents and in published information from the specialist press, but the MiG-29 performance capabilities quoted in this book relate to the aircraft operated in normal power mode. However, combat mode can be selected for additional thrust to the maximum afterburner operating position.

This is activated by the pilot or by ground crew prior to flight and requires attention to the combat selector switch, marked MAKC PIIT (Russian for 'normal combat'), which can be found situated in the left-hand landing gear bay. By selecting this switch to the PIIT position operation of the engine in flight provides additional thrust that causes an engine gas temperature value approximately 25°C (77°F) above the value of normal operation. To achieve this the throttle setting is at maximum afterburner at an air speed in excess of Mach 1.5. However, engine operation in combat mode must not exceed 2% of service-life time.

To enhance its service life, the engine is tuned to limited power mode which limits the ECU to affording a maximum exhaust gas temperature 20°C (68°F) below the value of normal operation. As a result the NH and NL values are reduced also. Maintaining a close watch on the engine running time is key to efficient and safe use of the engines, whether in limited power mode, combat mode or normal power mode. To accommodate this, six running-time meters are located in the left-hand gear bay to record engine operating times in combat and afterburner modes and for total running time irrespective of mode.

Auxiliary power unit

The auxiliary power system provides facilities for starting the engines on the ground and in the air and transmits electrical power to drive the various accessories. The system includes the APU itself, an accessory gearbox and two engine gearboxes, the accessory box being mounted between the latter. In operation the APU drives the accessory gearbox, which itself drives the two engine gearboxes through two angle drives.

The accessory gearbox also drives the DC and AC generator, two hydraulic pumps of the hydraulic system and an active fuel pump of the fuel system. Each engine gearbox drives four associated engine system fuel pumps, three oil

BELOW Access to the RD-33 engine is facilitated through removal of a single panel below the fuselage, without necessarily removing the entire engine from the airframe. The engines are inclined upward by 4° and have a 1.5° toe-in.
(Vitaly Kuzmin)

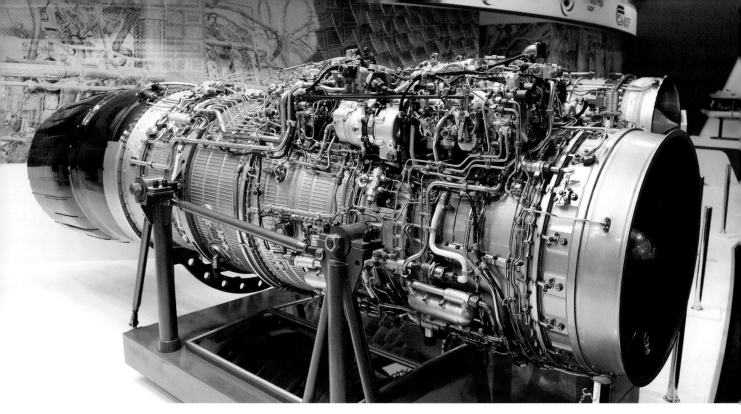

ABOVE The engine can be started on the ground by an NPP Klimov GTDE-17 auxiliary power unit, which is located between the engine nacelles. The intake is offset to port on most versions at frame 7, while the exhaust is located in the underside of the fuselage near the starboard nacelle.

(Vitaly Kuzmin)

pumps and two speed sensors to support the associated engine. The accessory gearbox can be driven by either engine via its engine gearbox through the angle drives or it can drive each engine gearbox and the associated engine for engine start.

The APU itself is a gas turbine using aircraft fuel and oxygen injection to get started. It drives the accessory gearbox through an exhaust gas coupled turbine. Apart from starting the engine the APU is also used for cold cranking to check the engine systems and it also provides power to drive the accessory equipment for checking aircraft systems.

To start the APU, a 28VDC starter motor is used with electrical power indicated on the voltmeter located on the pedestal panel in the cockpit. Pressing the GND START button activates the engine starter unit to supply oxygen and this energises the engine ignition unit. After one second the starter motor is switched on to wind up the APU compressor shaft. Simultaneously, engine fuel is injected into the oxygen atmosphere within the combustion chamber. At 35% rpm the starter motor, the ignition and the oxygen supply are switched off. At 100% rpm operating speed is controlled by a fuel-flow regulating governor. Power output is 77.7kW. If the exhaust gas temperature of the APU exceeds a pre-set value the engine fault

RIGHT The APU drives the accessory gearbox, which was the KSA-2 on early Fulcrum-A variants but the KSA-3 on the 9.13 variant and the MiG-29SE and SM variants.

(Vitaly Kuzmin)

indication unit will activate the information and warning equipment advising the pilot to shut down the APU immediately.

For engine or APU systems checkout, the engines and the APU can be cold-cranked by setting the APU switch to ENG COLD CRANK, positioning the throttle to the 'off' setting and the start-up mode switch to LH or RH. On depressing the GND START button, the high-pressure shaft of the selected engine will be driven by the APU. Fuel will not be injected into the engine combustion chamber and the engine ignition system will not be activated.

For cold-cranking the APU, the APU switch has to be set to APU COLD CRANK and the GND START button depressed. In this mode the electrical starter motor will drive the APU compressor shaft. Fuel, oxygen and ignition will not be supplied to the APU.

On the ground the APU can be used to generate electrical and hydraulic power. In this mode the two engine gearboxes are disconnected from the accessory gearbox to prevent engine rotation. For internal power supply, the ENG SYS switch on the system power panel is set to ON and the APU switch on the engine start panel is set to APU MODE. With this set-up, only the APU is started when the GND START button is pressed. The APU will drive the accessory gearbox and the associated equipment at a speed equivalent to 70% engine rpm. The APU is shut down with the ENG SYS switch located on the electric power panel.

In addition to driving aircraft accessories such as pumps and generators etc the accessory gearbox also transfers torque generated by the APU to the selected engine and controls drive from an engine to the accessory units. Torque is transferred between the accessory gearbox and the two engine gearboxes by angle drives. The lubrication oil unit and the two hydraulic pumps provide cooling and lubrication for the accessory gearbox and the APU. The oil quantity is 4.5 litres (8 gallons) and sensors for vibration and oil pressure are installed as standard.

A cross driveshaft and three friction clutches are engaged by oil pressure from the hydraulic pumps. The clutches are controlled by an internal control unit depending on the mode of operation and the engine selected for start. Normally the accessory gearbox is driven by the right-hand engine; however, if the left-hand engine rpm exceeds the right-hand engine rpm by 7% or more a free-wheel clutch will select the left-hand engine and drive the accessory gearbox instead.

All accessories except the AC generator are gear-driven by the accessory gearbox with a fixed transfer ratio. The AC generator is driven by a constant-speed torque converter. Malfunctions in the accessory gearbox and detected by the engine fault detection unit are issued to the warning equipment. These flag up flashing lights on the telelight panel indicating such anomalies as GBX FIRE or OIL GBX or ACFT ACCRY GBX VIBR. An indication of low oil pressure in the accessory gearbox indicates that quantity is sensed as being below the minimum required level for at least 20 seconds.

LEFT A rare view showing the underside panel and fuselage attachment for the engine and attachment lugs, effective for easy access, on the MiG-29 9.134 Fulcrum-C. *(MiG)*

A vibration-sensing alarm indicates that the level sensed exceeds a pre-set level by 35% for at least two to three seconds.

The two engine gearbox assemblies physically support the attachment of a low-pressure fuel pump, an engine control pump, an afterburner fuel pump with NH sensor unit, a lubrication oil unit, an oil centrifugal breather, a fuel filter unit and an additional NH sensor unit as a backup.

Fuel systems and associated subsystems

Fuel is carried internally in five interconnected internal fuselage tanks and two internal wing tanks. External fuel is carried in a single 1,500-litre (329-gallon) tank on the fuselage centreline position at station 7. All internal tanks may be refuelled on the ground through a single pressure refuelling point located in the left main landing gear well. The centreline tank must be refuelled separately through a pressure refuelling point located in the front section of the tank.

The fuselage tanks are arranged so that tank 1 is behind the aft bulkhead of the cockpit and limited by frames 4 and 5. Tank 2 (frames 5 to 6), the engine feed tank, tank 3 (frames 6 to 7) and the two tanks 3A complete the fuselage-mounted tank group. Tank 3 comprises the main structural elements of the fuselage and absorbs loads from the wings,

engines and main landing gear. The two tanks 3A are integral and in two separate structures between frames 7 and 7-Zh. A fuel accumulator is installed in tank 3 to supply engine fuel during situations of near zero-g flight.

On the Fulcrum-A the fuselage tanks hold 650 litres (142 gallons) in tank 1, 870 litres (191 gallons) in tank 2, 1,810 litres (398 gallons) in tank 3, 310 litres (68 gallons) in tanks 3A and 330 litres (73 gallons) in each wing tank. This provides a total fuel quantity of 4,300 litres (946 gallons), or 3,200kg (7,050lb) as defined by a specific gravity of 0.785g/cm^3 (0.028lb/in^3). The Fulcrum-C has an enlarged tank 1 that contains 890 litres (196 gallons) carried in the longitudinally bulbous dorsal back. This raises total fuel quantity to 4,540 litres (999 gallons), or 3,400kg (7,495lb).

The inner wing drop tanks on wet pylons carried by the Fulcrum-C carry 1,500 litres (253 gallons) each, which, with the centreline tank, increases total capacity on the fat-back versions to 8,340 litres (1,835 gallons). The MiG-29M has received several structural changes that increase internal capacity to 5,810 litres (1,278 gallons) and 5,670 litres (1,247 gallons) on the MiG-29K.

Tanks 1 and 2 are arranged so that fuel will gravity-flow into tank 2 if a transfer pump failure occurs. Flapper valves prevent reverse fuel flow. The two internal wing tanks are installed in the wing roots, one at each side. All fuel is

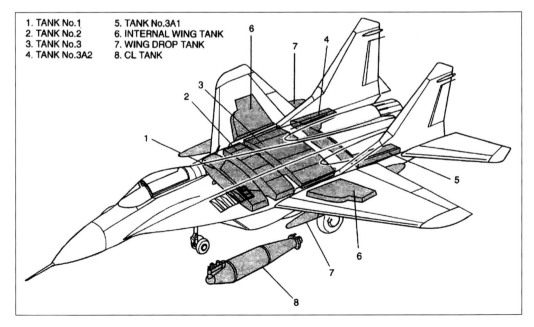

1. TANK No.1
2. TANK No.2
3. TANK No.3
4. TANK No.3A2
5. TANK No.3A1
6. INTERNAL WING TANK
7. WING DROP TANK
8. CL TANK

RIGHT This diagram shows the location and number allocation for the fuel tanks in the MiG-29 Fulcrum-A, with associated key.
(MiG)

transferred to the engine feed tank, tank 2, and from there fed to the engine check valves within the transfer lines to prevent reverse fuel flow in all aircraft attitudes. If the transfer rate to tank 2 is higher than the fuel consumption, a pressure relief valve opens and fuel is dumped to tank 1. A safety relief valve between tanks 2 and 3 permits dumping of fuel to tank 3. Both tanks 3A and the internal wing tanks contain a jet pump to transfer fuel to tank 3. Tank 3 contains a jet pump to transfer fuel to tank 1 and additionally a turbo pump to transfer fuel to the engine feed tank 2. Tank 1 contains a turbo pump to transfer fuel to tank 2.

The fuel transfer sequence is automatically controlled by a hydro-mechanical system. Regulated engine bleed air is used to transfer fuel from the external tanks to the internal tanks. Internal fuel transfer is accomplished by transfer pumps. Air pressure or nitrogen pressure is used to maintain positive pressurisation in all internal tanks, air pressure only being used for pressurisation of the centreline tank.

Fuel is also used as a cooling medium to cool hydraulic and lubrication oil as well as the cooling fluid for the radar equipment. Level control valves regulate the fuel levels in the tanks during transfer operations and fuel gauging units supply quantity and flow data to the indication system. Additional external fuel is carried in two 1,150-litre (329-gallon) wing drop tanks, each being suspended by pylons mounted to wing stations 1 and 2. Refuelling of the wing drop tanks is accomplished individually through external filler points. Regulated engine bleed air is used for wing drop tank pressurisation and fuel transfer.

The fuel transfer system serves two purposes: to transfer all fuel to the engine feed tank; and to maintain centre-of-gravity (cg) variation due to fuel consumption, within limits. The transfer system is self-sustaining. The engine accessory gearbox drives a centrifugal-type pump for active fuel delivery. Active fuel is used to drive and to control the associated

RIGHT After modification to carry underwing drop tanks, the fuel transfer sequence was changed to this arrangement for both G and GT variants. *(MiG)*

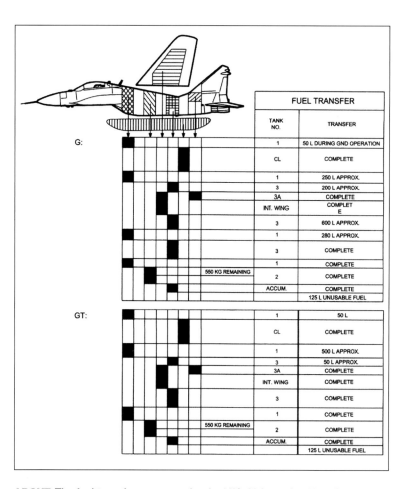

FUEL TRANSFER	
TANK NO.	TRANSFER
G:	
1	50 L DURING GND OPERATION
CL	COMPLETE
1	250 L APPROX.
3	200 L APPROX.
3A	COMPLETE
INT. WING	COMPLETE
3	600 L APPROX.
1	280 L APPROX.
3	COMPLETE
1	COMPLETE
2	COMPLETE (550 KG REMAINING)
ACCUM.	COMPLETE
	125 L UNUSABLE FUEL
GT:	
1	50 L
CL	COMPLETE
1	500 L APPROX.
3	50 L APPROX.
3A	COMPLETE
INT. WING	COMPLETE
3	COMPLETE
1	COMPLETE
2	COMPLETE (550 KG REMAINING)
ACCUM.	COMPLETE
	125 L UNUSABLE FUEL

ABOVE The fuel transfer sequence for the MiG-29 issued to East Germany before the collapse of the Warsaw Pact and the reunification of East and West Germany. Against the representation of the aircraft's fuel tank configuration are set the transfer sequence for the G and the GT variants. *(MiG)*

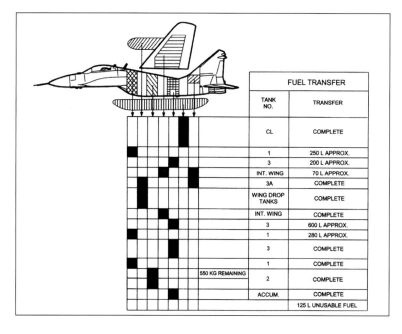

FUEL TRANSFER	
TANK NO.	TRANSFER
CL	COMPLETE
1	250 L APPROX.
3	200 L APPROX.
INT. WING	70 L APPROX.
3A	COMPLETE
WING DROP TANKS	COMPLETE
INT. WING	COMPLETE
3	600 L APPROX.
1	280 L APPROX.
3	COMPLETE
1	COMPLETE
2	COMPLETE (550 KG REMAINING)
ACCUM.	COMPLETE
	125 L UNUSABLE FUEL

RIGHT This fuel quantity data table indicates the tank quantities in litres calculated by subtracting 7% of the fully serviced fuel and the fuel remaining trapped in the tanks, amounting to 100 litres for internal fuel, 25 litres for the centreline tank and 10 litres for the wing drop tanks. Note 1 for the F-34 panel indicates measured value at 15°C and a specific weight of 8.03. Note 1 for the TS-1 fuel rates at 20°C and a specific weight of 0.780. (MiG)

TANK	FULLY SERVICED			USABLE FUEL		
	LITER	F-34 / kg *1)	TS-1 / kg *2)	LITER	F-34 / kg *1)	TS-1 / kg *2)
TANK 1	650	522	507			
TANK 2	900	723	702			
TANK 3	1 800	1 445	1 404			
TANKS 3A	300	241	234			
INTERNAL WING TANKS	650	522	507			
TOTAL INTERNAL FUEL	4 300	3 453	3 354	3 899	3 131	3 041
CL TANK	1 500	1 205	1 170	1 370	1 100	1 068
TOTAL INTERNAL FUEL PLUS CL TANK	5 800	4 658	4 524	5 269	4 231	4 110
WING DROP TANKS	2 300	1 847	1 794	2 129	1 709	1 661
TOTAL INTERNAL FUEL PLUS WING DROP TANKS	6 600	5 300	5 148	6 028	4 840	4 702
MAXIMUM FUEL LOAD TOTAL INTERNAL PLUS ALL EXTERNAL TANKS	8 100	6 505	6 318	7 398	5 940	5 770

components. These components include: level/pump control valves installed in tanks 1, 2 and 3 and the internal wing tanks at certain levels; empty sensors in tanks 1 and 3 and in the under-fuselage centreline tank; electromagnetic valves for control of external fuel transfer; turbo-type transfer pumps in tanks 1 and 3; and jet-type transfer pumps in tanks 3, 3A and the internal wing tanks.

Upon switchover to internal power supply, the electromagnetic control valve for centreline tank fuel transfer opens. After engine start, the turbo-type transfer pumps in tank 1 are run to transfer fuel to the engine feed tank (tank 2). The centreline tank fuel shut-off valve and the transfer valve open, allowing fuel to transfer. However, centreline tank fuel is not transferred at power settings below 80% rpm, but above that value all centreline tank fuel is transferred to tank 1.

As soon as all the fuel has been transferred a sensor sends a tank empty signal to the fuel indicator and to an electromagnetic check valve. The check valve interrupts control pressure to the transfer valve, causing the valve to close. During negative-g flight an inertia switch associated with the check valve causes the transfer valve to close momentarily to prevent pressurised air from entering tank 1 and forcing fuel into the drain lines. At altitudes above 9,100m (30,000ft) centreline fuel may or may not transfer due to design limitations. After transfer of a total 250 litres (54 gallons) of fuel from tank 1 the transfer pumps in tank 3 start transferring fuel to tank 1 and thence to the engine feed tank.

Upon depletion of approximately 200 litres

(43 gallons) from tank 3, the jet-type transfer pumps in tanks 3A and the internal wing tanks start transferring fuel to tank 3. Tanks 3A keep feeding until they too are empty. However, there is no indication for the exhaustion of tanks 3A. When the internal wing tanks are empty a sensor sends a tank empty signal to the fuel indicator. When all fuel is transferred from the internal wing tanks and tanks 3A, and approximately 600 litres (131 gallons) are depleted from tank 3, the transfer pumps of tank 3 are shut down. Consecutively, another 280 litres (61 gallons) are transferred from tank 1 to the engine feed tank.

Transfer from tank 3 is resumed, and when it is empty the empty sensor signals depletion to the fuel indicator. The turbo-type transfer pump in tank 3 and the transfer pumps in tanks 3A as well as the internal wing tanks are shut down, but the jet-type transfer pump in tank 3 continues to pump active fuel to tank 1, from where it is transferred to the engine feed tank. When tank 1 is empty the empty sensor causes the respective caption on the fuel indicator to illuminate. When the amount of fuel in the engine feed tank has diminished to 550kg (1,213lb), the caption 550 KG REMAIN lights up on the telelight panel.

After complete depletion of the engine feed tank, fuel is forced from the fuel accumulator to the engine feed line. A pressure differential sensor causes the AEKRAN to indicate NO BOOST when the entire fuel supply has been consumed.

With wing drop tanks installed, the transfer sequence is essentially the same. However, since the pressurisation system has been modified, centreline tank fuel is transferred immediately, regardless of engine rpm. When 70 litres (15 gallons) have been transferred from the internal wing tanks, the transfer valves of the wing drop tanks open and fuel is transferred to the internal wing tanks. Upon completion of fuel transfer from the wing drop tanks an empty sensor signals fuel depletion to the fuel indicator and to an electromagnetic check valve.

The check valve interrupts control pressure to the transfer valve causing it to close. During negative-g flight an inertia switch associated with the check valve causes the transfer valve to close momentarily to prevent pressurised air from entering the internal wing tanks. After depletion of all fuel from the wing drop tanks the transfer sequence continues the same way as it would with no wing tanks installed.

Procedures differ for the MiG-29 GT. Following engine start on this variant fuel is transferred from tank 1 to the engine feed tank. When approximately 50 litres (10 gallons) of fuel have been transferred the centreline tank transfer valve opens, allowing fuel to transfer to tank 1 as soon as rpm is increased above 80%. On completion of this transfer cycle an empty sensor signals fuel depletion to the fuel indicator and the transfer valve closes.

After depletion of another 500 litres (109 gallons) from tank 1 the transfer pumps in tank 3 start transferring fuel to tank 1 and to the engine feed tank. Upon depletion of approximately 50 litres (10 gallons) from tank 3, the jet-type transfer pumps in tanks 3A and the internal wing tanks start transferring fuel to tank 3. When the internal wing tanks are empty, an empty sensor signals fuel depletion to the fuel indicator.

Upon completion of fuel transfer from tanks 3 and 3A an empty sensor signals fuel depletion to the fuel indicator, shuts off the jet-type transfer pumps in tanks 3, 3A and the internal wing tanks, and closes the transfer valves in tanks 3A and the internal wing tanks. The turbo-type transfer pumps in tank 3 continue running. The transfer sequence is continued with tanks 1 and 2 and the accumulator tank, with the respective indicator/warning captions illuminating at the appropriate fuel level.

The fuel pressurisation and ventilation system uses air or nitrogen to pressurise the internal tanks, while regulated engine bleed air is used to pressurise the accumulator

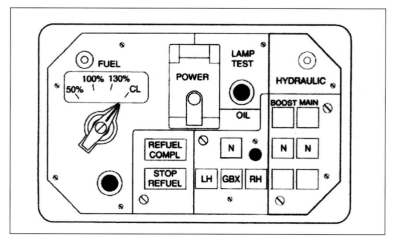

tank and all external tanks. Both systems are interconnected by check valves to permit pressurisation of the internal tanks by engine bleed air when the nitrogen supply is exhausted or when the electro-pneumatic nitrogen control valve is closed.

Four bottles contain the nitrogen at a pressure of 32,000kPa (4,640lb/in²). During engine start, at 55% rpm the electro-pneumatic nitrogen control valve opens and nitrogen is supplied via a pressure reduction valve to the venting unit at a pressure of 800kPa (116lb/in²). The venting unit controls pressurisation of the internal tanks between 3kPa (0.43lb/in²) and 25kPa (3.6lb/in²), depending on the altitude of the aircraft. It also provides pressure relief whenever a predetermined value is exceeded.

The circuitry for the nitrogen control valve is routed through the left main landing gear scissors switch to prevent closure of the valve in case of an engine failure during flight. As soon as engine bleed air from the low-pressure compressor is available, the fuel accumulator and the external tanks are pressurised. Engine bleed air is delivered at a pressure of 50Pa (0.007lb/in²) to 500Pa (0.07lb/in²) and reduced by safety relief valves to deliver a constant pressure of 55±5Pa (0.008±0.0007lb/in²) to the fuel accumulator and 90±10Pa (0.013±0014lb/in²) to the external tanks for pressurisation and fuel transfer purposes.

At high altitudes and at power settings below 80% rpm bleed air pressure can be insufficient to maintain fuel transfer from the centreline tank, resulting in intermittent illumination of the AEKRAN indication DROP TANK NO USAGE on the pilot's displays. If the nitrogen supply

ABOVE Control of the refuelling operation by ground crew or servicing technicians, filling or removing residuals, is through a panel located in the left main wheel well. *(MiG)*

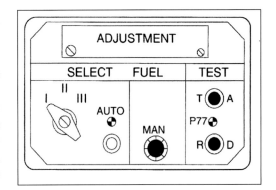

RIGHT Located in the rear cockpit beneath the instrument panel, the fuel signals calibration panel provides control over the selection of configuration for fuelling operations. (MiG)

is exhausted or the nitrogen control valve is closed, engine bleed air is supplied to the vent unit through the check valve for pressurisation of the internal tanks.

For aircraft modified to carry drop tanks, pressure from the fuel pressurisation and ventilation system is insufficient to transfer external fuel at low power settings and high altitude. To maintain positive pressurisation for fuel transfer, the fuel pressurisation and ventilation system was modified to use compressed air from the cockpit pressurisation system during high-altitude and low engine rpm conditions.

The fuel boost system supplies fuel for engine operation during positive and negative-g forces, supports operation of the active fuel system, provides cooling of the radar cooling fluid and assists with cooling of the engine oil. Two turbo-type boost pumps are located in the engine feed tank 2. The pumps are arranged so that at least one pump remains submerged in fuel regardless of flight attitude so as to deliver fuel to the engine low-pressure fuel pumps during positive- and negative-g flight.

A proportion of the fuel is pumped to the fuel accumulator in tank 3. The accumulator

BELOW The fuel signals calibration panel is different for the aircraft modified to carry underwing drop tanks. (MiG)

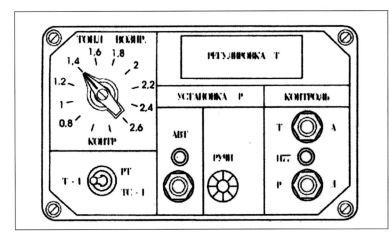

consists of two chambers separated by a membrane. The upper chamber is pressurised by compressed air from the fuel pressurisation and ventilation system. During negative- or positive-g flight, fuel is transferred to the lower chamber and the membrane is bent towards the upper chamber. The compressed air in the upper chamber forces the fuel from the lower chamber of the accumulator into the fuel supply lines in case pressure in these lines is insufficient during near-zero-g flight conditions.

A portion of the fuel is routed to the active fuel pump, a centrifugal-type device mounted to the accessory gearbox. It increases fuel pressure depending on engine speed to drive the transfer pumps and the boost pump. The active fuel is also used to control the level control valves, the transfer pumps and the external tank pressurisation valves and transfer valves.

Fuel from the lower boost pump is used to cool the coolant fluid of the radar equipment cooling system. After passing the heat exchanger the fuel is routed to the entrance of the upper boost pump. Active fuel is sent to the oil cooler and returned to the fuel supply line. Two temperature-controlled valves open a return line to the engine feed tank when the fuel temperature after the engine low-pressure fuel pump exceeds 105°C (221°F). The resulting increased fuel flow causes the temperature to decrease.

The motor-driven starter fuel pump sends fuel to the APU and to the engine supply lines during engine start. The pump remains in operation as long as either engine is running. It therefore provides a backup for fuel supply in case of an inactive fuel system and a resulting boost pump failure. The FUEL PUMP switch is located on the electric power panel on the right-hand console in the cockpit and is used to activate the starter fuel pump.

The centreline tank jettison button is located on the control stick. The button is safety-covered to prevent inadvertent actuation. Pressing the button causes an electromagnetic lock to open and releases the tank. The system is DC-powered by an external source, the DC generator or the batteries in the aircraft. Care is essential during ground operations as the centreline tank can be inadvertently jettisoned with DC power energised should the button be depressed.

To jettison the wing drop tanks the pilot activates the EMERG RELEASE button located on the front display panel in the cockpit. The button is covered and secured to prevent inadvertent actuation. Pressing the button causes the release cartridges to fire. A safety device automatically activates the firing circuit of the remaining wing drop tank upon separation of either tank, in order to prevent jettisoning of a single wing drop tank which would result in severe asymmetry of attitude and potentially momentary loss of control. The jettison circuit is live as soon as DC power in the aircraft is energised.

All internal tanks can be refuelled via a single pressure refuelling point or through external filler points. The single refuelling receptacle is located in the left main landing gear wheel well and external filler points are located on tanks 1 and 3. The centreline tank is not replenished during single-point refuelling and must be refuelled individually. The central refuelling process is controlled from the refuelling panel located in the left main gear bay and the following options are available: 50% partial load, for refuelling of tank 2 and partial refuelling of tanks 1 and 3; 100% fuel load for refuelling of all internal tanks; 10% full load plus centreline tank; or the centreline tank exclusively.

The refuelling process automatically stops when the selected fuel load is reached and the caption REFUEL COMPLETE lights up on the centre panel in the cockpit. When refuelling of internal tanks plus the centreline tank is selected, the central refuelling process automatically stops when the internal tanks are refuelled completely. In this instance the REFUEL COMPLETE does not illuminate until the centreline tank is full.

To refuel the centreline tank the respective position has to be selected. After completion of centreline tank refuelling, selection of the position for full load plus centreline tank is mandatory for adjustment of the indication system. If the refuelling vehicle is equipped with two connectors for single-point refuelling, simultaneous refuelling of the internal tanks and the centreline tank is allowed.

The wing drop tanks are always refuelled last. They can only be refuelled manually through filler caps. To obtain the correct amount of fuel the fuel indicator has to be adjusted manually for the amount of fuel in the wing drop tanks, which is approximately 1,800kg (3,970lb), with the MAN adjustment knob on the fuel signals calibration panel in the rear of the cockpit.

The internal tanks are de-fuelled through a drain valve located near tank 3, while the centreline tank is de-fuelled through its own drain valve. Remaining fuel can be drained by opening several drain plugs. The wing drop tanks are de-fuelled through the filler caps.

The refuelling panel is located in the left main landing gear wheel well, and in addition to being used for refuelling the aircraft it also provides for adjustment of the fuel indication and the verification of oil and hydraulic fluid quantities. The POWER switch is used to connect the DC power to the refuelling panel, but to accomplish this the BAT GND SUPPLY switch must be in the ON position. A LAMP TEST button is provided to check the light captions prior to refuelling to verify that they are in working order. The FUEL selector knob is a rotary selector which has four positions: 50% for refuelling of tank 2 and partial refuelling of tanks 1 and 3; 100% for refuelling of all internal tanks; 130% for refuelling of all internal tanks plus the centreline tank; and CL for refuelling the centreline tank alone. When the centreline tank is refuelled, the fuel selector knob must be positioned to 130% to obtain correct indications on the fuel indicator.

The refuelling panel also carries a STOP REFUEL button that is used to halt the refuelling procedure manually. The REFUEL COMPL caption illuminates when refuelling is finished in accordance with the selection of the FUEL selector knob. Oil indicators are carried by way of one green and three red options to indicate oil servicing requirements. The green caption lights up when the oil level is within limits; individual red captions indicate servicing requirements for the accessory gearbox and the left-hand and right-hand engines.

Hydraulic captions include three indicators for servicing requirements for the MAIN and BOOST hydraulic system. The green caption marked N indicates no servicing is required; the red caption shows that there is a servicing requirement; and the yellow caption indicates that the system has been overfilled.

The fuel signals calibration panel is located in the rear of the cockpit beneath the power distribution panel. It is used for adjustment, calibration and checkout of the fuel indication system but AC power must be available for the operation of this panel. After refuelling has been completed with battery power the power take-off switch (the DC/AC converter) must be set to the ON position before the indication system can be adjusted. Due to the limited capacity of the batteries, operation of the PTO is limited to 30 seconds.

In the rear cockpit the fuel signals calibration panel is located beneath the instrument panel in front of the control stick. The fuel selector knob has three positions labelled with Roman numerals to select the type of fuel used. The fuel computer receives the specific weight data for calculation of the remaining fuel quantity and the remaining flight distance. In aircraft

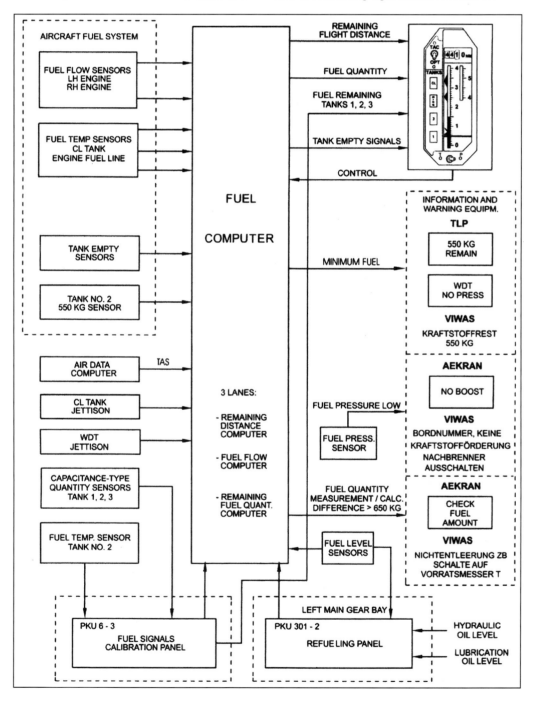

RIGHT This chart shows the integration of the fuel indication system with the fuel computer and three-way information to the cockpit displays, minimising the amount of information presented to the pilot. At upper left the aircraft fuel systems are grouped, with the integration and data flow with the air data computer and sensors at lower left. Information and warning indicators are categorised at lower right, with the instrument displays to the cockpit at upper right. (MiG)

equipped with wing drop tanks this rotary knob has been replaced by a three-position toggle switch. Pressing the push-button inputs the fuel quantity to the computer in accordance with the selection on the refuelling panel and an indicator light illuminates as soon as the quantity is displayed on the indicator.

The manual adjustment knob can be used for random adjustment of the fuel quantity. Prior to adjustment, the FUEL COUNTER circuit breaker must be pulled and the position P selected with the T/P switch on the fuel indicator. In aircraft with drop tanks this button is used to add the fuel quantity of the wing drop tanks in kilograms to the fuel indication system. Two test buttons and an LED are used for maintenance checkout, the buttons being labelled T-A and P(R)-(D), with the LED labelled п77(P77). The fuel return selector is used to select the desired bingo fuel (minimum to return safely to base) and a VIWAS warning is issued when the selected fuel level is reached, but the display of this warning may differ from the adjusted value by up to 190kg (419lb).

The fuel indication system consists of a remaining fuel quantity computer, a remaining distance computer, a fuel consumption computer and an indicator, all of which are in an integrated operational flow display found here on an adjacent illustration. The system is interconnected with the refuelling panel and the fuel signals calibration panel. Basic calculations such as total fuel depend on settings on the refuelling panel and on indicator calibration. Fuel consumption calculations depend on settings on the fuel signals calibration panel and on inputs from the fuel-flow sensors.

The system includes capacitance-type gauging units in tanks 1, 2 and 3, level control valves, full and empty sensors, fuel-flow sensors and temperature sensors. The fuel indicator displays the remaining fuel quantity in kilograms, the remaining flight distance (in kilometres or

nautical miles depending on customer) and empty tank signals. The initial fuel quantity is computed using inputs from the capacitance-type gauging units plus the quantities for the remaining internal and external tanks based on refuelling information from the refuelling panel and density information from the fuel signals calibration panel.

Consecutive fuel quantity data computation is based on the fuel flow level, corrected for density and temperature. When the centreline tank is jettisoned the computer corrects the remaining fuel quantity accordingly. Jettisoning of the wing drop tanks may lead to a false fuel quantity indication, usually higher than the actual value. The remaining flight distance computer calculates the remaining flight distance based on actual fuel consumption and data from the air data computer (ADC), but this distance is not corrected for wind factors, plus or minus.

LEFT The fuel indicator tape-meter integrates a wide range of parameters into functional information displays. Key: (1) remaining distance counter; (2) total quantity scale; (3) remaining quantity markers; (4) minimum quantity marker (550kg); (5) light-emitting diode; (6) two-position toggle switch; (7) tank 1 empty light caption; (8) tank 3 empty light caption; (9) wing tanks empty light caption; (10) centreline tank empty light caption; (11) distance computer mode switch, with TAC showing current fuel consumption, OPT showing optimised calculated fuel flow for maximum range. (MiG)

TANK EMPTY	REMAINING FUEL IN KG	ILLUMINATED CAPTION
CL TANK	3 000 TO 3 700	CL
WING TANKS	2 300 TO 2 800	WING
TANK 3	700 TO 850	3
TANK 1	550 TO 700	1
TANK 2	470 TO 630	TLP: 550 KG REMAIN
	0 TO 100	NO BOOST

LEFT The remaining fuel quantity and associated caption indicators to the pilot for an aircraft not carrying underwing drop tanks. (MiG)

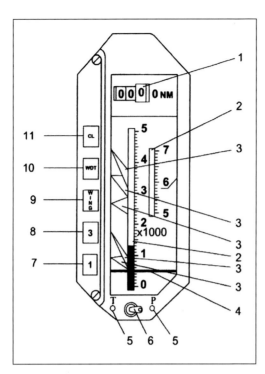

RIGHT The modified tape-meter fuel quantity indicator for the MiG-29 variants capable of carrying underwing drop tanks. Key: (1) remaining distance counter; (2) total quantity scale; (3) remaining quantity markers; (4) minimum quantity marker; (5) light-emitting diode; (6) two-position toggle switch; (7) tank 1 empty light caption; (8) tank 3 empty light caption; (9) wing tanks empty light caption; (10) wing drop tank empty light caption; (11) centreline tank empty light caption. (MiG)

counter at the upper part of the indicator shows the remaining flight distance based on actual or optimum flight conditions and a switch next to the counter selects actual or optimum range. The fuel indicator has a tolerance of ±3% of the maximum scale value.

In aircraft equipped with wing drop tanks the tape-type quantity scale has been modified to indicate the additional fuel available. Two markers are available for indicating the tolerable fuel quantity remaining when the centreline tank is empty. The triangular marker on the left scale is applicable with no wing drop tanks installed, the marker lines on the right scale are applicable when carrying wing drop tanks. During level, unaccelerating flight without afterburner, the tank 1 empty caption will not illuminate prior to an indication from the tank 3 empty caption lighting up.

After all fuel from the wing drop tanks has been transferred, the tank empty light is likely to flash. The counter at the upper part of the indicator shows the remaining flight distance based on actual flight conditions or current fuel flow. The selector switch for optimum or actual range available is removed from aircraft carrying wing drop tanks.

Several indications and warnings may be displayed to the pilot, for instance a fuel pressure drop at the output of the fuel pumps or when total fuel quantity falls below 100kg (220lb) triggering a NO BOOST indication, or when total fuel quantity falls below 550kg (1,212lb) and a telelight illuminates. This last indication can be triggered during negative-g loads. A CHECK FUEL AMOUNT indicator is illuminated if the measured quantity is below 1,800kg (3,970lb) and the internal wing tanks are not empty, or if the measured fuel quantity is below that value and a difference of 550–750kg (1,212–1,654lb) between the measured and the calculated fuel exists. It can also occur if

The fuel indicator consists of a tape-type quantity scale, a remaining flight distance counter and tank empty captions illuminated on the display panel. A two-position toggle switch marked T and P with indicator lights for selection of measured or calculated fuel is located at the bottom of the scale, triangular-shaped markers along the scale completing the indicator. In position T, the scale indicates fuel quantity sensed by the capacitance-type gauges in tanks 1, 2 and 3. In position P, the total fuel quantity is displayed as calculated by the fuel computer.

Four triangular-shaped markers along the scale indicate the tolerable remaining fuel quantity when the particular tank empty caption lights up. The markers point in the direction of the corresponding indicator caption. Illumination of a tank empty caption with the fuel quantity above or below the applicable marker indicates a transfer system malfunction or a fuel leak. The

RIGHT With underwing tanks the fuel quantity indicator captions are different, as shown in this chart. (MiG)

TANK EMPTY	REMAINING FUEL IN KG	ILLUMINATED CAPTION
CL TANK	5 000 TO 5 700	CL
WING DROP TANKS	2 800 TO 3 500	WDT
INTERNAL WING TANK	2 300 TO 2 800	WING
TANK 3	550 TO 1 000	3
TANK 1	550 TO 1 000	1
TANK 2	470 TO 630	TLP: 550 KG REMAIN

a difference of 200–350kg (441–772lb) exists between the measured and calculated fuel quantities with tanks 1 and 3 empty. The application of g-forces along the longitudinal axis with a duration in excess of 35 seconds can also cause the indication CHECK FUEL AMOUNT to illuminate and to remain so until the g-forces are off-loaded.

Cautionary warnings are also effected after a delay of 25–35 seconds, if the centreline tank is not pressurised or when 120–360kg (265–794lb) of fuel have been used and the centreline tank fuel has not transferred. For aircraft modified to carry wing drop tanks, the DROP TANK NO USAGE sign illuminates too, with exactly the same consumption levels noted. In the event of a wing drop tank pressurisation or fuel transfer failure the WDT NO PRESS sign lights up. If a bingo fuel setting has been selected with the fuel return selector knob on the fuel signals calibration panel, the flashing sign with those same words is displayed when the selected fuel quantity is reached. Furthermore, a flashing WDT TEST light illuminates if that button on the control and test panel on the right console is pressed without the engines running.

The MiG-29SMT has an internal fuel capacity of 5,300 litres (1,166 gallons) through the installation of the larger tank 1 fitted to the K and M variants. It is also capable of carrying larger, 1,800-litre (396-gallon) underwing drop tanks. All MiG-29 variants assume the use of RT, T-1, TS-1, JP-1, Jet A-1 and other fuels.

Electrical power supply system

The electrical system for the MiG-29 consists of the power generating system and the control and monitoring system. The power generating system is composed of the AC generator, the DC generator, the converter, the batteries and the distribution network. The control and monitoring system interacts with various other aircraft systems such as the engines, the fuel system and the fire extinguisher system, etc.

The primary source of alternating current is one three-phase 115/200V, 400Hz constant frequency generator, which is equipped with

a regulator and overload protection device. It is attached to the accessory gearbox. The GT30NZhCh12 generator is regulated by a hydrodynamic constant-speed drive to ensure stable rpm, regardless of engine rpm and the generator load. Maximum power output of the generator is 30kVA. A transformer supplies three-phase, 36VAC power at a maximum output of 1.5kVA. In case of a generator failure or a shutdown triggered by the regulator and protection device or in case of a transformer failure, the systems essential for flight are powered by the DC/AC converter, designated the PTO.

One 28.5V, ±0.5V, 400A, 12kW generator is the primary source of DC power. The generator is equipped with a regulator and overload protection device that ensures a DC-regulated power output and protects the generator and the DC busses against over-voltages as well as short circuits in the generator itself.

A DC/AC converter supplies emergency power in the case of an AC generator failure or a transformer failure. The PTO is capable of delivering 115VAC at a minimum output of 1.5kVa and three-phase 36VAC at a minimum output of 1kVa. If PTO operation is caused by a transformer failure, the laser range-finder, the angular rate sensors of the flight control system and course and glide-path indications of the approach mode are all rendered inoperative. In the case of a failure to the AC generator all systems not essential for flight are automatically disconnected.

Two 155STsS-45B silver-zinc batteries located in the starboard LERX are provided as an emergency power source and are used to start the auxiliary power units. Nominal voltage of the batteries is 27.6V/45Ah; however, under load (200A) a minimum of 22V is delivered. Since the charging voltage of the silver-zinc batteries is higher than the generator voltage, the batteries will not be charged when the generator power is available. The batteries supply power to the DC bus during engine start on internal power, when the DC generator voltage drops below battery voltage and during a DC generator failure.

External DC and/or AC power may be supplied to the aircraft for start-up or alignment purposes. Regardless of whether external

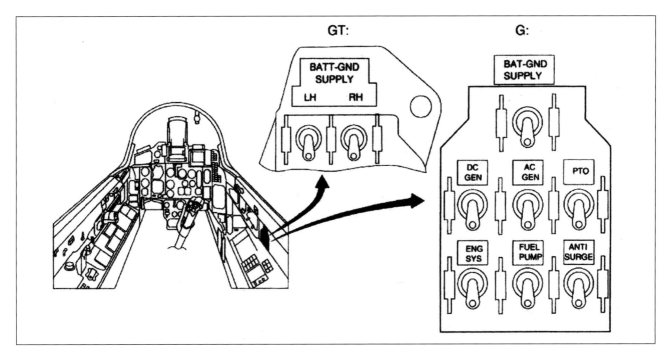

GT:

BATT-GND SUPPLY

LH   RH

G:

BAT-GND SUPPLY

DC GEN   AC GEN   PTO

ENG SYS   FUEL PUMP   ANTI SURGE

ABOVE The electrical
power panel is
situated on the right-
hand console in the
cockpit, providing
control over electrical
circuits and vital
engine control
components. (MiG)

ABOVE The electrical power panel is situated on the right-hand console in the cockpit, providing control over electrical circuits and vital engine control components. (MiG)

power is connected or not, the BAT-GND SUPPLY switch must be switched to the ON position to energise the DC bus of the aircraft. The voltmeter will indicate a voltage in excess of 22.5V in case the external power is connected and the engines are off.

Controls for the electrical power supply system are located on the electrical power panel. The DC power can be checked with a DC voltmeter located in the lower centre of the vertical panel. It measures the voltage of the DC source actually connected with the DC bus. The charge of the batteries can be checked on the amp-hours counter in the nose section.

The electrical power panel is located on the right-hand display console in the cockpit. It contains the switches for the electrical power system and for essential engine control components. The two-position toggle switches have several specific functions: engagement of the batteries through selection of BAT-GND SUPPLY; engagement of the DC generator with the DC GEN switch position; activation of the AC generator with AC GEN; engagement of the DC/AC converter at the PTO position; engagement of various engine control components at ENG SYS; activation of the engine fuel pump by switching to FUEL PUMP; and engagement of the anti-surge system by selecting ANTI SURGE.

In case of an AC generator failure or a shutdown triggered by the regulator and an

AZU-400A overload protection device, the most important consumer subsystems of electrical power are automatically shut off. To prevent a converter overload, several items of equipment are disconnected: heaters for the main and standby inertial navigation platform; the radar system and the optical sight with the exception of the navigation system; the infrared search and tracking system; laser range-finder and helmet-mounted sight; the left-hand angle of attack probe heater and sideslip vane heater; the windshield heaters for upper and lower section; the automatic flight control system; and the external armament and identification-friend-or-foe (IFF) altitude encoder.

The constant-speed drive of the AC generator is a hydrodynamic transmission with the generator driveshaft running at 12,000rpm. An electromagnetic clutch connects the driveshaft to the AC generator and provides for automatic or manual disconnect in case of a constant-speed drive failure. It will select automatic if the driveshaft speed is increased to 14,300–14,500rpm, equivalent to a frequency of 465–480Hz. It will opt for manual if the oil pressure of the constant-speed drive drops below 10kp/cm² (1,000kPa) or if the oil temperature is too high, with the GEN DRIVE EMERG SWITCH in the off position.

Illumination of the indicator DISCON GEN DRIVE indicates the need for disengagement of the constant-speed drive, and successful cut-off is shown by illumination of the AC GEN indicator. To avoid serious damage or destruction of the AC generator, the constant-speed drive has to be disconnected manually as soon as possible if the DISCON GEN DRIVE indication is displayed. The GEN DRIVE EMERG OFF switch on the emergency panel must be held to the spring-loaded position for a maximum of 25 seconds for generator cut-off and for the avoidance of damage to electrical circuits. Also, if over-voltage or short-circuit conditions occur in the DC power supply the regulator and overload protection device will disconnect the generator from the DC bus. This fail condition can only be reset by the ground crew.

Hydraulic power supply system

The hydraulic system for the MiG-29 consists of two independent systems: the main hydraulic system and the hydraulic boost system. The main system provides operation of the hydraulic actuators serving the tailerons, the ailerons, the rudders and the hydraulic actuator of the angle of attack limiter system (COC). It also provides extension and retraction of the landing gear, the trailing-edge flaps and the leading-edge flaps and speed brakes. The main system also provides control of the variable air intake ramps, the actuator for the APU exhaust door, the nose wheel steering and damper system and the hydraulic actuator of the rudder feel force system.

Each control surface actuator has two chambers, the main hydraulic system slaved to one chamber and the hydraulic boost system to the other, operating as an emergency backup. The two systems have separate hydraulic tanks pressurised to 275.8kPa (40lb/in²). The hydraulic fluid reservoirs are located inside fuel tank 3 and ensure normal operation of the NP-103A main pump and the N-58 self-contained backup pump under all flight conditions. The systems use AMG-10 oil-type hydraulic fluid.

Due to the arrangement of the two-chamber configuration, they will feed the pumps during negative-g flight conditions. The reservoirs are filled up as a closed system through filler caps in the return lines. To avoid cavitation at the inlet of the hydraulic pumps, the reservoirs are pressurised with low-pressure compressed air. The necessary compressed air is obtained from the main pneumatic system through a pressure regulator valve. Safety relief valves are incorporated to prevent over-pressurisation.

Both main and boost systems are powered by variable volume piston pumps, one per system, flanged to and driven by the engine accessory gearbox. The pumps operate at a pressure between 190kp/cm² (19,000kPa) and 220kp/cm² (22,000kPa). A pressure limiter and isolation valve is installed in the high-pressure lines of the main system. If the pressure drops below 130kp/cm² (13,000kPa), it will disconnect all systems except the flight controls and supply only one chamber of tailerons, ailerons, rudders, leading-edge flaps and angle of attack limiter actuator.

To protect the hydraulic lines, pressure relief valves are installed in the main and the boost hydraulic systems. The valves open at a pressure of 240kp/cm² (24,000kPa) and discharge hydraulic fluid into the return lines. An emergency hydraulic pump installed in the hydraulic boost system supports basic control functions of the aircraft at an rpm of both engines of at least 85%.

Although the pump delivers hydraulic pressure of up to 240kp/cm² (24,000kPa) the delivery rate permits only severely degraded control of the aircraft. This pump is driven by fuel pressure and is activated automatically whenever the system pressure of both systems drops below 100kp/cm² (10,000kPa). It can also be activated manually with the EMERGENCY HYDR PUMP switch located on the control panel next to the CHUTE JETTISON button.

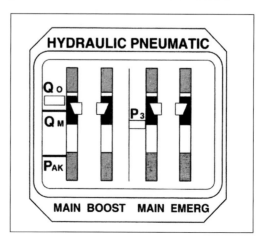

LEFT The combined pressure indicator for hydraulic and pneumatic status connected to the nitrogen gas side of the accumulators.
(MiG)

Accumulators in the main and boost systems store a supply of high-pressure fluid to damp pressure surges caused by sudden variations in flow demands. Both accumulators are charged with nitrogen at 80kp/cm^2 (8,000kPa), which corresponds with the marking P_{AK} on the combined pressure indicator, the CPI. Installation of the hydraulic reservoirs in fuel tank 3 ensures adequate cooling of the hydraulic fluid due to heat exchange with the fuel.

Both hydraulic fluid reservoirs are equipped with level transmitters connected to level indicators installed in the central refuelling control panel located in the left main wheel well; the actual hydraulic pressures of the main system as well as of the boost system are displayed on the CPI. The indicator utilises 115VAC power from the AC generator.

Transmitters for the combined pressure indicator, which is located in the cockpit, are connected to the nitrogen gas side of the accumulators. Therefore the CPI will indicate nitrogen pressure P_{AK} when the hydraulic system pressure is zero. Whenever one engine has reached a minimum of 20% rpm the hydraulic pressures must be within the green areas on the indicator. These green areas contain two markers, Q_o and Q_m, which indicate hydraulic pump performance.

Q_o is the marker for the system pressure with none of the actuators moving, that is, zero delivery of the pumps. Q_m is the marker for the system pressure with the hydraulic actuators moving at minimum velocity. During engine start at low ambient temperatures and increased hydraulic fluid flow rate, the hydraulic pressure indication may drop into the yellow area.

Whenever the pressure of one of the hydraulic systems drops below 100kp/cm^2 (10,000kPa) the respective warning indications are displayed. If hydraulic pressure is regained, the negative warning indications are extinguished. The automatic flight control system is disengaged if the pressure in both systems drops below 100kp/cm^2 (10,000kPa), until pressure is regained. With the emergency hydraulic pump running, pressure in the boost hydraulic system may increase up to 240kp/cm^2 (24,000kPa) at zero delivery rate. Whenever a pressure above 100kp/cm^2 (10,000kPa) is regained the DOUBLE HYD SYS indication on the telelight panel and the BOOST HYD SYS indication on the AEKRAN will extinguish.

With the emergency hydraulic pump running, boost hydraulic system pressure may be regained at low or zero delivery rates. Therefore extinguishing of the double hydraulic system indications must be considered temporary and the situation is generally treated as a double hydraulic system failure.

Pneumatic power supply system

The pneumatic power supply system consists of two independent systems, main and emergency. The main system supplies nitrogen pressure to operate the wheel brakes, the canopy and canopy seals,

BELOW This schematic shows how the pneumatic power supply system integrates separate mechanical operations around the aircraft and feeds into the hydraulic/pneumatic indicator in the cockpit. (MiG)

BELOW This schematic shows how the pneumatic power supply system integrates separate mechanical operations around the aircraft and feeds into the hydraulic/pneumatic indicator in the cockpit. (MiG)

the drag parachute, the fuel shut-off valves, the radio and radar receiver pressurisation and the venting of the hydraulic reservoirs. In the duel-seat GT version, this also operates the periscope system. The emergency system supplies nitrogen pressure to ensure emergency landing gear extension and emergency braking of the main wheels.

Several pressure bottles are charged to 150kp/cm² (15,000kPa) gaseous nitrogen. To ensure drag parachute operation an additional pressure bottle charged to 63kp/cm² (6,300kPa) is located close to the drag parachute compartment. A common charging valve and a pressure indicator are located in the left main landing gear bay. Cross-feed between the systems is prevented by check valves in the interconnecting lines. The pneumatic power supply is not charged during flight.

Pressure indicators are integrated in the combined pressure indicator, which is located at the right side of the main vertical cockpit console. Two scales display main and emergency pneumatic system pressure. For normal operation the pressure must remain in the green area.

A third, emergency system pressurises the hydraulic tanks and the avionics bay with air bottles charged to 14,776kN/m² (2,143lb/in²) but reduced to 6,205kN/m² (900lb/in²) for operation.

Landing gear system

The MiG-29 is equipped with a retractable tricycle landing gear, which is electrically controlled and hydraulically actuated by the main hydraulic system. DC power for the generator or the batteries is required for its operation. Retraction time for the landing gear is 9–10 seconds and extension time is 7–8 seconds. Simultaneously to the extension or retraction of the landing gear, the APU doors are opened or closed respectively.

Each main landing gear is hydraulically retracted and extended. In the extended position the gear is locked down by an internal mechanical lock in each gear-actuating cylinder. When the landing gear handle is in the position RETRACTED, the gear will retract. As the main gear retracts the wheels are automatically braked to a stop. When the gear is up and locked, brake pressure is automatically released. The main gear retracts forward and is enclosed by three fairing doors. The gear is mechanically locked in the wheel wells.

The right main gear strut is equipped with a shock detector plate to indicate evidence of a hard landing. It consists of a steel pin mounted in the upper track swivel arm and a small metal plate mounted in the lower track swivel arm of the shock absorber. The metal plate will be dented or pierced whenever the shock absorber is compressed beyond limits during a hard

ABOVE The MiG-29 landing gear was designed to levels of shock and vertical and lateral accelerations that on Western fighters would be characteristic of aircraft specifically designed for carrier-based operations. *(MiG)*

ABOVE The landing gear for the MiG-29K is modified for degree of travel and changes to the shock-absorbing system specifically catering for carrier operations, with few modifications being necessary. *(MiG)*

RIGHT A simple system for observing possible damage to the landing gear consisted of a steel pin in the upper track swivel arm and a metal plate that would be dented in the event of a high level of compression. *(MiG)*

landing. As a result, the landing gear has to be inspected and the plate has to be replaced.

The nose gear is hydraulically retracted and extended. The gear is locked in the down position by a mechanical lock inside the gear-actuating cylinder. A mechanical lock inside the wheel well locks the gear in the up position, after it has retracted aft into the forward fuselage. The nose gear is equipped with twin nose wheels, a nose-wheel steering and damper system and wheel brakes. As the nose gear retracts, the wheels are automatically braked to a stop and the strut is mechanically shortened. When the gear is up and locked, brake pressure is automatically released.

The nose-wheel steering system provides two steering modes, low and high. In low mode, used for take-off and landing, nose-wheel deflection up to 8° to either side is possible. For

taxiing the high mode may be selected, allowing nose-wheel deflection of up to 31° to either side. Activating the high mode causes the nose wheel brakes to be disabled.

Directional control is obtained by operating the rudder pedals. The nose gear is controlled mechanically and operated hydraulically. Additionally, electrical power is needed to engage the high mode and simultaneously disengage the nose-wheel brakes. A damper system prevents lateral oscillation of the nose wheels during take-off, landing and taxiing. High mode is engaged by pressing the LOCK ON button, provided the flaps are up and the MRK EMERG OFF switch is in the normal, safely wired, position. In case this switch is placed to the OFF position, the high steering mode cannot be activated. However, the nose-wheel brakes will be disabled as usual upon actuation of the LOCK ON button. When the nose gear is retracted, nose-wheel steering is disconnected mechanically.

The aircraft's pneumatic system provides compressed air to extend the landing gear, regardless of the landing gear handle position. Either the nose gear alone, or nose and main gear together can be extended. Pulling the EMERG GEAR handle aft directs compressed air to the nose-gear hydraulic actuator to extend the gear. A pneumatic shut-off valve closes the hydraulic lines to prevent inadvertent gear retraction in case hydraulic pressure is regained. After the nose gear is confirmed fully extended, rotating the EMERG GEAR handle

90° clockwise and pulling fully aft activates the main gear hydraulic actuators to extend the main gear. The hydraulic lines are shut off by pneumatically driven shut-off valves. Normal gear down indication on the landing system signal panel is achieved after all landing gears are fully extended.

The landing gear is controlled by a handle on the left side of the instrument panel. To move the handle up or down, it has to be pulled to override a detent stop position. Placing the handle in the RETRACTED or EXTENDED position uses the DC electrical power to actuate hydraulic valves to position the landing gear. A red handle, marked EMERG HANDLE, is located beneath the left front panel and is used to lower the landing gear pneumatically. After the landing gear has been extended with the emergency gear lowering system, normal gear retraction is not possible. The MRK EMERG OFF switch is used to disable the high mode of the nose-wheel steering system.

The main wheels and the nose wheels are equipped with a pneumatically operated brake system for normal operation. Additional features are a run-up brake and a nose-wheel brake handle to disable the nose-wheel brakes if required. An emergency brake handle is available for the main wheels in case of a normal brake system failure. Normal braking is accomplished by pulling the brake lever on the control stick aft. The braking force is proportional to brake lever displacement. Differential braking is achieved by displacing

the rudder pedals. Moving the right rudder pedal forward releases brake pressure from the left main-wheel brake and vice versa. For engine run-up, the run-up brake lever has to be pulled together with the brake lever to achieve a higher braking force to prevent the aircraft rolling forward.

The rims of both main landing-gear wheels are equipped with four fuse plugs each. Three of them, with a melting point of 126°C (259°F), ±1°C, are mounted in the wheel flange, spaced 120° apart. If any of these fuse plugs melts it is an indication of overheating in the brake system, requiring a system checkout. If all three plugs are found to have melted, the entire wheel rim is considered damaged beyond repair. The fourth fuse plug, with a melting point of 143.5°C (290°F), ±1.5°C, is mounted opposite the tyre retention valve. If this plug melts, the air from the tyre is released completely and the brakes will be considered defective.

The MiG-29 has an electromechanical controlled anti-skid system that consists of two basic units: a wheel-driven mechanical sensing unit and an electrically driven pneumatic valve. The units are designed to give individual anti-skid protection to each main wheel, and to both nose wheels if either one begins to skid. The system utilises DC power from the generator or the batteries and is activated by placing the BAT-GND SUPPLY switch to the on position.

Whenever a wheel starts to skid the wheel-driven mechanical sensor closes an electrical switch, which causes the electrically driven

ABOVE A close view of the nose landing gear for an Indian Air Force MiG-29K. (MiG)

pneumatic valve to release pneumatic air pressure from the adjacent brake. Once the wheel has regained its speed, the sensor reopens the switch and braking action is resumed. Applying the brake pressure during touchdown will cause the anti-skid system to be momentarily inoperative. The brakes should not be applied until all landing gear elements have contacted the runway.

Pulling the emergency brake handle disables the normal braking system and directs compressed air from the aircraft's pneumatic system to the main-wheel brakes only. Braking action is degraded approximately 40% compared to normal braking. Differential braking is not possible. The pressure applied to the brakes is linearly proportional to the displacement of the handle and releasing the brake handle relieves brake pressure. The anti-skid system is inoperative when the EMERG

BRAKE handle is pulled. Pilots are briefed not to use the emergency brakes for normal taxiing.

The pneumatic control pressures for the left and right main-wheel brakes are monitored by a double pointer instrument. Actual brake pressure is three times higher than the indicated control pressure. The nose-wheel brake handle is located on the front panel and is moved to the OFF position to disable the nose-wheel brake system. Nose-wheel brake pressure is twice as high as the control pressure. The red emergency handle is located on the upper left side of the instrument panel and is labelled EMERG BRAKE. Pulling the handle activates the emergency brake.

Drag parachute system

A drag parachute contained in the aft section of the fuselage between the speed-brake doors reduces landing roll-out distance. A red control pin is visible whenever the jaws of the attaching mechanism are open. It is pulled into the airstream by a pilot chute when the electrically controlled, pneumatically operated compartment door is opened. In case of main pneumatic system failure, the system is buffered by a reservoir of 1.2 litres (2.2 gallons). If the compartment door opens inadvertently during flight the chute is allowed to separate from the aircraft by means of a shear bolt connecting the chute to the attaching mechanism. The drag chute will separate from the aircraft when it is exceeding 175KIAS.

The drag chute is deployed by pressing the CHUTE DEPLOY button beneath the left canopy rail. Pushing the button activates a pneumatic valve to open the chute compartment door. The spring-loaded pilot chute pops out and pulls out the drag chute. The drag chute is jettisoned by pressing the CHUTE JETTISON button on the left side of the panel. To prevent unintentional chute release, the CHUTE JETTISON button is deactivated until the CHUTE DEPLOY button has been depressed. Use of the drag chute is considered mandatory for landing immediately after take-off, landing on a wet runway, short field landings, landing without leading-edge flaps, abort after nose-wheel lift-off and when the FEEL UNIT (see below) is in the heavy position.

BELOW The nose-wheel actuators, brake handle, emergency handle and indicators located in the cockpit. *(MiG)*

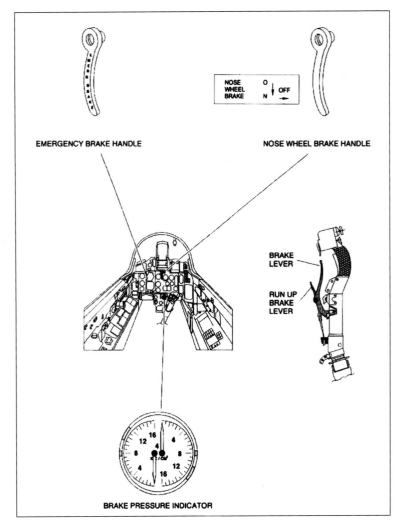

NOSE WHEEL BRAKE   O   OFF
                   N

EMERGENCY BRAKE HANDLE

NOSE WHEEL BRAKE HANDLE

BRAKE LEVER

RUN UP BRAKE LEVER

BRAKE PRESSURE INDICATOR

RIGHT The operation of the flaps is controlled
from the cockpit by three separate buttons, with
the relative position identified by a relevant light
on the landing system signal panel. *(MiG)*

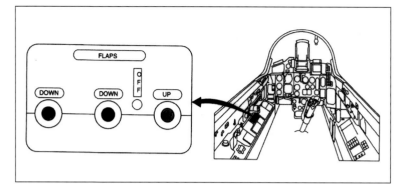

Wing flap system

The flap system provides an automatic leading-edge flap configuration for in-flight manoeuvring and a selective flap configuration for take-off and landing. Each wing has two independent leading-edge flaps, the root section consisting of three interconnected segments, and the unique end section. A single slotted flap is mounted on the trailing edge, adjacent to the fuselage.

The leading-edge flaps and the main flaps are electrically selected and operated by the main hydraulic system. The leading-edge flaps incorporate hydraulic locks, which lock them in either in or out position. The main flaps are locked in the up position only. The extender position depends on hydraulic pressure only and as air speed decreases the flaps are partially blown upward by the airstream.

For take-off and landing the leading-edge flaps and the main flaps operate together. Any time the flaps are selected down, the leading-edge flaps extend automatically. However, if the landing gear is extended the leading-edge flaps are extended too, regardless of the flaps position. With the flaps in the position UP, the leading-edge flaps operate automatically as a function of the angle of attack and the air speed.

When the angle of attack is increased to 8.7° or above and the air speed is below Mach 0.8, +0.2/-0.05, the leading-edge flaps extend automatically. The leading-edge flaps retract again when the angle of attack decreases to 7° or the air speed increases above the aforementioned Mach value. The exact Mach number is dependent on the switching point of the Mach sensor installed.

Flap operation is controlled by three push-buttons on the left console. Two are marked as FLAPS DOWN, one FLAPS UP. Pushing either FLAPS DOWN button extends all flaps. Pushing the FLAPS UP button will retract the main flaps and the leading-edge flaps, provided the landing gear is up. The position of each flap

and leading-edge flap is indicated individually by the corresponding light on the landing-system signal panel.

Speed brake system

Electrically controlled, hydraulically operated speed brakes are mounted above and beneath the drag parachute compartment. The two surfaces are operated simultaneously, but they are not synchronised. A blow-back feature is incorporated, providing structural problems of the actuators and speed-brake surfaces as air speeds above 540KIAS. The speed brakes are operated by a spring-loaded switch, located on the right-hand throttle. It returns automatically to the IN position upon release, and full extension is achieved within three seconds.

To protect the operation of the taileron, the speed brakes are electrically deactivated if main or boost hydraulic pressure decreases. If the boost hydraulic pressure drops below 100kp/cm² (10,000kPa), the speed brakes are retracted automatically by the main hydraulic system. If the main hydraulic pressure drops below this value, the speed brakes are pushed into closed position by the airstream. Speed-brake operation is not possible with the centreline tank installed or when the landing gear is extended. If total electrical failure occurs, the speed brakes will retract automatically.

Flight controls

The aircraft's primary flight controls consist of the tailerons, rudders and ailerons. Artificial feel systems provide simulated aerodynamic forces to control stick and rudder pedals. Secondary controls are the leading-edge

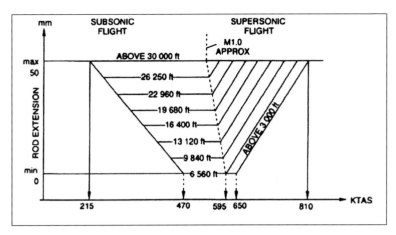

ABOVE The pitch feel control unit schedule which integrates signals from the air data computer to the electronic actuator gearbox assembly. The unit regulates the length of the rod to change the ratio of the stick to the taileron. *(MiG)*

flaps, the main flaps and the speed brakes. Mechanical linkages transmit control inputs to duel irreversible hydraulic actuators mounted next to the corresponding control surface. All primary flight controls are operated by the main and boost hydraulic systems. Full control command is retained if the main or boost hydraulic system fails.

If both systems fail, an emergency hydraulic pump supplies pressure to the boost system, provided hydraulic fluid is still available for that situation. If the emergency hydraulic pump has

to be used, however, control of the aircraft is severely degraded. In order to maintain aircraft control as long as possible the pilot is briefed to make the flight control inputs as smooth as possible and kept to a minimum.

Longitudinal control is provided by synchronised deflection of the tailerons. Partial lateral control is achieved by differential deflection. Maximum pitch authority is 15° nose down and 35° nose up. Differential taileron deflection is limited to ±5°. Taileron authority is varied as a function of air speed and altitude. It is limited to a minimum of 5° 45' nose down and 17° 45' nose up near ground level at speeds between 470KIAS and 650KIAS. Differential taileron operation is disabled when the leading-edge flaps are extended.

Lateral control is provided mainly by the ailerons, assisted by the tailerons if the leading-edge flaps are IN, and by the rudders at high angles of attack, provided the stability augmentation system is operating. Maximum aileron deflection is 25° up and 15° down from the neutral position. To prevent excessive yaw during rolls the neutral position is 5° up from the aircraft's horizontal reference line and, for the same reason, taileron authority is reduced above 18° angle of attack.

The aircraft vertical stabilisers are equipped with small rudders, deflecting 25° to either side. The rudder feel gradient is increased by 30kp (4.35lb/in²) at a rudder pedal deflection of 24mm (0.94in) from the trimmed position at air speeds above Mach 0.8, or for the GT variant with the landing gear up. Pilots are strongly advised not to override the artificial stop position. To prevent overstressing of the vertical stabilisers pilots are prohibited from overriding the rudder artificial stops at air speeds above 485KIAS, or 432KIAS for the GT variant.

Artificial feel is provided by a system of springs. The artificial feel applies centring forces to the stick and the rudder pedals toward the trimmed position. The pitch feel control unit utilises signals from the air data computer to control an electric actuator gearbox. This gearbox varies the length of a rod by up to 50mm (1.97in) to change the stick-to-taileron linkage ratio. This results in alteration of the taileron deflection range and required stick force with respect to

BELOW The feel and trim controls and indicators are displayed on this arrangement of stick and feel control switch unit with the rudder trim switch and the indicators on the telelight panel. *(MiG)*

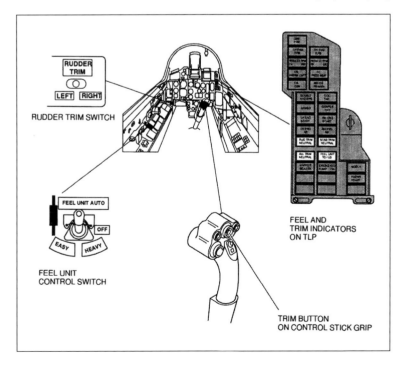

aerodynamic forces, that is, air speed and altitude. The FEEL UNIT TO/LD light on the telelight panel illuminates whenever the feel control unit is in the easy position, for example during take-off and landing.

At altitudes below 914m (3,000ft), the length of the variable rod depends on air speed only. At 215KTAS, the rod starts to retract and it is fully retracted at 470KTAS, and stays fully retracted up to 650KTAS. At 650KTAS the rod starts to extend again and is fully extended at 810KTAS, and the FEEL UNIT TO/LD light illuminates again. At altitudes above 914m (3,000ft), rod retraction becomes smaller with increasing altitude. If the feel control unit fails, it can be controlled manually with the FEEL UNIT control switch on the left console. If it does fail, stick movements have to be minimised to prevent pilot-induced oscillations.

Roll-feel forces are generated by a mechanical spring unit with linear force characteristics. Non-linearities are induced with the stability augmentation system engaged to provide low sensitivity for small control inputs and high sensitivity for large control inputs. Pedal-feel forces are generated by a spring unit system with linear force characteristics. When the landing gear is retracted, a hydraulic actuator adds additional centring forces at air speeds higher than Mach 0.8 and rudder pedal displacements of more than 24mm (0.94in), equivalent to 6° rudder deflection. The trim system is used to relieve control-stick pressure. Actuating a trim switch causes the appropriate trim actuator to move either in yaw, roll or pitch.

Pitch trim is affected by a trim actuator incorporating an electric motor. When operated, the trim actuator varies the translation ratio of the taileron linkages, which in turn provides a new stick centre position. Trim authority is 80% of available taileron deflection. Roll trim is similarly effected by an electric motor driving a trim actuator. Trim authority is 60% of available taileron deflection. Yaw trim is also effected by an electric motor driving the trim actuator, which is 60% of the available rudder deflection.

The trim button on the control stick grip consists of a pyramidal cap that houses two toggle switches. It provides trim control in the pitch and roll axes. The trim button

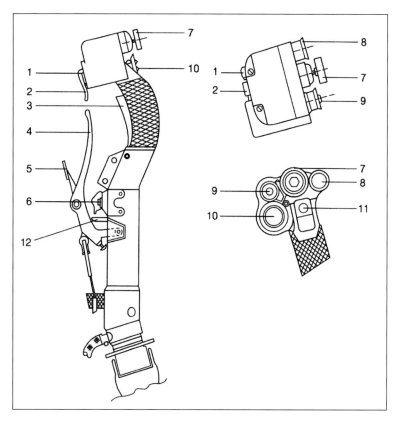

is spring-loaded to the centre and can be moved forward, aft, left and right. The rudder trim switch is located on the left vertical panel of the cockpit. Three lights on the telelight panel indicate the neutral position of the corresponding trim actuator.

The control stick consists of a grip with an adjustable hand-rest and provides several key functions, including the gun trigger, missile trigger, the autopilot cut-out button, brake lever, run-up brake lever, centreline tank jettison button, trim button and levelling button. It also supports the automatic flight control system (AFCS) modes-off button, the target acquisition symbol button, the break-lock button and the rudder pedal adjustment handle.

The AFCS modes-off button interrupts the power supply to the automatic flight control system. The autopilot cut-out lever disables all automatic flight modes of the AFCS as long as it is pressed. The control stick also supports a ring-type handle for adjusting the rudder pedals, which are used for differential braking during ground operations. Primary control for the rudders consists of conventional rudder pedals mechanically linked to hydraulic actuators.

ABOVE **The control stick supports a variety of levers and buttons for activating various systems and subsystems on the MiG-29. Key: (1) gun trigger; (2) missile trigger; (3) autopilot cut-out lever; (4) brake lever; (5) run-up brake lever; (6) centreline tank jettison button; (7) trim button; (8) levelling button; (9) automatic flight control system modes-off button; (10) target acquisition symbol button; (11) break-lock button; (12) rudder pedal adjustment handle.** (MiG)

Angle of attack and limiter system

The angle of attack and limiter control system (COC) measures and indicates angle of attack (AOA) and g-force levels. It controls automatic leading-edge flap operation and prevents inadvertent stalls by moving the control stick forward. The system is powered by 28.5VDC and two-phase 115VAC. The system consists of the AOA computer and the combined AOA/g meter, as well as warning and indicator lights. It utilises inputs from the AOA vanes, Mach sensors, the g-sensor and the leading-edge flaps-down limit switches to perform several tasks, including: display of actual and maximum g-forces; display of actual angle of attack; automatic leading-edge flaps operation considering pitch velocity; computation of the maximum AOA, considering leading-edge flap position and pitch rate; operation of the pitch-kicker (see below) considering pitch rate and AOA; and display of system malfunctions.

The g-sensor measures g-forces between

BELOW The operating interactions between the angle of attack and g-force computer and the integrated control system is depicted in this schematic of power, signal and command flow paths, with electrical circuits indicated. (MiG)

-2g and +10g. The signals are amplified in the computer and displayed on the g-scale of the combined AOA/g meter at a rate of at least 5g/sec with an accuracy of ±0.3g, or ±0.4g under extreme weather conditions. Actual AOA is measured by the left-hand and right-hand AOA vanes from -1.5° to +29°. The computer selects the higher value, amplifies the signals and displays the angle of attack on the AOA scale of the combined AOA/g meter at a rate of at least 20°/sec with an accuracy of ±1° or ±1.5° in extreme weather situations.

The AOA/g computer utilises signals from the AOA vanes and the Mach sensors to position the leading-edge flaps and to actuate the pitch-kicker. The system is disabled when the nose landing gear is not up and locked. Leading-edge flap extension limits in response to varying angle of attack values are found in the subsection above ('Wing flap system'). The signals from the leading-edge flaps-down limit switches are used to switch the AOA/g computer from the low AOA value of 15° (or 14° in the case of the GT variant) maximum to the high AOA value of 26° (24° for the GT) maximum.

The pitch-kicker is designed to prevent inadvertent stalls by moving the control stick forward of neutral when either pitch rate or the angle of attack, or a combination of both, reaches the critical value for stability and control. The computer triggers solenoid valves to operate the hydraulic actuators, which causes the taileron to assume an aircraft nose-down deflection and the control stick to move forward. Thus the pilot is immediately alerted to an approaching stall condition of the aircraft.

Full-aft trim reduces the forward force on the control stick considerably. Under this condition, the pilot is briefed to apply caution when applying back-stick pressure. Due to an extremely reduced stability margin at high angle of attack, an AOA reduction of approximately 4° is strongly recommended prior to initiating any roll manoeuvre. Overriding the pitch-kicker intentionally is prohibited. System redundancy is achieved by using dual actuators operated by the main and the boost hydraulic systems and by duplicating the computer channels.

The AOA limiter system contains a continuous built-in test that monitors the heating system of the AOA vanes, AOA signal inputs

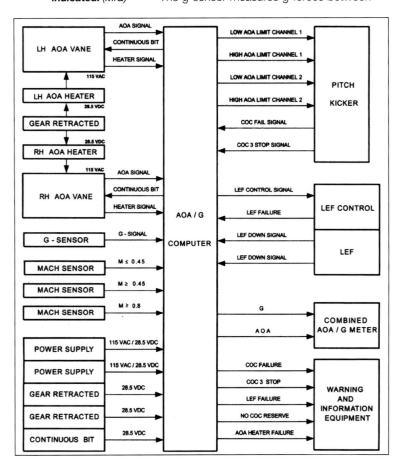

and DC electrical power. The heating system will operate with reduced power when the pilot heat switch is positioned to ON; however, full heating power is automatically provided when weight is off the right-hand main landing gear, regardless of switch selection. A test button on the control and test panel can be used for initiating an extended self-test for maintenance purposes. A complete failure of the AOA limiter system will be indicated on the telelight panel, when both AOA limiter channels of the AOA/g computer have failed. With a complete and total malfunction, pitch-kicker warning is not available. Consequently pilots are repeatedly warned to exercise extreme caution when operating near the allowable angle of attack limit.

Automatic flight control system

The automatic flight control system (AFCS) is an electro-hydraulic system designed to provide automatic, semi-automatic and manual flying modes without interfering with manual control. The system requires DC power and 36VAC power. It consists of the AFCS computer, the stability augmentation system and the trim actuators.

The AFCS computer receives signals from the gyro platforms, the accelerometers, the g-meter, the control stick position and the navigation system. The signals are corrected for altitude, Mach number, angle of attack and pitot pressure. The AFCS is capable of performing several separate modes of operation including: DAMPER for stability augmentation; ATT HOLD providing attitude hold; AUTO RECEIVER for altitude hold; automatic launching approach control; and levelling, for automated unusual attitude recovery.

Stability augmentation is obtained for pitch, roll and yaw by placing the AFCS switch to the ON position. The computer controls electro-hydraulic actuators within the mechanical control linkages to compensate for any tendency of the aircraft to oscillate in roll, yaw and pitch. Aileron-rudder-interconnect is provided at high angle of attack by the stability augmentation

BELOW Development of the MiG-29 automatic flight control system forced an evolution in Russian automated control systems, which for long had focused on electro-mechanical systems, until a new generation of electronic and computerised control systems gave the MiG-29 the flexibility to maximise the advantage of its superior aerodynamic design.
(German Air Force)

system to improve lateral stability. The automatic longitudinal stability control adjusts the taileron actuator to counteract pitch moments during leading-edge flap operation but is disengaged when the leading-edge flaps are in, the flaps are down or the dampers are off.

The dampers are disengaged if hydraulic supply to the actuators fails, if any phase of the 200V, 400Hz electric power fails, if the AFCS computer fails, or if the AFCS MODES OFF button on the control stick is pressed. If the AFCS MODES OFF button is depressed less than three seconds the stability augmentation system is re-engaged automatically upon release. If the button is pressed for more than three seconds it disengages completely. The DAMPER push-button on the AFCS mode control panel must be pressed to re-engage the system.

The attitude hold mode is designed to maintain the attitude of the aircraft. At bank angles from 7° to 80° and pitch angles of ±80° the aircraft attitude is maintained, and at bank angles below 7° and pitch angles of ±40° attitude and heading are maintained. To engage the attitude hold mode, the ATT HOLD button on the autopilot control panel is pressed. If the damper is off, it will automatically be engaged. The ATT HOLD light will flash until the autopilot (AP) cut-out lever is released. Releasing the lever starts mode operation, and the light becomes steady.

Aircraft attitude is changed by pressing the AP cut-out lever, attaining a new attitude and releasing the lever. Stick forces have to be trimmed to balance prior to releasing the lever. Engaging the attitude hold mode automatically disengages the levelling mode. The attitude hold mode is automatically disengaged if the levelling mode or auto recover are engaged. The trim condition may be slightly out of balance when disengaging the attitude hold mode.

The auto recover mode is designed to recover the aircraft to a minimum altitude setting on the radar altimeter during flight below 914m (3,000ft) above ground level. It is engaged by pressing the AUTO RECOVER push-button on the AFCS control panel. However, engagement should not take place when flying below the pre-set minimum altitude. Operation is indicated by illumination of the AUTO RECOVER light.

If the aircraft descends below the pre-set altitude, the low-altitude warning light on the radar altimeter illuminates. The AEKRAN displays ALT ALERT. The aircraft starts an 8° climb, initiated with 1.5g to 5.0g. The wings are set level and the levelling button light on the control stick illuminates continuously. On reaching the pre-set altitude, the levelling mode is engaged automatically. When the aircraft is in level flight, ATT HOLD mode is engaged automatically.

If the AP cut-out lever is pressed, or if trim is applied during the descent, the aircraft does not recover automatically. However, the low-altitude warnings are displayed and an aft stick force is applied within three or four seconds. Auto recover mode is disengaged by pressing the AUTO RECOVER button again on the AFCS control panel or by pressing the AFCS MODES OFF button for more than three seconds. In this case the dampers disengage simultaneously and must be re-engaged by pressing the DAMPER button on the AFCS control panel.

BELOW Toggle switches and indicators for the automatic flight control system are situated in the cockpit, on the right-hand panel and on the lower left of the left front console position, as shown. *(MiG)*

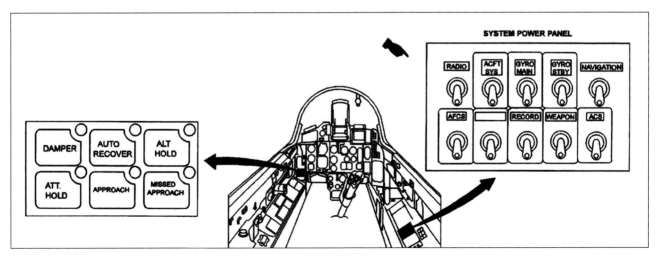

The auto recover mode is restricted to a minimum altitude of 183m (600ft) above ground level, a maximum bank angle of 30° and a maximum descent rate of 610m/min (2,000ft/min). During AUTO RECOVER, flying with the parameters mentioned above, an altitude loss of up to 91m (300ft) is possible. With a descent rate less than 61m/min (200ft/min) with wings level, no restrictions apply. However, due to radar altimeter restrictions the AUTO RECOVER mode is not reliable at bank angles greater than 30°.

The approach mode provides instrument landing system (ILS) information and command steering. It can be engaged by pressing the APPROACH button on the AFCS control panel as soon as reliable ILS signals are received for course and glide slope. Operation is indicated by the illumination of the APPROACH light and the disappearance of the pitch and course OFF flags on the attitude director indicator (ADI). To prevent violent control transients, the AFCS mode ATT HOLD must be disengaged prior to engagement of the APPROACH mode.

Bank and pitch commands are provided by the course and pitch steering bar on the ADI and the command circle in the head-up display (HUD). Bank steering commands are based on a roll rate of 5°/sec to 8°/sec. The pitch steering bar provides steering towards the engagement attitude of the APPROACH mode until glide path interception. Centring the pitch and course steering bar, as shown by the command circle in the HUD, ensures proper steering.

Failure of the glide slope indication will cause a level-off command by the pitch steering bar on the ADI. The pitch OFF flag on the ADI and the ILS glide slope OFF flag on the horizontal situation indicator (HSI) will appear. When the OFF flag on the HSI or the ADI appears, the pilot has to level off immediately and execute a missed approach. The approach mode can be deselected by pressing the AFCS MODES OFF button for less than three seconds.

The altitude hold mode is designed to maintain the aircraft at a specific barometric altitude and is engaged by pressing the ATT HOLD button first and then the ALT HOLD button on the AFCS control panel, with illumination of both lights indicating proper operation. To engage the mode, the pitch attitude must not exceed ±5°. If the pitch angle

does exceed that value the aircraft will stabilise at the given angle and the ALT HOLD light will flash until the angle is decreased below 5°. After correction to the engagement altitude, the aircraft is stabilised in bank angle and altitude. If the bank angle is less than 7° during engagement, heading and altitude are stabilised.

Altitude hold can be cut intermittently by pressing the AP cut-out lever, which is indicated by flashing of the ATT HOLD and ALT HOLD lights. Pressing the AFCS MODES OFF button for less than three seconds disengages the altitude hold mode. After recovery to level flight with the levelling mode ALT HOLD is engaged automatically. Altimeter variations while accelerating through the transonic range will produce transient fluctuations, which, although not violent, may cause the reference altitude to slip. The pilot is discouraged from using the ALT HOLD at altitudes below 914m (3,000ft).

The automatic landing approach system can be engaged after the approach mode has been selected and the pitch and course steering bars on the ADI have been centred. For smooth operation, air speed should be below 215KIAS, but automatic throttle adjustment is not available. To engage automatic landing approach control, the ATT HOLD button has to be pressed in addition to the APPROACH button on the AFCS control panel. Illumination of the ATT HOLD and the ALT HOLD lights as well as the disappearance of the OFF flags on the ADI/HSI indicate to the pilot that the system is operating correctly.

Level flight is maintained until glide-slope interception, whereupon the ALT HOLD light extinguishes and the aircraft begins to descend. Course corrections are performed with bank angles of up to 5° glide-slope corrections with pitch angles up to 2°. The automatic landing approach systems can be temporarily disengaged by pressing the AP cut-out lever and are automatically re-engaged as soon as this lever is released. The automatic landing approach has to be discontinued if the pitch or course steering bar on the ADI indicate a difference to the course or glide-slope indication on the HIS, or the minimum altitude of 46m (150ft) is reached.

The automatic landing approach control is disengaged by pressing the AFCS MODES

ABOVE Another shot of the Polish Air Force MiG-29 performing stunning aerobatics at RIAT-2015, helped to some degree by the automated flight control system and augmentation electronics.
(Steve Rendle)

OFF button for less than three seconds or by engaging the AFCS levelling mode. The autopilot may trim the aircraft considerably out of balance, in which case when disengaging the automatic landing approach mode the pilot must be prepared to counteract large control transients.

The levelling mode is designed to recover the aircraft to straight and level flight in the event of the pilot experiencing spatial disorientation. Pressing the levelling button on the right side of the trim button disengages all other AFCS modes and engages the levelling mode, provided that the AP cut-out level is released. If the dampers are off, they are automatically engaged. Levelling operations are indicated by steady illumination of the button light.

At bank angles below 80°, bank and pitch attitude are recovered to level flight simultaneously. At bank angles of more than 80°, bank is recovered to below that value before simultaneous recovery. The recovery rate varies from 10°/sec to 45°/sec in bank and -1g

to +5g in pitch, depending on altitude, attitude and air speed. Once the aircraft is recovered to ±7° angle of bank and ±5° in pitch or below, the ALT HOLD mode is automatically engaged within three to four seconds, as indicated by the ATT HOLD light. If the pilot interferes during levelling operations by pressing the AP cut-out lever or using the trim button, the levelling mode disengages momentarily, which is indicated by flashing of the levelling light.

Levelling mode is disengaged either by pressing the AFCS MODES OFF button for less than three seconds or by engaging the attitude hold mode. During levelling operations the rudder pedals must be neutralised and maintained in the neutral position. Throttle adjustments may be required according to air speed and altitude. If a forward trim condition exists prior to engagement of levelling, negative-g may be experienced momentarily before positive recovery. During recovery operations from negative pitch angles, or bank angles of 40° to 50°, the bank angle may increase up to 70° but not with an additional loss of altitude.

Placing the AFCS switch to ON initiates the built-in test, provided weight is on the nose gear, the inertial platforms are ready and the hydraulic pressure is available. Prior to engagement the control surfaces must be trimmed to neutral, as shown to the pilot by appropriate indicator lights. During the test phase, controls must be released to allow unrestricted movements. The DAMPER OFF light illuminates on the telelight panel and the MASTER CAUTION light flashes. The DAMPER light flashes continuously at a rate of 1.5–2.0Hz and all other lights on the AFCS control panel may illuminate temporarily, except for the MISSED APPROACH light.

On completion of the built-in test, the DAMPER OFF light extinguishes and the DAMPER light illuminates steadily to indicate satisfactory completion of the test and the stability augmentation system engaged. If the control stick is out of the neutral position it must be trimmed back to neutral. An AFCS malfunction is indicated by flashing of all the lights on the AFCS control panel, except for the MISSED APPROACH light. If the malfunction is not within the stability augmentation system the dampers can be engaged by pushing the DAMPER button, in which event only the damper function is usable and none of the other AFCS modes may be engaged.

A normal test cycle lasts 90 seconds but the dampers can be engaged after 40 seconds, in which case the built-in test is interrupted and none of the other AFCS modes can be engaged. After neutralising the control stick the built-in test may be reinitiated by pressing the AFCS MODES OFF button momentarily. For some aircraft modified for operation in the West, the installed ICAO (International Civil Aviation Organisation) II requires the course pointer to be set to a vertical position before the AFCS self-test can be initiated.

The AFCS switch is located on the system power panel and is used to turn it on or off. The control panel is situated in front of the left console and has five push-buttons to select the AFCS modes, each of which illuminates a green light on activation. The button MISSED APPROACH is used to obtain steering information from the navigation system. The AP cut-out lever is integrated into the control stick and disables the AFCS flying modes while pressed and the associated modes indicator lights begin to flash.

The AFCS MODES OFF button on the left side of the trim button disengages all AFCS modes. However, the stability augmentation system will be re-engaged if the button is pressed for less than three seconds. If it is pressed for more than three seconds the AFCS system is switched off, the DAMPER OFF light on the telelight panel lights up and the AFCS is disengaged completely. The levelling button with an integrated indicator light located to the right side of the trim button is used to engage the unusual attitude recovery mode of the AFCS. When an AFCS mode is selected, the pilot has to be prepared to manually counteract abrupt movements in the event of a malfunction.

Pitot static system

Two pitot booms, main and emergency, supply impact and static pressures to various flight instruments and aneroid switches. The main pitot boom provides pressure to the

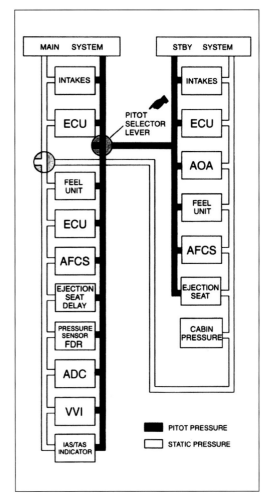

LEFT The pitot static system consists of a main and an emergency unit with the separate pitot pressure and static pressure sides indicated in this schematic. (MiG)

indicated air speed/true air speed (IAS/TAS) indicator, the vertical velocity indicator (VVI), the air data computer (ADC) and the identification-friend-or-foe (IFF) equipment. The emergency boom provides pressure for the Mach transducer, the leading-edge flap controls, the ECU, the AFCS, the engine intake ramp control and the ejection seat.

If the main system fails, the emergency pitot boom can be selected to provide pressure to the main systems users. Controls and displays include the pitot selection lever, which is located at the pedestal panel with the positions MAIN and STBY. The pitot heat switch is located on the right-hand side-wall and controls operation of the heating elements in both pitot booms, the AOA probes and the windshield.

The heater elements are energised any time 28VDC power is applied and the pitot heat switch is in the ON position. AOA probe and windshield heater elements are energised

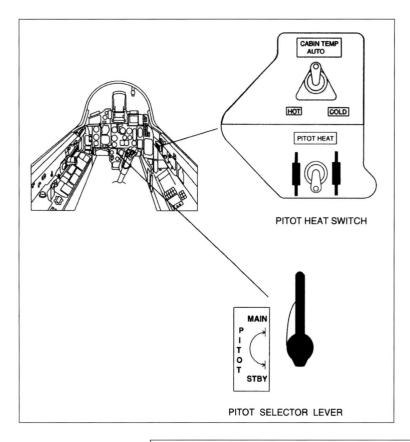

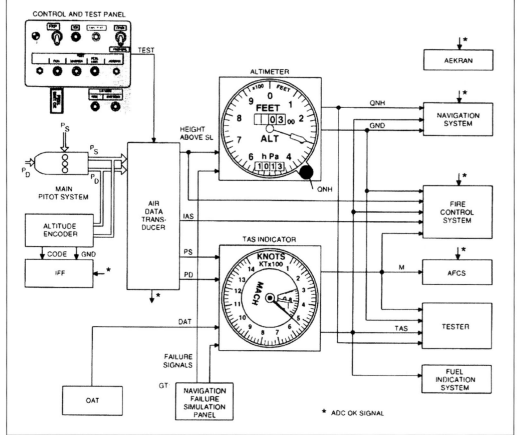

when the weight is off the wheels and the 115VAC/400Hz power is available. Technicians are advised against applying heat for more than one minute during operations on the ground to prevent damage to the system.

Air data computer

The air data computer (ADC) is part of the pitot static system and embraces the air data system, the pressure altimeter and the TAS indicator. It utilises inputs from the pilot and static pressure from the main pitot system and the outside air temperature sensor. The computer provides electrical outputs representing true air speed, Mach number, pressure altitude and density altitude. Data are supplied to the navigation system, the AFCS, the fire control system and the fuel indication system. The ADC utilises DC power from the generator or the batteries, 36VAC and 115VAC. A built-in test is provided to check system readiness during pre-flight preparation and checkout for maintenance purposes.

ABOVE The pitot static system controls, heat switch and selector lever are located as shown here. *(MiG)*

RIGHT An integrated part of the pitot static system, the air data computer directs information to the navigation system, to the automatic flight control system and to the fuel indication system as shown here, with associated control and test panel integrated with the air data transducer. *(MiG)*

Instruments

The indicated air speed (IAS) indicator USM-2AE displays indicated air speed. Single-pointer indicated air speed values between 0kt (knots) and 800kt are shown on a non-linear scale with Mach number indicated on an inner scale. The pneumatic inputs for the indicator are impact and static pressure supplied by the main or the backup pitot tube. Since the indicator is directly driven by the pneumatic outputs of one of the pitot tubes, the indicated Mach number may differ from the real value by as much as 0.05 due to non-linearities of these pitot tubes.

The UMS-2.5-2U true air speed (TAS) indicator provides a combined display of true air speed and Mach number. Electrical power is supplied from the ADC, since it is part of the system. The longer pointer rotates at the linear outer scale to indicate values between 100kt and 1,400kt, with the shorter pointer traversing the inner Mach number scale. The input signals for the indicator are supplied by the ADC and the ambient air temperature sensor.

The altimeter is an electrically operated instrument, indicating from zero to 30,000m (100,000ft), and is powered by the ADC system of which it is an integral component. An adjustable barometric scale is provided so that the altimeter may be set at the corrected sea-level pressure. The two-seat GT variant has an altimeter in the rear cockpit which is a pneumatically operated instrument incorporating a vibrator that reduces mechanical friction of the gear trains and linkages of the mechanical assembly. The vibrator is powered by 28VDC from the generator, or in the case of failure by batteries. A barometric setting knob adjusts the barometric setting on the hPa counter of the altimeter between 700hPa and 1,080hPa (hectopascals being a unit of atmospheric pressure equal to one millibar, or 14.503×10^{-5}lb/in^2).

The combined angle of attack/g-force (AOA/g) meter is a combined instrument with two different indicating systems. Since it is part of the AOA limiter system it receives electrical power via this unit. The AOA pointer, moving along the left scale, is electrically connected to AOA probes located at the left and right forward section of the aircraft. Recorded g-loads are indicated on the right scale by a main pointer

indicating instantaneous g-loads and an index tab driven by the main pointer. The index tab remains on its maximum indication until resettled. The g-meter is electrically connected to an external g-sensor transducer.

The attitude direction indicator (ADI) provides a pictorial display of the aircraft's attitude in pitch, roll and turn and utilises 36VAC and 28.5VDC received from the gyro system. A slip indicator is integrated at the bottom part of the instrument. Attitude is indicated by the aircraft symbol in relation to the horizon, pitch is indicated by the attitude sphere. The pitch and bank of the aircraft are displayed by the pitch scale on the spheroidal surface and the centre

ABOVE The cockpit of the 9.12 Fulcrum with a clear view of the right console panels, with map retainer clip. This configuration could change within block designations for production line upgrades and minor modifications. (MiG)

ABOVE

Instrumentation in the
MiG-29 is somewhat
different to the
traditional displays
found in cockpits
of Western aircraft,
relying on dials,
telelight panels (to the
right), toggle switches
and tape-meters.
(David Baker)

of the aircraft symbol. The vertical position of the aircraft symbol can be adjusted with the aircraft symbol setting knob. The bank angle is displayed by the aircraft symbol rolling on the spheroidal surface to indicate the magnitude of the aircraft's bank angle on the bank scale.

During the navigation mode RETURN, a 7° glide slope is displayed on the ADI glide-slope deviation indicator for an extended runway centreline interception at 610m (2,000ft) above ground level. During the navigation mode MISSED APPROACH, deviation from this altitude is displayed. In the AFSC mode LANDING, deviation from the ILS glide path is displayed. The ADI course deviation indicator provides steering for extended runway centreline intercept when the navigation modes RETURN and MISSED are selected and in the AFCS mode LANDING, deviation from the ILS course is displayed on this instrument.

During an ILS approach, with the AFCS mode APPROACH selected, command steering information is available by the pitch steering bar and the bank steering bar. When the aircraft is exactly on the desired flight path, the intersection of the two bars coincides with the

centre dot. The bars will be parked in the centre when the system is not engaged. However, the pitch and azimuth OFF flags will be visible.

Two red flags are incorporated in the upper left and right part of the ADI. The pitch OFF flag marked T and the azimuth OFF flag marked K will be visible when either channel of the ILS system fails or is not activated. As soon as the AFCS mode APPROACH is selected and no malfunction exists, both OFF flags will disappear. During an automatic landing approach the appearance of either OFF flag will initiate an automatic levelling off by the AFCS.

Aircraft slip is indicated by a ball inside a tubular case located at the lower part of the instrument face.

The horizontal situation indicator (HSI) provides a horizontal view of the aircraft with respect to the navigational situation. The compass card rotates so that the aircraft heading is always under the course index. Three OFF flags provide warnings for course and glide-path indicator failures and navigation or gyro/platform malfunctions. Depending on the selection of the NAV panel, indications on the HSI vary. The HSI utilises 36VAC power.

The mechanical clock allows determination of normal daytime and elapsed (mission) time and has a stopwatch facility. The indications may be read on three individual scales: normal daytime is displayed on the outer scale with an hour and a minute pointer; elapsed time is displayed in hours and minutes on the upper inner scale; and elapsed time is displayed in minutes and seconds as a stopwatch on the lower inner scale.

A red winding and setting knob is provided on the left lower corner of the clock. Rotating the knob anticlockwise winds up the clock. Pulling the knob allows the pilot to set the clock. Pushing the knob starts the small elapsed time scale on the upper portion of the face and a small status indicator window within the scale changes colour from white to red. Pushing the knob again stops the small clock and the indicator turns red/white. Pushing the knob a third time resets the elapsed time and the status indicator turns white.

A setting knob on the lower right corner of the clock is used to start and stop the seconds pointer of the normal daytime scale and to operate the stopwatch on the lower portion of

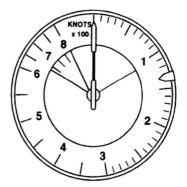

The indicated air speed non-linear dial provides impact and static pressure levels from the main or the emergency pitot channel. *(MiG)*

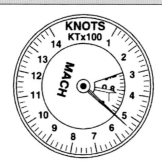

The true air speed (TAS) UMS-2.5-2U indicator integrates the Mach number value as an inset with the long pointer on the outer scale indicating knots and the inner pointer showing Mach number. *(MiG)*

An optional alternative to the UMS-2.5-2U TAS display is the UIS-1250 AE, which gives air speed between 100kt and 1,250kt. *(MiG)*

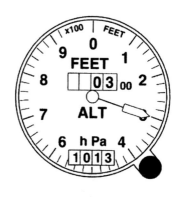

The altimeter is operated electronically and provides an adjustable barometric scale in hPa and feet. *(MiG)*

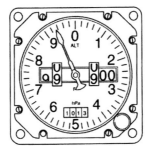

The altimeter provided in the rear cockpit of two-seat variants is a pneumatically operated instrument and provides a setting knob (bottom right on the square face), which incorporates a vibrator powered by the direct-current generator. *(MiG)*

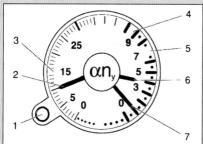

The combined angle of attack and g-force meter shows AOA on the left side of the instrument, with the g indication on the right. Key: (1) reset button for the g-index tab; (2) AOA pointer; (3) 15° marker (in red); (4) red region on the face; (5) g-index in red; (6) maximum g-index tab; (7) g-pointer. *(MiG)*

The cockpit clock with a red winding knob to the lower left and a setting knob on the lower right, functional use of which can be found in the accompanying test. *(MiG)*

The combined vertical velocity and turn and slip indicator provides information on rate of climb and direction of turn, but not turn rate. *(MiG)*

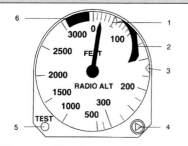

The radar altimeter is a continuous-wave instrument that feeds the avionics and the system indicator, shown here. Key: (1) 45ft test mark; (2) off flag; (3) minimum height set marker; (4) minimum height set/warning light; (5) test button; (6) black sector. *(MiG)*

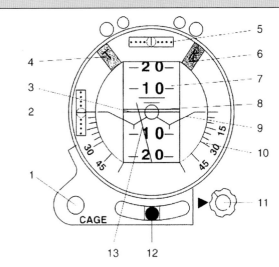

The attitude correction indicator, which provides the pilot with a pictorial display of attitude in pitch, roll and turn. Key: (1) gyro cage button/gyro fail light; (2) glide-slope deviation indicator; (3) pitch steering bar; (4) pitch off flag; (5) course deviation indicator; (6) azimuth off flag; (7) attitude sphere; (8) centre dot; (9) aircraft symbol; (10) bank scale; (11) aircraft symbol setting knob; (12) slip indicator; (13) course steering bar. *(MiG)*

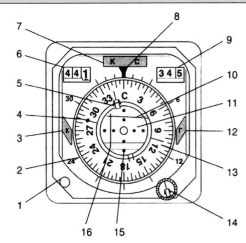

The horizontal situation indicator provides a horizontal view of the aircraft in a navigational situation. Key: (1) test button; (2) fixed compass card; (3) ILS course off flag; (4) bearing pointer (yellow); (5) course pointer (white); (6) range counter; (7) HSI of flag; (8) course index; (9) bearing counter; (10) ILS glide-slope indicator; (11) ILS course deviation scale; (12) ILS glide-slope off flag; (13) compass card; (14) course selector knob; (15) ILS guide-slope deviation scale; (16) ILS course deviation indicator. *(MiG)*

RIGHT Operation of the horizontal situation indicator shows the relevant information for each mode setting (left column) with the relevant functional display information on the rows across. *(MiG)*

MODE SETTING	COURSE POINTER	BEARING POINTER	BRG COUNTER	RANGE COUNTER	COURSE INDEX	ILS COURSE INDICATOR	ILS GLIDE SLOPE INDICATOR
NAV	Course to selected navigation point	Bearing to selected TACAN / NDB	Course to selected navigation point	Distance to selected navigation point	Aircraft HDG	-	-
NAV RETURN	An offset point to intercept final	Bearing to TACAN / NDB	Aerodrome reference point	Distance to aerodrome	HDG	-	-
NAV RETURN without TACAN update	Course to the aerodrome reference point	Unreliable	Course to the aerodrome reference point	Distance to the aerodrome reference point	HDG	-	-
NAV landing approach	Final course	Bearing to selected NDB	Final course	Distance to touchdown	HDG	Deviation from final course, max deviation is indicated 0.5˝ (4 dots) on the course deviation scale	Glide slope deviation, max deviation is indicated 0.5° (4 dots) on the glide slope deviation scale
NAV missed approach	Course to an offset point to intercept final approach	Bearing to TACAN / NDB	Course to the aerodrome reference point	Distance to the aerodrome reference point	HDG	-	-
MANUAL TACAN / RSBN for non programmed aerodrome	Course set by the course selector knob	Bearing to selected station	Course selected	Distance to selected station	HDG	-	-
BIT initiated by pressing the TEST button	Will rotate 20° ±5° CCW	-	-	Indicates 43 ±2.5 NM	Will rotate 20° ±5°	-	-

the clock face. Rotating the knob clockwise stops the seconds pointer of the normal daytime scale and operates the stopwatch on the lower portion of the clock face. Rotating the knob clockwise stops the seconds pointer, rotating the knob anticlockwise starts it again. Pushing the knob starts the stopwatch located at the lower portion of the face, pushing it again stops it and pushing a third time resets both pointers to the zero position.

The vertical velocity indicator (VVI) provides information on the rate of climb or descent of the aircraft. The indicator is connected to the static pressure system and actuation of the pointer is controlled by the rate of change of the atmospheric pressure. It can register a rate of gain or loss of altitude that would be too small to cause a noticeable change in the altimeter reading. The turn and slip indicator is incorporated in the VVI. The turn needle indicates direction of turn but does not provide accurate turn rate. The instrument receives three-phase 36VAC from the gyro system.

The continuous-wave radar altimeter (RAD ALT) measures the height of the aircraft above the surface. It supplies information to the avionics equipment and the radar altimeter indicator. The height marker may be set to the desired minimum height. If the aircraft is below that height the radar altimeter forwards inputs to the AFCS, AEKRAN, the voice information and warning system (VIWAS) and the RAD ALT indicator warning light. Accuracy of the minimum height selected is 0.45m (1.5ft) from zero to 18m (60ft) and ±3% above 18m. The radar altimeter is switched off with the ACFT SYS switch. After a warm-up period, the indicator OFF flag disappears and an altitude of zero ±0.9m (3ft) is indicated.

The RAD ALT contains a built-in test capability and is powered by 28VDC current and 115VAC. If the DC generator fails, power is supplied from the aircraft batteries, and if the AC generator fails power comes from the DC/AC converter. The system provides height information from zero to 914m (3,000ft) above ground level within bank angles of up to 15° and the system accuracy is ±0.9m (3ft) from zero to 9m (30ft) and ±10% above 9m. At bank angles above 30° or when over rough terrain RAD ALT can occasionally give incorrect

information, and at bank angles from 15° to 40° it is generally considered unreliable. At heights above 9,140m (30,000ft) an OFF flag appears on the indicator and the pointer is rotated to the black sector. Identical indications occur with a malfunction. A test button is provided to check the instrument and when this is pressed the pointer moves to the test mark at 14m (45ft).

Head-up display/head-down display

The HUD/HDD consists of the head-up display and the head-down display for image processing, synchronisation and power supply. The system is powered by 28.5VDC and 115/200VAC power. It displays information originating from the navigation system and the fire control system (FCS). Signals from the AFCS, AOA and sideslip vanes and from the radar altimeter are processed. The HUD projects information in symbolic and numeric form into the pilot's field of view and this source of information

BELOW The cockpit contains a head-up display (HUD) and a head-down display (HDD) with associated image processing and display optics on information from the automatic flight control system, the angle of attack and sideslip vanes and from the radar altimeter. (David Baker)

RIGHT The HUD incorporates brightness adjustment, a test button, reticle illumination for day or night and a filter control handle. *(MiG)*

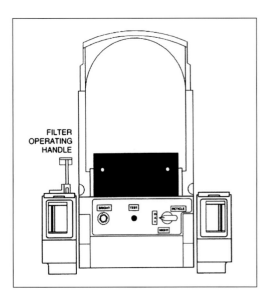

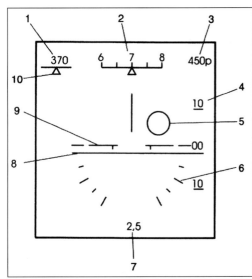

ABOVE The HUD incorporates a range of navigational symbols as shown here. Key: (1) indicated air speed; (2) heading reference; (3) present altitude/radar altitude; (4) pitch angle; (5) steering circle; (6) bank angle; (7) navigation range; (8) artificial horizon; (9) aircraft symbol; (10) indicated air speed trend index. *(MiG)*

provides steering commands in the navigation mode and constitutes the primary source of information during the attack phase.

The image-processing unit receives inputs from the navigation system, the FCS and additionally from the AFCS, AOA and sideslip vanes and from the radar altimeter. It generates signals that are displayed on a cathode ray tube (CRT) and projected on to the pilot's line of sight by means of a collimator and a combining lens. The collimator focuses the HUD picture to infinity. The combining glass projects the symbology within a space of 13° in azimuth and 18° in elevation, resulting in a circular field of view of 24°. A light filter may be raised to ensure readability of the HUD display against a bright background.

The filter operating handle on top of the left mirror unit of the helmet-mounted sight is used to erect the light filter to the vertical position. Brightness control is adjusted by a BRIGHT

LEFT With several minor changes, the cockpit of the MiG-29SMD for the Slovak Air Force *(MiG)*

knob that alters the brightness of the HUD, and in addition, a light-dependent resistor on the front side of the HUD display unit automatically adjusts the brightness of the display depending on ambient light conditions. The brightness of the image as seen by the pilot is the result of the setting of the BRIGHT knob and the intensity of the ambient light.

The HUD selector has three positions: NIGHT, where the colour of the image is amber; DAY, when the colour is green; and RETICLE, where the HUD image is blanked off and a fixed reticle displayed for air-to-air weapon employment. A test button is provided for equipment test and when depressed the boresight cross appears in a square on the HDD and on the HUD, identical crosses appearing in the centre of each quadrant of the display indicating system readiness.

Several navigational symbols can be displayed on the HUD, including: indicated air speed; heading reference; pressure altitude/ radar altitude; pitch angle; steering circle; bank angle; navigational range; artificial horizon; moving aircraft symbol; and indicated air speed trending indexer.

The HDD is a television monitor situated on the right side of the instrument panel. It displays essentially the same picture information as the HUD. A light-dependent resistor in the lower right corner of the front panel automatically

LEFT Configuration and layout of the MiG-29UB two-seat trainer incorporates some duplication and dedicated control and monitoring equipment and systems installation. *(MiG)*

adjusts the brightness of the display depending on ambient light conditions. In combination with the setting of the CRT brightness control knob, it renders the displayed information readable even in direct sunlight.

Canopy

The canopy consists of a rigid curved front section, the windshield fixed to the fuselage and a section that can be raised and which is hinged aft. Normal canopy operation is controlled by a handle and powered by the pneumatic power supply system. The operation ensures raising and lowering of the hinged

BELOW The canopy is a one-piece moulding on both single- and two-seat variants, with pressure seal and internal and external manual actuation. *(David Baker)*

portion corresponding to the position of the canopy handle, downlock of the canopy in the closed position, and sealing of the canopy for cockpit pressurisation.

The internal handle has three position detents: open, taxi and closed. To open the canopy, the handle must first be set in the taxi position and then in the open position. When the handle is in the taxi position, the seal is deflated and the canopy will be released and lifted approximately 0.8cm (2in) from the cockpit rim. When moving the handle further into the open position the canopy will be raised and held by a pneumatic actuator. It is prohibited to taxi the aircraft with the canopy in the open position and the maximum speed for taxiing with the canopy in the taxi position is 16kt.

For two-seat MiG-29 variants identical internal cockpit handles are located in both cockpits, with the rear cockpit canopy safety-wired to the closed position, since normal canopy operation is performed from the front seat.

Opening the rear cockpit canopy control handle to the taxi or open position overrides

the front cockpit canopy control handle and positions the front cockpit canopy control handle accordingly. When the canopy control handle in either cockpit is moved from the open position towards the taxi or the closed position, the other handle is automatically positioned accordingly. The canopy is lowered to the taxi position or the closed position respectively.

The external canopy-operating handle is mechanically linked to the internal handle and is located on the left-hand side of the front fuselage. It is used to open or close the canopy from the outside. To open the canopy without pneumatic pressure available, the control handle has to be set in the open position to disengage the locks and the canopy has to be raised manually and held in the open position with the canopy retaining rod.

The canopy emergency jettison provides release and separation from the cockpit if the emergency jettison handle on the right cockpit sill is pulled, or automatically if ejection is initiated in flight. A pyro-mechanical system is used to jettison the canopy, with explosive cartridges used to open the locks. In two-seat versions of the MiG-29, canopy emergency jettison handles are located in both cockpits on the right cockpit sill and pulling either handle jettisons the canopy. In the event of a canopy downlock failure, a canopy warning light LOCK CANOPY will appear on the telelight panel and a message arrive via the voice information and warning system.

Ejection seat system

The NPP Zvezda K-36DM ejection seat provides emergency escape from a variety of situations from the ground and at zero speed up to a specified series of altitudes and velocities, and can be used in conjunction with the KKO-15 protective and oxygen equipment and with a total installation weight of less than 103kg (227lb) inclusive of the parachute system, the survival kit, emergency oxygen system and associated pyrotechnic charges.

The seat is propelled from the aircraft by a cartridge-operated twin-barrel ejection gun assisted by a rocket motor, both located at the back of the seat. The ejection system is designed to function at all altitudes at air

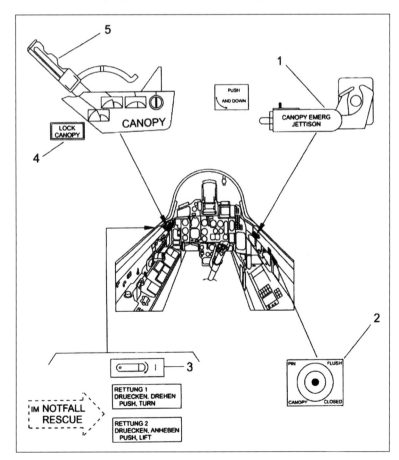

BELOW The internal and external controls for the cockpit canopy. Key: (1) internal canopy emergency jettison handle; (2) canopy closed control pin; (3) external canopy operating handle; (4) lock canopy control light; (5) internal canopy control handle. *(MiG)*

speeds up to 700kt. However, during ground operation a minimum of 40kt (80kt for the trainer version) is required for safe canopy separation. On two-seat variants the ejection sequence can be triggered by either front or rear cockpit occupants, but the rear seat ejects first followed one second later by the front seat.

Pulling the ejection handle initiates the ejection sequence, causing the canopy to be released and the ejection gun to fire. The handle must be subject to a continuous pull until full travel of the ejection handle is reached and the seat fires. The ejection sequence continues until a normal parachute descent of the occupant is accomplished. After the initial firing of the seat the operation is completely automatic and requires no additional action by the occupant. Canopy jettison malfunctions will not interfere with the seat firing system, but should it fail to jettison after the sequence has been initiated the seat fires through the canopy after a delay of one second.

Ejection is initiated by pulling the seat firing handle and the sequence is electrically controlled until the firing of the ejection gun. A mechanical backup provides fail-safe operation. As the main cartridge of the pyro-mechanical system is fired, gases are ducted to the canopy lockdown mechanism to jettison the canopy, to retract and lock the shoulder harness and lap belt by means of the retraction units, and to activate both leg raisers and arm protectors. Simultaneously a backup system is activated to open the canopy locks after 0.5sec in case of a main breach unit failure. It allows the seat to fire through the canopy after a further 0.5sec.

As the canopy is jettisoned, the canopy cable is pulled, allowing the twin-barrel ejection gun to fire and to accelerate to at least 13.6m/sec (44.6ft/sec, or 30mph). As the seat rises along the canopy rails, the emergency oxygen supply is tripped, a body windshield is activated above 485kt and the leg restraint lines are retracted. The rocket motor fires to propel the seat to a greater height. The seat is stabilised and decelerated by two rotating drogues on telescopic struts during descent through the upper atmosphere with the occupant securely restrained in the seat.

Automatic operation of the delay-release mechanism occurs after reaching the barostat

altitude of 4,877m (16,000ft) or, in ejections below this altitude, when the seat is decelerated to parachute-opening speed. The headrest/parachute container is fired from the seat to pull out the parachute. The recoil produced is also used during the process of man/seat separation.

The ejection seat is mounted on the guide rails and the telescopic ejection gun and the firing handle are connected to an electromagnetic igniter unit that starts the ejection sequence. Electromagnetic igniter cartridges are installed for initiating the ejection, for activating the retraction units and for raising the windshield. Percussion cartridges are installed for the ejection gun, the drogue gun and the firing mechanism of the rocket motor.

The ejection gun provides the initial power for seat ejection by means of a single percussion-fired cartridge. The gun consists of three major assemblies, which include the breech firing mechanism, a fillet transition piece and a telescopic launch tube. The gun assembly is mounted to the structure of the seat except for the inner barrel of the launch tube, which is mounted to the bulkhead of the cockpit. After ignition the gun develops thrust for 0.2sec.

ABOVE The NPP Zvezda KM-1 ejection seat, developed initially for use in the MiG-21 and the MiG-23, which formed the basis for an evolution to the K-36DM for the MiG-29.
(Via David Baker)

RIGHT An early
design of K-36D that
formed the prototype
for the K-36DM
selected for the
Fulcrum family, with
basic restraints but
lacking the necessary
safety restraints later
evolutions would
introduce.
(Via David Baker)

FAR RIGHT The left
side of the K-36D with
dual-ring activation
pull handle.
(Via David Baker)

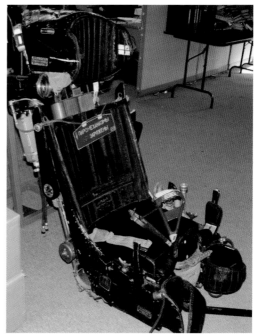

As the seat rises along the rails it extends an initiator cable that fires the rocket motor when the seat has been raised between 104.5cm (41in) and 107.5cm (43in).

The thrust of the ejection gun is sustained by the rocket motor, located under the seat pan, and is ignited as the seat leaves the ejection gun. A static line, incorporated in the rocket firing unit, cocks and triggers a firing pin to fire the ignition cartridge. The gas pressure generated by this cartridge ignites the rocket propellant. The rocket motor develops a thrust of 14.68kN (3,300lb). Two drogue arms are mounted on the right and left sides of the headrest and consist of a firing mechanism and a telescopic rod with built-in drogue chute. The unit is triggered as the ejection seat rises along the guide rails. The gas pressure of the cartridge extends each rod at an angle of 15°, and deploys the drogue chute with an area of 0.06m² (0.64ft²). The drogue chutes are ribbon-type with opposite direction of rotation, thus actively stabilising the seat.

Two independent time-release mechanisms are installed to the right and left sides of the main beam assembly. Their function is to delay deployment of the personal parachute and separation of the occupant from the seat until

LEFT A newly serviced K-36D ejection seat on its wheeled handling frame. *(MiG)*

it has descended from high altitude and/or slowed enough to prevent excessive opening shock of the personal parachute.

A barostat assembly prevents operation of the time delay above a pre-set altitude. The barostat of one delay unit is set to an altitude of 4,877m (16,000ft) at mean sea level and 5,790m (19,000ft) when flying above 3,960m (13,000ft) across mountainous terrain. The associated time-release unit is set to four seconds. The barostat of the second delay unit is set to an altitude of 1,980m (6,500ft), or 3,048m (10,000ft) when flying above 5,490m (18,000ft) mountains and in this the time delay is 0.7sec.

Although both time-delay units operate independently, each unit triggers the parachute deployment mechanism of both units. At altitudes below 1,980m (6,500ft) the time-release mechanism of the second delay unit is adjusted for the air speed at the time of ejection, depending on the speed, readjusting from 0.1sec at 375KTAS up to 1.75sec at 750KTAS.

The ejection seat contains a powered inertia lock that provides a velocity (g-sensing) system and a power retraction system. The inertia lock provides safe restraint during violent aircraft manoeuvres, and restraint is achieved by a g-sensor functioning in accordance with acceleration of 2g. Manual locking of the inertia reel lock can be accomplished by the shoulder harness release handle on the left side of the seat bucket. The powered retraction system provides automatic retraction of the shoulder harness for ejection. The device is gas powered and functions only when the ejection handle is pulled.

LEFT The top rear of the K-36D with ejector gun rail and seat deployment links. *(Via David Baker)*

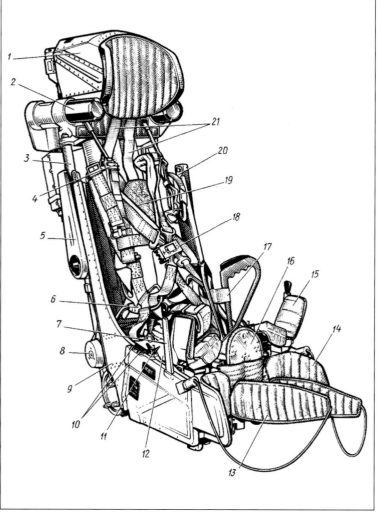

RIGHT The definitive K-36DM. Key: (1) headrest; (2) telescopic stabilisation boom; (3) stabilisation gas cartridge; (4) shoulder restraint strap; (5) right arm paddle; (6) pelvic restraint strap; (7) manual pelvic restraint strap adjustment handle; (8) waist restraint mechanism; (9) propulsion rocket housing; (10) seat vertical adjustment switch; (11) leg lifting mechanism; (12) right leg restraint padding; (13) left shin cradle; (14) wind blast deflector; (15) left thigh protector; (16) padding; (17) ejection handle fastening strap; (18) restraint straps lock and tensioner; (19) right over-shoulder harness; (20) left shoulder harness; (21) parallel parachute harness. (MiG)

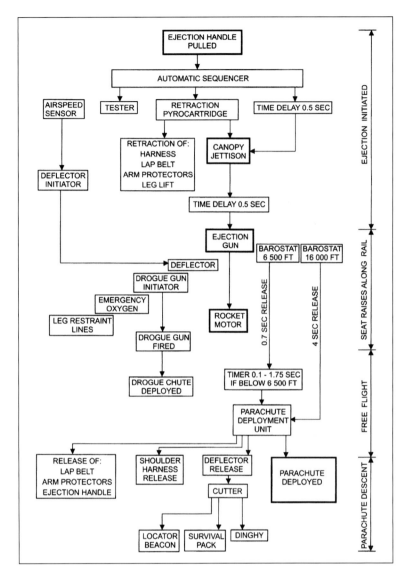

```
                    ┌──────────────────┐
                    │ EJECTION HANDLE  │
                    │      PULLED      │
                    └──────────────────┘
                             │
         ┌───────────────────────────────────────────┐
         │            AUTOMATIC SEQUENCER             │
         └───────────────────────────────────────────┘
```

| AIRSPEED SENSOR | TESTER | RETRACTION PYROCARTRIDGE | TIME DELAY 0.5 SEC |

RETRACTION OF:
HARNESS
LAP BELT
ARM PROTECTORS
LEG LIFT

CANOPY JETTISON

DEFLECTOR INITIATOR

TIME DELAY 0.5 SEC

EJECTION GUN

| BAROSTAT 6 500 FT | BAROSTAT 16 000 FT |

DEFLECTOR

DROGUE GUN INITIATOR

EMERGENCY OXYGEN

LEG RESTRAINT LINES

ROCKET MOTOR

0.7 SEC RELEASE

4 SEC RELEASE

DROGUE GUN FIRED

DROGUE CHUTE DEPLOYED

TIMER 0.1 - 1.75 SEC IF BELOW 6 500 FT

PARACHUTE DEPLOYMENT UNIT

RELEASE OF:
LAP BELT
ARM PROTECTORS
EJECTION HANDLE

SHOULDER HARNESS RELEASE

DEFLECTOR RELEASE

PARACHUTE DEPLOYED

CUTTER

LOCATOR BEACON | SURVIVAL PACK | DINGHY

EJECTION INITIATED · SEAT RAISES ALONG RAIL · FREE FLIGHT · PARACHUTE DESCENT

ABOVE The ejection sequence events timeline from time of pulling the ejection handle to seat release, free flight and parachute descent, together with associated mechanical activation. (MiG)

A lap arrestment unit provides the pilot with safe restraint in the seat during normal flight. Manual adjustment can be accomplished by the lap adjustment level on the right-hand side of the seat bucket. A gas-powered retraction system is automatically activated when the ejection handle is pulled.

To prevent injury to flailing arms during ejection, an arm protection system has been installed consisting of two metal blades mounted to the side of the backrest. As ejection is initiated, the arm protectors are rotated down to a horizontal position. The device is gas powered and operated simultaneously with the shoulder harness and the lap retraction system.

The leg restraint lines are routed along the cockpit side-wall, the instrument panel and the control stick casing, fixed into position with clips. Paddings are fixed to the section of the restraints that actually retract the legs. When the seat is ejected the occupant's legs are firmly pulled against the seat bucket and, simultaneously, the thighs are lifted to optimise body position during ejection.

A windshield is mounted to the front of the seat bucket to protect the pilot from the windblast during high-speed ejection. The unit consists of two telescopic rods that extend and raise a shield of Kopran ribbons in front of the pilot. The system is designed to extend even when one of the rods fails. The windshield is activated above 485KTAS only and is raised by electro-pyrotechnic charge.

A 60m^2 (645ft^2) personal parachute is packed into the headrest container, located on top of the seat beam. Upon release from the delay units, two cartridges are fired to separate the container and pull out the parachute. The gases of the cartridge are also used to operate cutters for simultaneous separation of the man from the seat and activation of the emergency locator beacon and the survival pack.

The personal parachute is connected to the shoulder harness by canopy quick-release connectors, which can be opened by pressing the latches on both sides simultaneously after a safety guard located between these latches has been pulled forward. The purpose of the safety guard is to prevent inadvertent operation of the quick disconnect.

An emergency oxygen bottle is installed in the ejection seat bucket and activation is accomplished automatically on ejection. The bottle can be activated manually by pulling on the red emergency knob. The pressure bottle contains 0.7 litres (0.15 gallons) of compressed oxygen at a pressure of 180kPa/cm^2 (26.1lb/in^2), indicated on the pressure gauge. The bottle supplies 100% oxygen for about six minutes during emergency descent, three to four minutes during high-altitude ejection and three minutes at low altitude. The emergency oxygen knob is located on the right side of the seat bucket and once pulled it cannot be shut off.

The seat may be adjusted only in the vertical, accomplished by actuating a momentary contact switch located on the right side of the seat bucket. The seat can be adjusted up or down through a total range of 135mm (5.31in)

but it is not necessary to adjust the height before ejection.

The survival pack contains the survival equipment, the emergency locator beacon, the emergency rations, the first-aid kit and the distress signalling kit. It is stored in the seat pan, side by side with the dinghy. A cushioned profile seating face, designed and shaped to give maximum support to the crewmember, covers the equipment. The survival pack is released automatically after the occupant is separated from the seat, thereby activating the self-inflating flotation device of the emergency locator beacon and the dinghy automatically.

Air conditioning and pressurisation system

This consists of two major systems, one for the cockpit and one for electronic equipment compartments. The cockpit air is conditioned so that it will have a defined temperature and pressure. The air conditioning system for the avionics provides cooled air for the various equipment compartments.

Engine bleed air for both systems passes through a common line to a pair of identical pressure reducer valves, arranged in series for fail-safe operation. It is routed through a parallel arrangement of two air–air coolers and an evaporative cooler. Behind the evaporator cooler the airstream is divided for equipment cooling and for cockpit air conditioning. The air for equipment cooling is passed through a turbo cooler, and as a cooling medium through a heat exchanger/dehumidifier for the cockpit air before being supplied to the equipment compartments.

The air for the cockpit is passed through the heat exchanger/dehumidifier and cooled down in a second turbo cooler. After being mixed with hot air from the pressure reducer valves, it enters the cockpit through several manifolds. Hot bleed air used for windshield defogging is taken from the pressure reducer valves and routed to a motor-driven valve which remains open at speeds below Mach 0.8.

The temperature of the air supplied to the cockpit and/or the canopy is controlled by regulating the mixture ratio of cold and hot air. Normally the ratio is adjusted automatically to maintain the selected cockpit temperature.

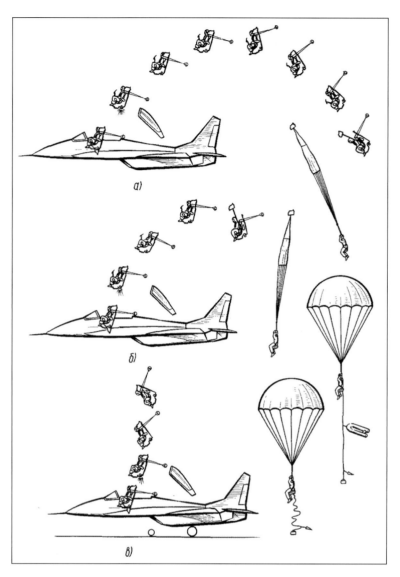

However, manual adjustment is possible. DC power is required for temperature control.

Pressure in the cockpit is controlled by a cabin pressure control valve. When the aircraft is below 1,980m (6,500ft) the valve automatically maintains a pressure differential of 0.05kp/cm^2 (50hPa) or less. Above that altitude, differential pressure increases up to 12,120m (40,000ft). The differential pressure of 0.29kp/cm^2 to 0.31kp/cm^2 (300±10%hPa) obtained between 9,144m (30,000ft) and 12,120m is maintained constant at higher altitudes. A safety relief valve controls the cabin pressure at a nominal 0.33kp/cm^2, 33kPa above ambient pressure in case the cabin pressure control valve fails. If ambient pressure exceeds cabin pressure, a vacuum valve opens to allow pressures to be equalised.

ABOVE A graphic depiction of the visual sequence of ejection events from activation through terminal parachute descent.
(Via David Baker)

RIGHT The cabin
pressurisation
schedule relating
cockpit altitude in the
vertical scale with
aircraft altitude in
rows. (MiG)

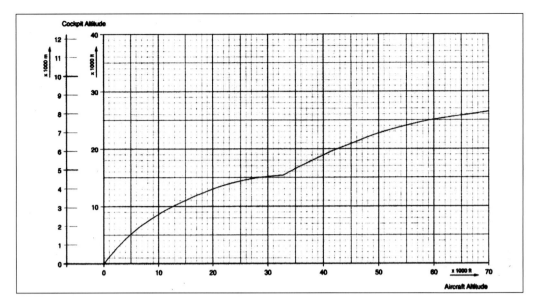

Cabin pressure on the GT variant is controlled by the cabin pressure control valve. Prior to take-off and immediately after landing, the cockpit is not pressurised. In flight it is pressurised to a cockpit altitude equivalent to an altitude below mean sea level immediately after take-off. As altitude increases, differential pressure increases so that a cockpit altitude equivalent to mean sea level is maintained up to approximately 1,230m (4,000ft), above which altitude the differential pressure increases continuously until a differential of 290hPa is reached at 3,657m (12,000ft) mean sea level. Above that altitude a differential pressure of 290hPa is maintained. A safety relief valve controls the cabin pressure at a nominal 315hPa to 340hPa above ambient pressure in case the cabin pressure control valve fails. If ambient pressure exceeds cabin pressure, a vacuum valve opens to compensate for the differential.

Fogging of the windshield is prevented by heating the inside surface of the glass with hot air from the pressure reducer valve, which is delivered through defogging manifolds at air speeds below Mach 0.8. Cold air is automatically mixed with hot air to prevent inconvenient cockpit temperature. When the mixing valve is fully open, windshield defogging is automatically shut off to prevent an over-temperature. Manual shutdown is possible with the CABIN AIR lever.

The anti-g valve controls air delivery to the anti-g suit. Air is trapped from the air–air coolers, passed through a regulator valve and an anti-g valve and delivered to the suit via the personal equipment connector (PEC). Below 2.5g no pressure passes through to the suit but above that value an anti-g valve controls the suit pressure in proportion to the g-forces experienced. For proper inflation of the anti-g suit, the pressure regulator must be set to minimum. Any other position will result in premature pressurisation. The ventilation suit valve controls air delivery to the suit where air is trapped downstream of the turbo cooler, passed through an ejector valve and mixed with hot air, delivered via the PEC.

The cabin temperature switch is located on the right-hand side-wall. The four-position switch permits selection of the automatic temperature control system or manual adjustment of cockpit temperature. In the AUTO position, cockpit temperature is adjusted in accordance with the setting of the cabin temperature control knob on the main vertical console. In the centre or neutral position, electrical power is removed from the mixing valve. As a result it freezes the valve in its last position. In the HOT/COLD position the mixing valve is driven in the appropriate direction, but the switch should only be moved to the position momentarily to prevent the valve from driving to an extreme temperature position.

The cabin temperature control knob permits selection of the desired cockpit temperature, provided that the CABIN TEMP switch is in the AUTO position. Indications and warnings provide an AEKRAN indication of NO COOLING if the temperature of the air towards the equipment compartment exceeds 80°C (176°F). A reduction of the temperature in the equipment compartment can only be achieved by reducing the air speed.

The cabin air lever regulates the volume of air delivered from the air conditioning system, and in the CLOSED position windshield defogging is manually shut down. The air lever routes the air either to the manifolds directed towards the pilot or those orientated in the direction of the canopy in the open position. The pressure regulator controls volume and pressure of the anti-g suit in MIN, or the partial pressure suit in MAX. The suit vent knob adjusts temperature and flow of air routed to the ventilation suit. The uppermost right scale of the combined oxygen indicator displays differential pressure between cockpit pressure and outside air pressure.

Oxygen system

The oxygen system is a pressure-demand system and consists of a main system, located in the fuselage, an engine supply system and an emergency system on the ejection seat. The oxygen supply for the main oxygen system and for the engine supply is replenished through one single-charging connection and the emergency oxygen is charged directly to the bottle.

The main oxygen system consists of three 4-litre (0.88-gallon) high-pressure gaseous oxygen bottles charged at 150kPa/cm² (21.7lb/in²). The MiG-29GT carries seven bottles. Further components are an oxygen flow valve, a pressure reduction valve, an oxygen flow regulator, a personal equipment connector, a pressure regulator, the combined oxygen indicator and the oxygen control panel. The system is mechanically controlled but 115VAC power is required for operation of the indicator.

The oxygen flow valve, which controls the supply of oxygen to the system, is a rotary knob marked OPEN/CLOSE on the left-hand console. The blue-coloured MIX-100% switch allows the selection of either an oxygen/air mixture or a supply of pure oxygen. The red EMERGENCY ON-OFF switch permits selection of 100% oxygen with positive pressure or normal oxygen supply. The switch remains in the OFF position

at all times, unless an unscheduled pressure increase is required. Moving the switch to EMERGENCY ON provides 100% oxygen with continuous positive pressure to the face mask.

When EMERGENCY ON is selected, use of oxygen is two or three times higher than normal and the pilot is advised to continuously monitor the quantity remaining. The black HELMET VENT ON-OFF switch is provided for the pilot to control the helmet ventilation system.

The pressure regulator comprises an air mixture and a 100% oxygen demand regulator. With MIX selected, the air/oxygen ratio is determined by an air inlet valve, and this varies according to cabin altitude. Below 2,012m (6,600ft) pure cabin air is delivered, but above that altitude the air inlet valve reduces the air percentage until 100% oxygen is delivered at 7,925m (26,000ft). Above 12,190m (40,000ft) pressure breathing is introduced, with pressure increasing with altitude. The EMERG OXYGEN

BELOW The oxygen-related instrumentation and levers situated in the cockpit are displayed on this diagram with indicator and control equipment where appropriate. *(MiG)*

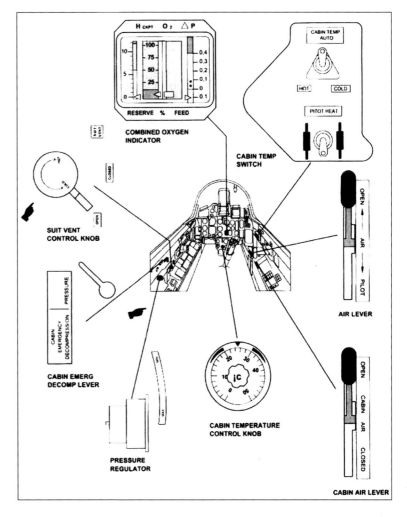

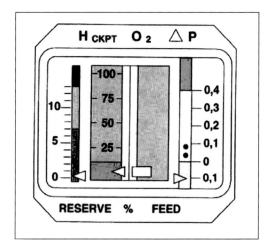

RIGHT The combined oxygen indicator has three thermometer scales with pointers for displaying cabin altitude, oxygen quantity, oxygen flow and cabin pressure differential. *(MiG)*

RESERVE warning is presented when the quantity remaining falls below 15%. Between ground level and 7,925m, with 100% selected, the regulator delivers 100% oxygen.

Operation of the oxygen system can be monitored on the combined indicator located in the centre of the front panel. The instrument has three thermometer-type scales with triangular pointer and one rectangular pointer for oxygen flow. The system can monitor cabin altitude, where the scale is calibrated in kilometres, as long as the cabin is not pressurised where the pointer indicates actual flight altitude. It also controls oxygen quantity, where 100% is indicated at a pressure of 150kPa/cm² (21.7lb/in²) in the bottles, but as the pressure decreases the indication drops proportionately. During normal oxygen flow the pointer moves up during inhalation and down during exhalation, a steady pointer indicating that no oxygen is being supplied. It also monitors cabin pressure differential.

Lighting system

The lighting system provides both external and internal lighting, the external provision including navigation lights, anti-collision lights, landing lights and taxi lights, all powered by the DC system. Two navigation lights are installed at the wing tips, a green one to the right and a red one to the left, with a white one at the left vertical stabiliser. All navigation lights are controlled by the NAV LTS switch located on the forward lighting-control panel. The selectable modes are OFF, 100%, 10%, and FLASH. On the ground the navigation lights will

RIGHT The oxygen system controls and displays are shown here, with the location of the combined oxygen indicator together with the control panel and the flow valve, the latter two located on the left side-panel in the cockpit. *(MiG)*

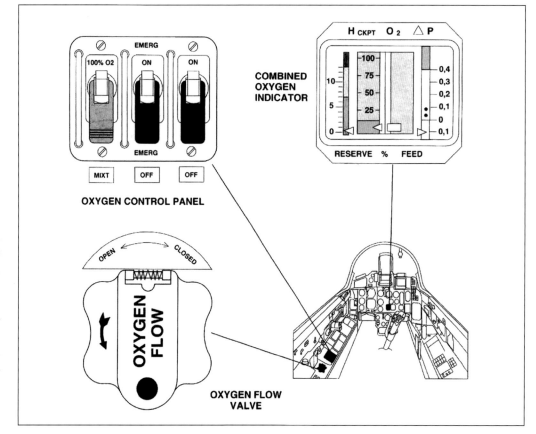

be in the 10% intensity mode regardless of the mode switch setting.

Anti-collision lights are installed behind the cockpit and on the left engine bay. These lights are controlled by the ANTI COLL switch. Two landing lights are installed, one on each main landing gear door, and a single taxi light is attached to the nose-wheel strut. The light beam of the right landing light is angled down 10° with respect to the horizon, and offset by 12° to the left with respect to the aircraft's centreline. The beam of the left landing light is angled down 8° and offset 14° to the left. The light beam of the taxi light is aligned parallel to the horizon and to the centreline of the aircraft.

The landing and taxi lights are powered by the DC supply system and are controlled by the LAND LIGHT/TAXI switch located on the left side of the instrument panel. With the switch in the TAXI position, only the taxi light will be illuminated, whereas both taxi and landing lights are on when the switch is in the LAND LIGHT position. The landing lights are disabled when the landing gear is retracted, regardless of the position of the control switch.

The internal lighting equipment comprises console panel lights, instrument lights, console floodlights, map-reading light and associated controls. The control panels and indicators are powered by the AC system and the console floodlights for the panels, instruments and the map-reading light by the DC system. The instruments are illuminated with shielded light fixtures located adjacent to each indicator. The major left and right console control panels are indirectly illuminated. The lights are controlled by rheostat-type switches located on the aft lighting-control panel.

The control knobs are assigned to the various illumination systems. The PANEL control knob has dual functions: if pushed in it allows manual intensity control of all cockpit information and warning lights except AEKRAN; if pulled out, intensity is controlled automatically by a photodiode according to ambient brightness. The MAP ILLUM control knob switches and dims the map-reading light located near this panel. Instrument lighting is switched and controlled with the INSTRUMENT control knob. The CONSOLE control knob switches and controls the intensity of the

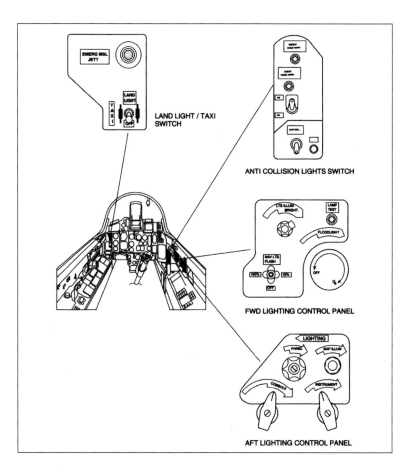

indirect illumination of various switches and control knobs. Two more control knobs are located on the forward lighting-control panel to control the floodlights and the brightness of the landing system signal panel illumination.

Communication and avionic equipment

Voice communication is provided by the VHF/UHF radio with 2,000VHF and 7,200UHF frequencies available using 29 pre-set frequencies, all with UHF guard monitoring. Due to the wideband antenna location in the right fin tip, communication can be interrupted momentarily during turns exceeding 45° angle of bank.

The radio switch is located on the right console with power to operate the VHF/UHF radio supplied by the DC generator or the batteries. A VHF/UHF frequency control panel is installed on the left-hand console. With the pre-set/manual switch on MAN, five toggle switches are used to select the desired frequency. Physically, frequencies from 100.000MHz to

ABOVE Lighting system controls are located on the right side-panel and on the upper left of the main display console. *(MiG)*

399.975MHz in increments of 0.025MHz can be selected. However, only frequencies from 100.000MHz to 149.975MHz and 220.000MHz to 399.975MHz can be used. The selected frequency is displayed on the VHF/UHF radio indicator panel. However, the last digit (0 or 5) is not displayed and if an unusable frequency is selected the indication flashes.

The PRE/MAN (pre-set/manual) switch controls the frequency selection method. In MAN, the frequency is selected with the toggle switches; in PRE, the frequency is selected with the channel selector knob on the indicator panel. A VHF/UHF radio panel is installed on the left-hand console, with the following functions: volume control knob, clockwise rotation of which increases the volume of the communication receiver; the guard receiver select switch, which monitors the UHF guard frequency when GUARD RCVR is selected; the squelch switch, which enables or disables receiver squelch; the guard received control light, which provides an illuminating light when guard transmissions are received, irrespective of the position of the guard receiver; and the automatic direction finder (ADF) switch, which allows transmissions on the ADF frequency to be received.

A VHF/UHF indicator control panel is installed on the instrument panel with the following functions through each control position: the channel selector knob allows access to any one of 29 pre-set frequencies; the channel display reveals the selected frequency; the frequency display shows the frequency of the selected channel when the pre-set/manual switch is in the PRE position or, if in MAN, the manual selected frequency; the dim knob adjusts brightness of the channel and the frequency displays; and the store push-button enters the frequency selected with the toggle switches to the indicated channel.

The VHF/UHF equipment is activated by switching the RADIO switch to ON. Transmission is accomplished by pressing the throttle-mounted microphone button. The receiver signal can be controlled with the volume knob on the control panel. The manual frequency selector allows the pilot to set the pre-set/manual switch to MAN to enter a six-digit frequency via the toggle switches in the order 00-25-50-70, with the last two digits selected with one toggle switch. The channel selector knob allows selection of the desired channel with the channel number displayed on the channel display panel and the corresponding frequency on the frequency display. If a stored frequency needs to be changed, the pilot selects the desired channel, inserts the new frequency via the toggle switches and after pressing STORE the new frequency is shown on the frequency display and stored simultaneously.

The XT-2000 emergency UHF radio provides air-to-air and air-to-ground communication on the UHF pre-set distress frequency of 243.0MHz and two further pre-set channels.

RIGHT The location of primary communication and avionics equipment on the MiG-29. Key: (1) radar; (2) infrared search and track system; (3) TACAN; (4) automatic direction finder; (5) radar homing and warning; (6) VHF/UHF radio; (7) XT-2000 emergency UHF radio; (8) IFF/SIF; (9) radar altimeter; (10) marker beacon; (11) available for optional equipment on different variants. *(MiG)*

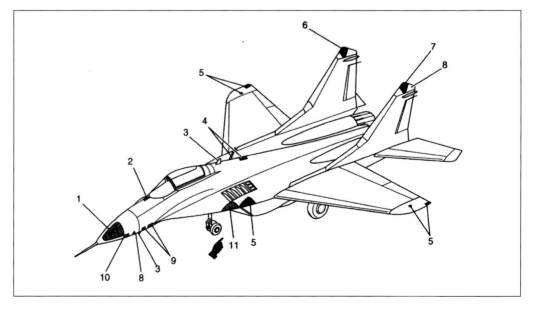

The radio can also be used as guard or auxiliary receiver in the airborne communication system. The radio is powered by 28.5VDC and utilises the emergency UHF antenna in the left vertical fin. The emergency UHF control panel is located on the forward left-hand console and supports a function selector, volume control knob and channel selector. The test push-button activates the built-in test to verify that the system is operating properly. The indicator light illuminates and remains lit as long as the button is held and a short tone is heard if the system is operating properly. In the event of a system malfunction, the indicator light flashes momentarily and then extinguishes and the audio tone is not heard.

The intercom system enables communication between the ground crew and the pilot and in the two-seat MiG-29GT the system allows communications between the two cockpits. All audio warnings produced by various aircraft systems and identification signals from radio and navigation equipment are routed to the pilot's headset. Volume of the radio and navigation equipment can be adjusted by the relevant volume control and aircraft warnings are transmitted at an audio level high enough to attract attention.

Flight recorder

The flight data recorder stores flight parameters from the operation of critical aircraft systems and has high survivability, with a requirement to withstand accelerations of up to 1,000g, temperatures up to 1,000°C for 15 minutes, exposure to sea water for up to five days and exposure to the corrosive effects of fuel for up to two days. The recorder is powered by a 28.5VDC current and the stored data represents the last three hours of the aircraft's operation.

The recorder is activated manually with a switch labelled RECORD on the right-hand console, and if not activated manually automatic recording starts at or above 85% engine rpm with the trailing-edge flaps down, or if the weight is off the right main landing gear at any rpm. Data is extracted from the recorder by the ground evaluation system at a rate 8–12 times the record speed for rapid analysis of aircraft systems and operational performance.

The recorder stamps all recordings with the aircraft serial number, flight number, date of

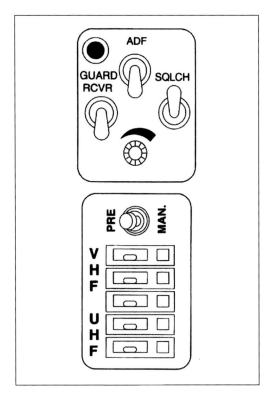

LEFT The VHF/UHF frequency control panel is located on the left-hand console and provides toggle switches for the guard receiver, automatic direction finder and squelch. The pre/manual switch allows the pilot to select frequencies. (MiG)

BELOW The VHF/UHF indicator control panel incorporates a selection knob to the left, a selected channel display, the displayed frequency and a dimmer. (MiG)

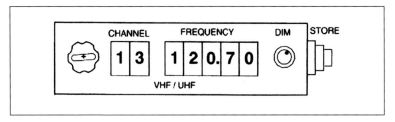

BELOW The emergency UHF radio (XT-2000) provides an emergency signal transmitted on 243.0MHz. Key: (1) function selector; (2) volume control knob; (3) channel selector; (4) test push-button; (5) test indicator light. (MiG)

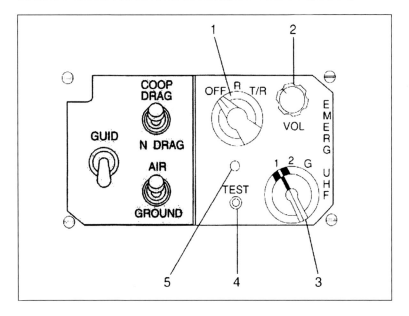

flight, sequence number of the malfunction, channel number for recorded data and start and end time of occurrences or malfunctions. Data includes all aircraft velocities, rates and control surface positions, storing a wide range of parameters, including barometric altitude, altimeter setting, g-forces in all three axes, true course, angle of bank, pitch angles, angle of attack, deflection of tailerons and rudders, control stick deflection, pedal position, aileron position and Mach number.

Engine parameters stored by the recorder include the rpm of high-pressure and low-pressure compressors, air temperature of engine intake, fuel pressure at the first stage of the turbine, fuel quantity, oil pressures in the engines and engine gearboxes, position of the exhaust nozzle flaps, pressure at the intakes of both engines and at the exhaust of both turbines, throttle positions, and vibration in the engine gearbox and in the engine turbines. A wide range of parameters of the automatic flight control system are recorded, together with bus voltage of both AC and DC systems, and a broad spectrum of measurements to capture malfunctions and unexpected occurrences.

BELOW This block diagram shows the major elements of the MiG-29 navigation architecture with the navigation computer, the central element in the processing flow from sensors, gyroscopes and radar.
(MiG)

Navigation system

The MiG-29 navigation system consists of the gyro platform reference system, navigation computer, air data computer (ADC) and radio navigation equipment. The gyro platform reference system consists of a main and a standby platform, the radio navigation system of TACAN, ADF and marker beacon receiver. All systems are closely interfaced to supply complete navigational information throughout all phases of the flight.

The gyro systems are used to measure bank and pitch angles, course and acceleration along the axis of the platform. They supply the primary azimuth and attitude references and in addition supply velocity, direction and distance inputs to the navigation computer. The system uses DC power from the generator or the batteries, with 115VAC and three-phase 36VAC supplied by the AC generator and the transformer or the DC/AC converter. However, the converter capacity is insufficient to supply heating power to the gyro system.

The gyro unit consists of the main and standby gyros, an analogue/digital computer,

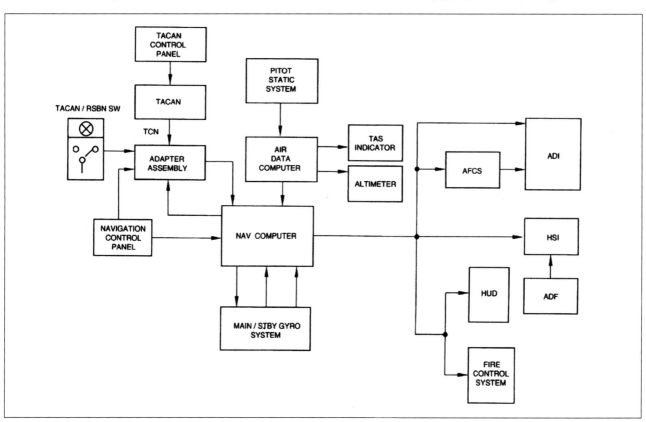

operating controls for variation (which are located behind the ejection seat) and latitude, a flux valve and built-in test equipment. Each system uses a gyro-stabilised platform upon which three accelerometers are mounted. With the platform stabilised in pitch and roll by gyros and oriented along the aircraft axis, the accelerometers sense acceleration in any direction. This acceleration is processed by the analogue/digital computer to provide course reference, attitude information, main gyro platform stabilisation and signals for the navigation computer. A circuitry loop corrects for apparent precession, based on pre-set latitude.

With the BAT-GND-SUPPLY switch and the generator and navigation switches placed to ON, power is applied to bring the gyro platforms to operating temperature. MAIN and STBY switches are selected for stabilisation of the platforms, but prior to selection the appropriate airfield has to be chosen. The alignment cycle is started by placing the MAIN and STBY gyro switches to ON, and the PREPARE/OPERATE switch in PREPARE.

After approximately 30–40 seconds, heading reference is inserted to the analogue/digital computer by pressing the mag heading slave button and COURSE CMPTR ZERO push-button simultaneously for 10–15 seconds. The PREPARE/OPERATE switch has to be placed to OPERATE within 90 seconds after switching both gyros to ON. After a total of three minutes, the fast prepare light on the right console rear panel illuminates, indicating completion of the alignment and system readiness. The light extinguishes during take-off when the weight is off the main landing gear.

The PREPARE/OPERATE switch is left in the PREPARE position until the NAV READY light illuminates on the right console rear panel after 15 minutes, indicating completion of the alignment, which may last up to 20 minutes at temperatures between -30°C (-22°F) and -60°C (-76°F). When switching the PREPARE/OPERATE switch to OPERATE, the light extinguishes, indicating system readiness. If the long alignment has been selected, and circumstances dictate switchover to fast alignment, at least five minutes should elapse prior to switching from PREPARE to OPERATE.

The gyro system can be operated either

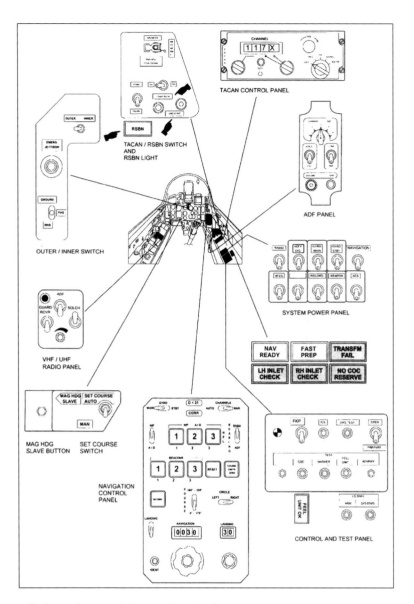

with the main gyro platform or the standby gyro platform. However, the main gyro platform is more accurate since digital integration is provided to the main gyro platform only. In case of a main gyro system failure, switchover from main to standby has to be accomplished manually.

The navigation computer is the central unit of the navigation system. It processes data from the inertial navigation unit and from the air data computer (ADC) to compute the present position and to correct it according to TACAN signals, to compute azimuth and distance information to a selected, programmed navigation point and altitude deviations as well as ground track information. Additionally, the navigation computer produces discrete control signals for automatic control of the complete

ABOVE The navigation system controls are located on the right side-panel of the cockpit, with the communication controls on the left side. (MiG)

RIGHT The control panel for the navigation systems is set in the right face of the main instrument panel and consists of input stations and flight route settings. *(MiG)*

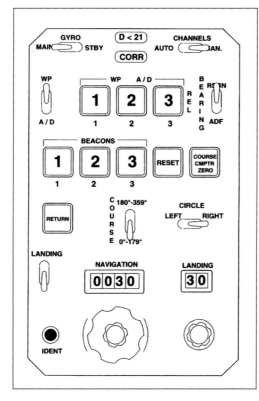

navigation system. The navigation computer is provided with 28.5VDC, 115AC and three-phase 36VAC electrical power supplies.

To reduce computational capacity, a relative coordinate system is used, restricted in latitude and longitude. The zero point of the system is in the lower left corner. Required navigation points are entered into the navigation computer via the navigation computer programming panel, located on the left side of the nose section. Two different types of navigation computers are available, the CWU A-340-071M version 2204 and the 2205. Computational capability of the CWU version 2204 is restricted in latitude and longitude to an area of 36° and one set of coordinates, while the CWU 2205 is restricted to an area of 40° and two sets of coordinates.

Four operating modes are possible, the normal mode being dead-reckoning with TACAN update. This mode is available after fast alignment; only analogue integration of both gyro platforms is performed. Accuracy is a minimal 4% of distance travelled per hour of circular error probability, 1.5° precession per hour. However, since no meteorological wind information data are processed, large computational errors may be present. The inertial navigation operating mode is available

after long alignment with the main gyro platform. From selection of precise alignment, maximum error is 8.33kph (5.17mph) of circular error probability, precession 1° per hour.

Automatic continuous navigation computer update is available in both operating modes. System inaccuracy is reduced to ±0.37km (0.685 miles), +0.1% of distance to the station used for update. Three individual TACAN stations can be programmed prior to flight for update purposes. The channel select switch must be placed to AUTO, the REL BEARING switch to RSBN, and the landing switch to OFF. TACAN is selected on the right-hand console and the CORR light illuminates if proper signals are received and automatic update is performed. For update with a TACAN station, the programmed station must be selected on the TACAN control panel in addition.

The navigation computer can be manually updated by pressing the COURSE CMPTR ZERO illuminated push-button and releasing it upon overflight of a selected and programmed waypoint. Update is not possible, however, if a discrepancy of more than 39km (24 miles) exists between the present position computed and the actual position.

Various navigational options are operated according to the setting on the navigation control panel, including point-to-point navigation, return, landing approach, traffic re-entry after a missed approach, and manual station selection.

In point-to-point navigation mode six points can be programmed. These are selected by setting the WP-A/D (waypoint/aerodrome) switch and selection of one of the three WP-A/D illuminated push-buttons. The course to the selected coordinate is displayed by the course pointer and the course window, distance being displayed by the range indicator on the horizontal situation indicator and on the head-up display. As the aircraft closes on the selected coordinate the D<21 NM (21 nautical miles, or 38.9km/24 miles) light illuminates. Passing the coordinate, the lost bearing indication will be shown exceeding 5.9km (3.7 miles) distance outbound.

For the return mode, pressing the RETURN illuminated push-button provides bearing information to a lead point for the nearest 17km (10.5 miles) final intercept to the nominated airfield, provided the correct landing direction is selected with the COURSE switch and the update function is operating. Slant range is indicated to the selected A/D coordinates. If automatic navigation computer update is inoperative, course and distance to the airfield reference point are provided. During the approach, glide-path information is displayed on the attitude director indicator for a 7° glide-slope to the final intercept point at 1,128m (3,700ft) above ground level or the barometric pressure at airfield level.

If the traffic re-entry (missed approach) mode button is pressed, the navigation computer supplies steering information for a traffic pattern, provided the landing select switch is off and TACAN correction is in operation. Steering is provided for a 10km (6.2-mile) downwind leg and final intercept. Pattern direction left-hand or right-hand is selected by placing the circular left–right switch to the corresponding direction. Glide-path information is displayed for a pattern altitude of 610m (2,000ft) above ground level or the barometric pressure at airfield level.

In manual select mode the channels MAN/ AUTO switch is set to MAN, with bearing and distance to a selected TACAN station displayed. With the CHANNELS switch in manual, the final course must be dialled in on the horizontal situation indicator to be in a configuration to receive steering commands.

The navigation control panel contains all the switches for selection and required input for the four primary operating modes, for the gyroscopes, channel selection, relative bearing and landing position indications. Three combined push-button and indicator lights marked 1, 2 and 3 allow selection of a beacon for navigation system updates. A reset button and indicator erases existing beacon lock-on information to allow selection of another beacon. A combined push-button and indicator light also allows reset of the navigation computer, and manual selection of the instrument landing system is displayed through a landing channel window and operated by the appropriate selector knob.

Programming the navigation computer is achieved through a panel located on the lower left side of the nose section. It is used for programming the reference latitude for the coordinate sphere, relative coordinates for three

airfields, three waypoints and three beacons, the heading for four visual reference points, runway directions for three airfields, and three ILS channels. A second set of data has to be programmed with the CWU 2205 version, which is restricted to a 40° area; however, it cannot be selected from the cockpit.

Programming is performed with an eight-digit code consisting of a two-digit address number, a single-digit prefix number and the five-digit programming code. The reference latitude has to be entered into the computer to adjust the relative coordinate system. In the northern hemisphere the lateral geographic coordinate is complemented by three zeros; in the southern hemisphere this is subtracted from 360 and the result complemented by two zeros.

The programming code for headings consists of the geographical heading with the arc minutes and arc seconds expressed in hundredths of degrees. For programming of runway directions, the value between 0.00 and 179.99 has to be selected. For programming of coordinates, the relative coordinate is calculated to an accuracy of four decimal places, rounded to the third decimal and expressed as an unfragmented number. The relative coordinates

BELOW The navigation programming panel provides the pilot with options for entering course and bearing information and for landing-position information. Key: (1) data input display; (2) repeater display; (3) built-in test; (4) enter button; (5) lamp test button; (6) on/off button; (7) keyboard for data input. (MiG)

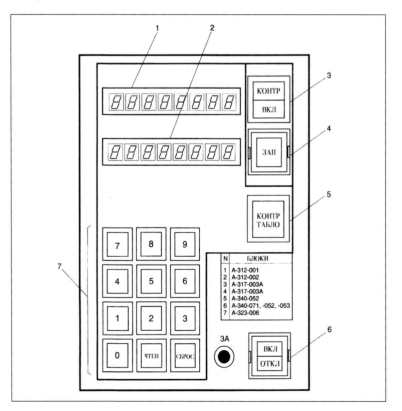

are obtained by subtracting the reference coordinates of the relative coordinate system from the geographical coordinates.

To receive the five-digit programming code, the relative coordinate has to be converted to a decimal number by the following formula: arc degrees + arc-minutes/60 + arc-seconds/3600 = five-digit code. The five-digit code has to be combined with the address and the prefix number. For example, with a waypoint 3 relative latitude of 24° 20' 22", an address number for waypoint 3 latitude of 41, a prefix number of 0 and a five-digit code for the latitude of 24339 (because 20' 22" is 33.9% of one degree), the programming code would be 41024339.

To enter the data set, DC and AC power must be available and the NAVIGATION switch on the system power panel has to be placed in the ON position. The navigation computer programming panel is switched on with the ON button and illumination of the data input display indicates system readiness. Pressing the RESET button on the keyboard sets the data input display to zero. Before entering the data set in random sequence, the opening code 77127777 has to be entered and after entering each eight-digit code the ENTER push-button has to be pressed for data input. After resetting the system with the RESET push-button, the next code can be entered. The RESET button can also be used to delete the displayed code in case of an input failure or error. After input of the complete data set the closing code 77139999 has to be entered to complete the action.

When the computer CWU 2205 version is in use, the code 25100001 has to be entered after the opening code for input of the first data set, and code 25100002 will input the second data set.

BELOW The TACAN controls and indicators panel, providing magnetic bearing and slant range to ground stations selected by the pilot. Key: (1) navigation channel window; (2) volume control; (3) TACAN function selector knob; (4) channel selector control knob (X/Y selection); (5) channel selector control knob (unit digit selection); (6) test indicator light; (7) test button; (8) channel selector control knob. (MiG)

The same code is used for switching sets between two sorties. The READOUT button can be used to check out valid codes. After entering the two-digit address number and the prefix number and pushing the READOUT button the valid code will be displayed on the data input display.

TACAN

Developed during the 1950s as an evolved form of both the VHF Omnidirectional Range (VOR) and the Distance Measuring Equipment (DME) system, adopted by civil aviation for bearing and range information, the TACAN system provides magnetic bearing and slant range to the selected ground station, or to a suitably equipped cooperating aircraft in air-to-air mode. A suitably equipped cooperating aircraft is one equipped with bearing transmitting equipment. The TACAN system can transmit only distance information when interrogated in the air-to-air/transmit mode and determines the identity of the transmitting station and indicates the dependability of the transmitted signal.

The system utilises radio navigational frequencies, the propagation of which is virtually limited to line-of-sight distances. In the case of co-channel interference in the transmit mode, the interfering channel identifier is garbled. When a temporary loss of signal occurs, a memory keeps range tracking for 15 seconds and bearing tracking for 3 seconds. The TACAN automatically self-tests after a temporary signal loss and displays its status on the control panel. The system is supplied with 115VAC and by the AC generator or the DC/AC converter.

The TACAN system uses an upper and lower antenna to receive TACAN signals. Antenna switching to the antenna with the greatest signal strength is automatic. A two-position REL BEARING toggle switch on the NAV panel allows the pilot to select the appropriate system for navigational display. The TACAN function selector knob has five positions: OFF, REC, T/R, A/A REC and A/A T/R.

In REC (receive) mode, no interrogation pulse is transmitted. The bearing identification of a selected ground station is received but range information is not available. In T/R (transmit/

receive) the transmitter and receiver are active, generating range and bearing information from a selected ground station. In A/A REC (air-to-air receive) mode, the system receives and decodes bearing information from a suitably equipped cooperating aircraft. The channel of the receiving aircraft must be either 63 channels above or 63 channels below the suitably equipped cooperating aircraft channel, but must be within the 1 to 126 X or Y channel range. Both aircraft must be either in the X or Y channel at the same time.

The A/A T/R (air-to-air transmit and receive) mode allows the TACAN system to interrogate a reference aircraft, and the slant range to the cooperating aircraft is displayed according to channel selection (see above). In this mode the TACAN system provides distance replies to other aircraft when interrogated. Bearing to a suitably equipped cooperating aircraft is also displayed. The TACAN AN/ARN-118 system can transmit only distance information when interrogated in the air-to-air, transmit and receive mode. The maximum number of aircraft to receive range information simultaneously is limited to five.

In the air-to-air modes, to prevent possible interference with IFF or transponder signals, channels 1 to 11, 58 to 74 and 121 to 126 are not used. To reduce the possibility of interference from distance-measuring equipment, the use of Y channels is recommended if the suitably equipped cooperating aircraft is provided with that capability.

The channel selector control consists of two rotary knobs that are used to select the desired TACAN channel. The left knob selects the tens and hundreds digits of the operating channel, the right knob selects units of digits and contains an outer knob which selects the X or Y channel. Placing the knob to X provides the capability for 126-channel operation and placing it to Y adds an additional 126 channels. The dial system is numbered 0 to 129, each number from 1 to 126 representing a specific pair (transmitting and receiving) of frequencies. Numbers 0, 127, 128 and 129 on the channel dial are not usable.

The TACAN test button can be used to test the primary function modes as well as the function knob and takes 90 seconds to warm up before it can be pressed and

released to start the process. The test does not check the antenna interface and TACAN accuracy would usually be reviewed against a ground checkpoint. If the TACAN bearing signal becomes lost or is unreliable, the TACAN system switches to automatic self-test. The indicators of the self-test correspond to the manual test. If there is a dedicated malfunction in the system, the test indicator light comes on and remains steady. If the indicator light illuminates steady during the test cycle in both the T/R and REC modes, the bearing and distance information on the horizontal situation indicator is invalid. The self-test can be terminated any time by turning either the TACAN function selector knob or any of the channel selector knobs.

If TACAN indicator readouts become suspect during flight, the pilot would perform an inflight confidence self-test of the system by setting the TACAN function selector knob to T/R and then pressing the TACAN test button, whereupon the test indicator light will flash momentarily. If the test indicator light illuminates steadily during the test cycle in both the T/R and REC modes, the bearing and distance information are invalid. If the test indicator light comes on in the T/R mode but not in the REC mode, the distance information is invalid and the bearing on the horizontal situation indicator is valid.

Automatic direction finding

The ADF system provides direction finding or radio monitoring in the high-frequency band (150–1299.5kHz) and eight different stations can be channelled for inflight use, although a standard setting is usually programmed. The system is powered with 28.5VDC and 36VAC from a transformer. The battery and DC/AC converter supply the system with power in case of a generator failure.

The controls consist of the ADF selector switch on the radio panel, the REL/BEARING/ADF switch on the navigation panel, the INNER/OUTER switch and the BEACON INNER light on the instrument panel above the radar altimeter, as well as of the ADF channel select knob, the VOICE/CW switch, the COMPASS/ANTENNA select switch, the VOL control knob

RIGHT The automatic
direction finding
control panel with
channel selector and
toggle switches for
voice or computer
selection. (MiG)

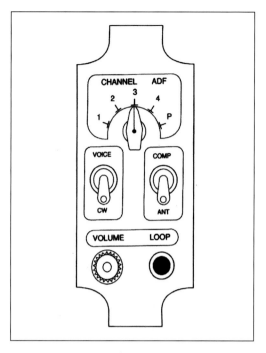

and the LOOP push-button on the ADF panel. On the MiG-29GT the INNER/OUTER switch and the BEACON INNER light are located on the left-hand side-wall.

To operate the ADF the pilot sets the ADF select switch (radio panel) to off, sets the RSBN/ADF switch (navigation panel) to ADF and sets the COMPASS/ANTENNA select switch to CMP. Then he sets the INNER/OUTER switch to the desired position, according to the required channel, and checks that the BEACON inner light is illuminated if the INNER position is selected. Then the desired channel is set with the ADF channel selector knob and the VOICE/CW switch is set as required.

The ADF receiver operation first requires the operator to set the ADF select switch to ADF, the RSBN/ADF switch to ADF and the COMPASS/ANTENNA to ANTENNA, and to select the desired channel via the INNER/OUTER switch and ADF channel select knob, followed by the VOICE/CW switch as required. The ADF self-test is initiated by setting the RSBN/ADF switch to ADF, setting the channel select knob to position P, checking that the bearing pointer rotates to approximately 195°, setting the VICE/CW switch to CW and checking for the 800Hz tone transmission. Manual rotation of the ADF loop antenna is facilitated manually by pressing the LOOP button, and after release the antenna will return to its original position.

Radio marker receiver

The radio marker receiver indicates the overflight of a marker beacon. According to ICAO standards the frequency is 75MHz, with overflight indicated by illumination of the MARKER BEACON light on the telelight panel and by an audio signal at 3,000Hz. The device is operated by 28.5VDC from the DC generator or battery power and is turned on by placing the ACFT SYS switch to the ON position. The marker beacon receiver will switch the ADF from a selected OUTER channel to INNER channel when passing a marker beacon within 15° of the final course, providing the landing gear is down.

IFF equipment

The MiG-29's identification system STR-700 provides automatic identification of aircraft in which it is installed when challenged by surface or airborne IFF interrogation sets. It identifies the aircraft position momentarily upon request, reports the altitude of the aircraft and indicates any emergency. Altitude is given from the air data computer. In operation, the identification system receives coded interrogation signals and transmits coded response signals to the source of the challenging lock. Five modes of operation are provided for interrogation and response to interrogation signals: 1, security identification; 2, personal identification; 3/A, traffic identification; C altitude reporting; and 4 crypto identification.

The codes for modes 1 (00–73) and 3/A can be set in the cockpit during flight, but the code for mode 2 must be set on the ground. Modes 2 and 3/A can be set from code 0 000 to 7 777. When mode C is selected, coded altitude information from the altitude encoder is applied to the IFF system for reply to mode C interrogation. The code represents aircraft altitude and there are no provisions for manually setting mode C code. Failure of mode 4 to reply is indicated by optical and audio signals. The system is supplied with 28.5VDC and 115VAC, 400Hz for the altitude encoder.

The IFF control panel is located on the right console, or, in the case of the MiG-29GT, in the front cockpit only. There is also a mode 4

RIGHT The IFF control panel is situated on the right console and on two-seat variants in the front cockpit only. An explanation of the modes and selections can be found in the accompanying text. *(MiG)*

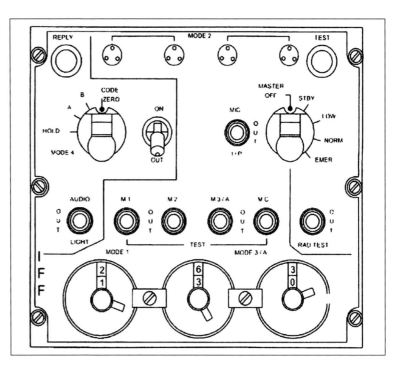

light on the telelight panel. A comprehensive set of function switches and selector switches provides a wide range of optional configurations and test options. Prior to each flight several checks are made to ensure functionality and to verify operability, and a run is made of the built-in test equipment to ensure that the transponder is working correctly. The checks also evaluate the IFF and the associated selective identification feature.

Warning and information equipment

To keep the cross-checking of instruments to a minimum, warning and indicator lights are incorporated throughout the cockpit. Additional voice warning is provided for abnormal conditions. The warning system complex consists of three independent systems: the telelight panel (TLP), the AEKRAN and the voice information and warning system (VIWAS). A MASTER CAUTION light flashes whenever a red warning light illuminates on the TLP or an AEKRAN warning signal is displayed. All the warning equipment is operated with 28.5VDC from the generator or from battery power.

The MASTER CAUTION light is located on the instrument panel, and whenever a warning signal is displayed on the TLP or the AEKRAN the MASTER CAUTION light starts flashing. Brightness of the light can be adjusted by rotating the light case. Pressing the MASTER CAUTION light extinguishes the light; the warnings on the TLP continue steady, but AEKRAN displays are not affected.

The telelight panel provides immediate warning of an abnormal condition which could

RIGHT The warning and information systems provide telelight displays on the cockpit panels depicted here, together with the VIWAS system. *(MiG)*

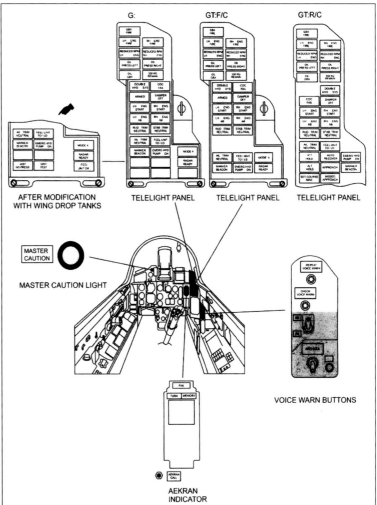

AFTER MODIFICATION WITH WING DROP TANKS

TELELIGHT PANEL   TELELIGHT PANEL   TELELIGHT PANEL

MASTER CAUTION LIGHT

VOICE WARN BUTTONS

AEKRAN INDICATOR

affect the safety of the aircraft, and these are in red illumination. Additional information shows green lights indicating system operation or condition. A malfunction is shown by a flashing warning light in conjunction with the flashing MASTER CAUTION light. After reset of this alarm the warning light illuminates steadily until the problem is solved. A photodiode automatically adjusts the brightness of the lights according to environmental conditions. A rheostat on the lighting panel provides for manual adjustment of brightness.

The AEKRAN system is part of the aircraft warning and recording system. It monitors and controls the operation of aircraft systems and self-test equipment and displays and records corresponding messages if malfunctions occur. After landing, additional information about the aircraft's systems, equipment limits exceeded during the flight but not relevant to the safety of flight, and illumination of warning lights are all recorded by discrete signals.

The AEKRAN system is activated automatically when the NAVIGATION switch is placed to the on position. During engine start, both generators' failure indication may be displayed until external power is disconnected. After take-off the FLIGHT light illuminates momentarily. If a malfunction is detected, the corresponding message is displayed. Simultaneously, the MASTER CAUTION light

flashes and the VIWAS gives the appropriate message, but if this is not available VIWAS signals the pilot to CHECK AEKRAN.

The AEKRAN indication is displayed until the problem indicated is solved, a signal with higher priority is received or the AEKRAN CALL button is pressed, an action which extinguishes the indication and the MASTER CAUTION light. However, the signal is stored in the memory circuit indicated by a memory light. If two or more systems fail the turn light illuminates; the highest priority signal is displayed first.

Depressing the AEKRAN CALL button stores the displayed signal in the memory circuit and permits display of the next signal in the priority sequence. After all signals have been displayed the turn light goes out. If required, the signals in the memory circuit can be repeated by pressing the AEKRAN CALL button. After landing, all stored signals are copied to a control slip after engine shutdown, and AC GEN is displayed on the AEKRAN.

Self-test is initiated by pushing the AEKRAN CALL button. The fail light should not illuminate. After 15 seconds the SELF TEST sign followed by OK are displayed in the display window. A system failure may be indicated by a fail light or by a distorted SELF TEST and AEKRAN FAIL light in the display window.

Voice information and warning system

The VIWAS provides voice warning to focus the pilot's attention on a problem indicated on the warning panel or AEKRAN. Depending on the type of emergency, an advisory for initial action to be taken is added. The system is powered by 28.5VDC. In case of multiple malfunctions, voice warnings are expressed according to a priority sequence. The VIWAS is switched on with the battery and two push-buttons are provided for this purpose on the right-hand console. The CHECK VOICE WARN button is used to initiate a self-test, and pressing the REPEAT VOICE WARN button repeats the last warning. To ensure reliability of the warning system, the light bulbs of all warning and indicator lamps are function tested. Pressing the LAMP TEST button on the lighting panel illuminates all lights.

REPEAT VOICE WARN

CHECK VOICE WARN

AM

FM

ANTI COLL

RIGHT The voice and information warning system (VIWAS) is one of the essential equipment lists in the warning and information systems inventory. It provides a fault director for further amplification through the telelight or AEKRAN panels. (MiG)

LEFT The gun port and associated gas vent forward of the air intake louvres characterise early variants of the Fulcrum. The gun has never been relinquished as a means of close-in air combat when the missiles run out and dogfighting is the only remaining option. *(David Baker)*

ABOVE Key to the MiG-29's effectiveness in air combat or ground support roles is its radar and the active electronically scanned array that was based on the N-31 Sokol range. This early version of the FGA-29 had a 575mm antenna. *(Via David Baker)*

BELOW The FGA-35 has gone through a similar series of upgrades and modifications and at one point was withdrawn from sales to foreign customers, but in some trade shows it has been redesignated as the FGA-29, from which it certainly evolved. *(Vitaly Kuzmin)*

LEFT The FGA-29 was developed in a series of modified configurations and improvements and the system was produced with clearance for export. *(Via David Baker)*

BELOW The Zhuk ME has similarly been marked up as an FGA-29, the designation applying to the export version. Developed as a pulse-Doppler radar, it was introduced into the MiG-29SMT. *(Via David Baker)*

ABOVE The covered radar compartment for the MiG-29 9.13 Fulcrum C displays the twist-cassegrain antenna for the N019E. *(MiG)*

ABOVE Elements of the N019E radar assembly on its handling dolly prior to installation. *(MiG)*

BELOW Weapons and armaments control panels located on the front side of the main cockpit console include the HUD/HDD optical screens, the radar homing and warning panel, the control stick, the weapon control panel, the radar control panel, emergency missile jettison station and the flare control panel. *(MiG)*

BELOW Weapons control panels for the left side (consisting of emergency UHF panel, throttle assembly switches and external stores switch) and the right side (radar homing and warning panel, flare indicators and the system power panel). *(MiG)*

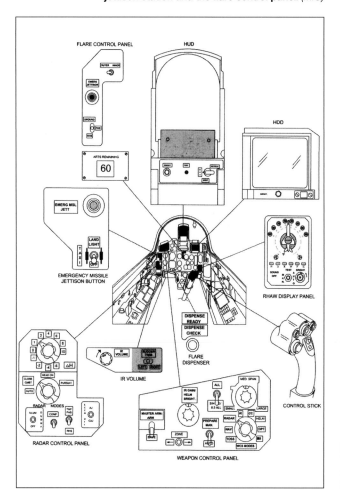

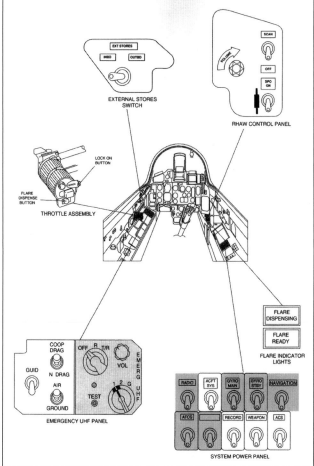

LEFT The Vympel Kh-29 (AS-14) air-to-surface missile has a range of up to 30km (19 miles) and is seen on the MiG-29M and MiG-29K. *(David Baker)*

LEFT The Kh-31A (AS-17) air-to-surface missile has a range of up to 110km (70 miles) and is most effectively employed as an anti-radiation weapon. With a top speed of Mach 3.5 it was the first supersonic anti-ship missile launched by aircraft of the MiG-29 class. *(Via David Baker)*

BELOW A *Luftwaffe* MiG-29 fires an R-17 (AA-10) air-to-air missile. Manufactured in the Ukraine and Russia, the R-17 has a range of up to 130km (81 miles) and comes in a variety of variants including infrared homing and semi-active or active radar homing. *(USAF)*

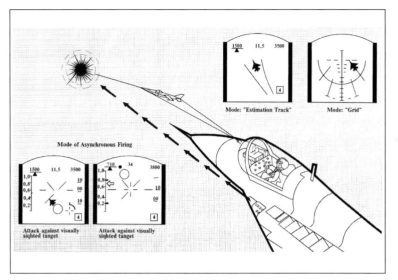

ABOVE Asynchronous firing in both estimation track and grid modes for the gun allows calculated as well as computed offset firing displays providing automatic deflection information for accurately placing the rounds on the target at a distance determined from radar tracking of the target. *(MiG)*

ABOVE The MiG-29K simulator alongside the MiG-35, a device which is also used to synchronise electronic signals between the functioning aircraft and the displays on the simulator. *(MiG)*

BELOW Weapons load capability for the MiG-29 9.12B and SD/SE variants. *(MiG)*

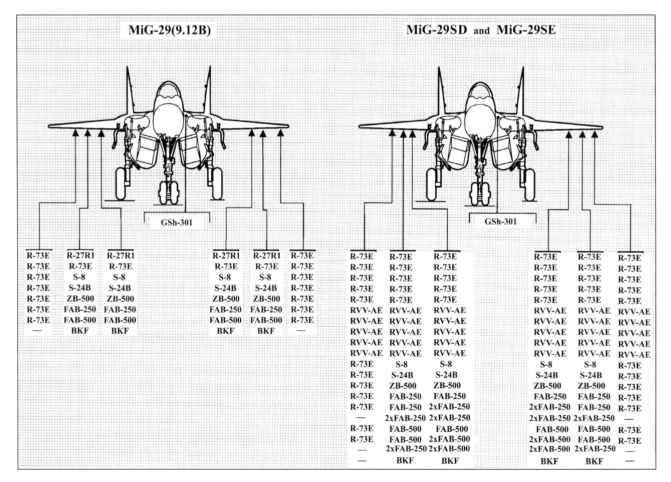

MiG-29(9.12B)

GSh-301

R-73E	R-27R1	R-27R1	R-27R1	R-27R1	R-73E
R-73E	R-73E	R-73E	R-73E	R-73E	R-73E
R-73E	S-8	S-8	S-8	S-8	R-73E
R-73E	S-24B	S-24B	S-24B	S-24B	R-73E
R-73E	ZB-500	ZB-500	ZB-500	ZB-500	R-73E
R-73E	FAB-250	FAB-250	FAB-250	FAB-250	R-73E
R-73E	FAB-500	FAB-500	FAB-500	FAB-500	R-73E
—	BKF	BKF	BKF	BKF	—

MiG-29SD and **MiG-29SE**

GSh-301

R-73E	R-73E	R-73E	R-73E	R-73E	R-73E
R-73E	R-73E	R-73E	R-73E	R-73E	R-73E
R-73E	R-73E	R-73E	R-73E	R-73E	R-73E
R-73E	R-73E	R-73E	R-73E	R-73E	R-73E
R-73E	R-73E	R-73E	R-73E	R-73E	R-73E
RVV-AE	RVV-AE	RVV-AE	RVV-AE	RVV-AE	RVV-AE
RVV-AE	RVV-AE	RVV-AE	RVV-AE	RVV-AE	RVV-AE
RVV-AE	RVV-AE	RVV-AE	RVV-AE	RVV-AE	RVV-AE
RVV-AE	RVV-AE	RVV-AE	RVV-AE	RVV-AE	RVV-AE
RVV-AE	RVV-AE	RVV-AE	RVV-AE	RVV-AE	RVV-AE
R-73E	S-8	S-8	S-8	S-24B	R-73E
R-73E	S-24B	S-24B	S-24B	ZB-500	R-73E
R-73E	ZB-500	ZB-500	ZB-500	FAB-250	R-73E
R-73E	FAB-250	FAB-250	FAB-250	2xFAB-250	R-73E
R-73E	FAB-250	2xFAB-250	2xFAB-250	2xFAB-250	R-73E
—	2xFAB-250	2xFAB-250			
R-73E	FAB-500	FAB-500	FAB-500	FAB-500	R-73E
R-73E	FAB-500	2xFAB-500	2xFAB-500	FAB-500	R-73E
—	2xFAB-250	2xFAB-500	2xFAB-500	2xFAB-250	—
—	BKF	BKF	BKF	BKF	—

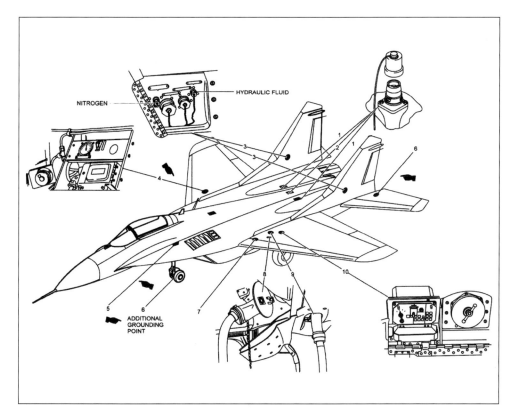

LEFT The primary access points for servicing the MiG-29. Key: (1) engine oil (IPM-10); (2) gearbox oil (IPM-10); (3) nitrogen with a purity density of 98% and hydraulic fluid (AMG-10 or H-515); (4) radar cooling (LENA-65); (5) gaseous oxygen at a pressure of 150 (±5) bar; (6) grounding cable; (7) compressed air at a pressure of 150 (±5) bar; (8) external AC power at 117.5/202VAC, 400Hz, three-phase; (9) external DC power at 28.5VDC, 15kW; (10) engine fuel (JP8, RT, TS-1 or T-1). *(MiG)*

BELOW A production line of MiG-29 aircraft in servicing bays. *(MiG)*

Chapter Four

The pilot's view

Pundits have diverging views about the MiG-29 and its flying qualities, and about its ability to survive in an environment of fifth-generation combat aircraft. But in an age of electronic net-centric warfare, the pilot is still an important part of the man-machine interface and flying characteristics are more important than ever. The pilot's view is paramount and the ability to fly and fight in the combat-ridden skies of 21st century warfare is essential.

OPPOSITE A fine study of the MiG-29SMT, which combines all the attributes of a superbly manoeuvrable dogfighter with the load and targeting capabilities of a ground-attack or strike aircraft. *(MiG)*

A pilot's perspective on flying the MiG-29 UB from John Farley

Noted for services to aviation and test flying in particular, John Farley trained as an apprentice at the Royal Aircraft Establishment, Farnborough, and joined the RAF in 1955. Initially flying Hawker Hunters with No 4 Squadron, he became a flying instructor at RAF Cranwell and took an Empire Test Pilots' School course in 1963. With a distinguished pass, John took up a position as test pilot at the RAE's Aerodynamics Research Flight, Bedford.

In 1964 he began an association with Harrier development from the P.1127 to the Kestrel and then the Harrier, an association which would last 19 years. Eventually, he retired from Dunsfold as Chief Test Pilot before starting a second career involved with marketing and displaying the Harrier overseas, helping the US induct the AV-8A and then the AV-8B. Despite the obvious contributions to the development and refinement of the flying qualities of the Harrier, a notable achievement was when he managed to maintain an AV-8B in soaring flight for two hours!

John Farley has flown more than 80 different types of aircraft and has gained international respect for his apolitical approach to aviation development, engaging with the Russians in constructive dialogue with their test pilots and design engineers. When quoting the exploits of John Farley to Russian engineers at TsAGI, it was made known to this author that he was highly respected in Russia's aeronautical circles. Keenly interested themselves in V/STOL, they knew him but from a distance.

That openness and dialogue, and an ability to cut through entrenched prejudice which has on so many occasions condemned a Western readership to hostile comments regarding the capabilities of Russian aircraft, opened the way for John to get closer and to fly the MiG-29 in 1990. At a time when the USSR was about to collapse, he finally got the chance to fly this aircraft for himself and his experience bears testimony to the outstanding design aspects and flying qualities of this fine combat aircraft. (*John Farley*)

If you are a fighter pilot and you are ever called upon to fly against the MiG-29, you should be aware that this aircraft may have a superior aerodynamic performance to the one you are flying. For those private pilots who can stall-turn a Tiger Moth, take my word for it, you would be able to stall-turn the MiG-29 as easily and reliably as the Tiger.

The above two sentences are the best I can do to give a brief introductory flavour of a very remarkable aeroplane. Neither is in any way an exaggeration, although, following my report of the flight in 1990, some people clearly felt I was overstating how well it flew. Indeed, one – after reading my views in *Flight International* – wrote to the Editor and accused me of 'having snow on my boots'.

It was back in 1988 when the Mikoyan Design Bureau and their test pilots stole the Farnborough show with the first-ever Western display of their MiG-29. That occasion was truly a political and commercial watershed, but for the aerospace professionals the display was technically remarkable, as it included manoeuvres that required a combination of engine handling, intake design and wing aerodynamics that no in-service Western fighter could offer at that time.

I had many questions but two examples will suffice at this stage. How had they developed their aircraft to pull considerably more g than ours at low speeds? And how did the engines and the aerodynamics allow the pilot to start a tailslide at 5,900m (19,356ft) and take the wings and intakes to 90° alpha (as angle of attack is normally called) during the recovery? I should add that this latter manoeuvre was flown in such a repeatable way that it seemed the aircraft was on rails.

As an aviation buff whose day job allowed privileged access behind the scenes at Farnborough, I went out of my way to make personal contact with the MiG pilots. However, this was not as easy as you might think, because the Berlin Wall was not consigned to history until 13 months later. Consequently well-built minders were very much in evidence whenever one met the pilots, and since any conversation required an interpreter the whole exercise lacked the easy informality that normally exists between pilots at air shows.

It will be difficult for youngsters today to appreciate the atmosphere of suspicion and fear (even dread on some people's parts) that existed between the East and West during the Cold War. This atmosphere was the normal stuff we breathed even a decade before the wall went up in 1961. Therefore in 1988, make no mistake, both the Russians and the Brits were very much feeling their way during personal contacts.

However, we don't want to talk about that! Suffice to say that I invited three MiG pilots to the traditional dinner for the Red Arrows in the BAe chalet on the Sunday evening after the show. Things progressed further at Paris the following year, such that I felt able to write to Michael Waldenberg, their chief designer, to see if there was any chance I could fly the aircraft at the next Farnborough. This resulted in a telex (those were the days ...) in which he agreed to talk about it when he got to the show.

Right from the beginning of the first tentative contacts with the MiG team, I had reasoned that they had no more control over their political circumstances than we had over ours, so I went out of my way not to put them on the spot in front of their minders. I felt the best approach was to concentrate on medium- and low-speed handling characteristics and not to push things by asking about military weapons fit and performance.

Walking to the MiG flight-line caravan for my first meeting with Waldenberg, I saw no reason to change that approach. It seemed to me he had to be proud of what he had achieved and would naturally want to talk about it, providing I stuck to aerodynamics. Thus after introductions, I simply took the initiative and volunteered how I had been a fan of vortex lift since my HP115 days at Bedford. I chatted slowly on through the interpreter for what must have been ten minutes or so, asking no questions and just explaining my views on vortex lift and the frustration I felt at having to limit our research on the HP115 to angles closer to 40° alpha than the 90° they were showing with their MiG.

Sketching in my notebook I went on to explain the problems we found with sideslip at high alpha. Although I was well aware that

Waldenberg would know all about the HP115 programme, I wanted to give him time to size me up and decide what to say, before I said to him, 'You have clearly solved all these issues with the MiG-29 and I would like to know how you did it and then experience such good handing at first hand.'

As he did so he was talking about how the wing and engine intake could cope with the high alphas of their display, especially the 90° alpha present during the recovery from the tail-slide manoeuvre that was a feature of the MiG-29 display. When he finished he turned to his chief test pilot, Valeriy Ye. Menitskiy, and told him to fly me – but 'in the back seat'.

Valeriy and he then had a long conversation in Russian, where Valeriy – a real bear of a man, and like most in his job no shrinking violet – was clearly deferring to his boss in a big way. Following this conversation Waldenberg left the caravan. Valeriy then apologised to me and said he had tried to get me cleared for the front seat 'because the view is poor in the back', but the rear seat it would have to be. I was actually delighted with this because I knew that if I had been in the front I would have been distracted by the need to operate the aircraft systems and deal with any related issues, whereas in the back I had nothing to do except concentrate on the handling.

ABOVE John Farley with aircraft design engineer John Fozard in front of a Sea Harrier at the 1978 Farnborough air show. Working for Hawker Siddeley since 1950 after seven years with Blackburn Aircraft, Fozard was instrumental in the development of the Harrier, and chief designer on that type from 1965 to 1978. He worked closely with John Farley to develop an aircraft unique in its time. *(John Farley)*

ABOVE John Farley in the back seat of the MiG-29 during his 1990 flight at the Farnborough air show, with a BAe Hawk 200 (ZH200) in the foreground taking pictures. This Hawk had made its first flight on 24 April 1987 before being stored at Warton, eventually finding its way to Loughborough University in March 2012. On the ground and to the left, preparing to depart for the runway, is the Antonov An-225 in the cockpit of which was this author, inducted as a flight engineer for the demonstration flight, but that is another story! *(John Farley)*

I then went away to sort out what tests I wanted to do. The next day Valeriy and I went through my plan, which was aimed at allowing me to be able to jot down some meaningful data as the trip progressed – not quite the same thing as going through a list of manoeuvres and reading the instrumentation after the flight!

Valeriy's brief was outstanding. Two examples serve to give an idea of his approach to the sortie. Firstly he said the trip would be governed by three rules. 'Rule one – maximum safety. Rule two – maximum information for you. Rule three – maximum fun for us.' Secondly, when I asked Valeriy to take into consideration that I had stopped testing high-performance aeroplanes seven years earlier, his reply was that he wanted me to do as much as possible and that the trip would proceed on the basis of 'your experience and my currency'. You can warm to a guy like that.

Because we had no common language we agreed to limit our essential communication in the air to 'Valeriy fly' and 'John fly', with me doing all the R/T.

Clearly such an operation needed good planning and the help of a reliable interpreter. Having agreed the tests and their sequence

RIGHT For three decades the MiG-29 has been at the top of front-line Russian aviation and the type has become a legendary symbol of fourth-generation fighter design, emerging at a time when Cold War challenges stimulated new ways to look at Russian aircraft design. The MiG-29 has been acquired by many air forces around the world, including the Peruvian *Fuerza del Perú*, which operates 19 MiG-29S/SE/SMP/UBP variants with the *Escuadrón Aéreo 612* of *Grupo Aéreo No 6* at the Chiclayo air base. *(David Baker)*

in the flight, we went back through them all again and discussed the details. As we did so, Valeriy covered appropriate aspects of the flight controls, aircraft systems and limits, but only in the context of this specific and necessarily limited flight.

There were two modes of nose-wheel steering available from the rudder bar. Fine for normal taxiing, take-off and landing (plus or minus 8°) and coarse for slow speed in confined areas (plus or minus 30°), chosen using a changeover selector. Valeriy briefed me that he would line the aircraft up on the runway, do checks on the brakes at full cold power, release the brakes, engage full reheat and say 'John fly'.

He went on to say that I should start pulling the stick back at 185/190kph (100/103kt) aiming to un-stick at 220/230kph (119/124kt). He would select gear-up. Then I should aim for 13 alpha until passing through 30° angle of climb, when the alpha should be increased to 15. After the aircraft reached the inverted I was to roll out and turn 180 towards Boscombe. He said that would be 'the fun before we work'. I suggest you need confidence in various aspects of your aircraft to brief a stranger to do a roll off the top after his first take-off, especially if he is seven years out of touch.

As soon as these MiGs came to Farnborough, we realised that the intakes had internal doors to protect the engines from foreign object damage (FOD) when using rough strips. These were hinged at the top, came down and slammed shut on start-up and were still shut during the take-off ground roll.

Therefore at this point I asked about their operation. I was told that the doors closed automatically as each engine started and the hydraulics came live. They opened fully on take-off as air speed increased through 200kph (108kts). I queried what would happen if one stuck shut and Valeriy replied, with a big grin, 'No practice.'

When I pressed him to say what would happen next he said 'We find out.' I was concerned about any possible asymmetric effects but clearly their chief test pilot was not. The reason for his calmness became clear when I queried how fast they had flown with the doors shut and was told 800kph (432kt). He went on to say that at this speed with the doors shut one should limit alpha to 22°. Clearly there was more to the intakes in the top of the wings than was apparent for the engines to be happy flying effectively with their 'intake blanks in' at that sort of speed!

The next day we were allocated a take-off slot at the end of the show. At the appointed time a patch of bad weather was going through and we walked out under a 90–122m (300–400ft) base with complete cover and cloud tops reported as 3,650m (12,000ft), although the base was forecast to improve for our return. I pointed to the cloud, put my thumb down and indicated with my hand (how else?) that I intended to pull briefly before rolling inverted, pull again to level just under the base, roll erect again and climb towards Boscombe.

BELOW A MiG-29SMT on the flight-line at Moscow's MAKS 2009, alongside a MiG-31. Beginning in 1997, MiG engaged on a major upgrade to the design through the 9.17-type modification to improve range, and designating the letter 'T' to *toplivo*, Russian for fuel. With a convex upper decking on the fuselage, a true multi-role capability and improvements of 35–40% in direct operating costs, the aircraft has kept pace with expanding requirements.
(David Baker)

ABOVE The East German Air Force acquired 20 MiG-29As and four MiG-29UB variants just before the collapse of the Berlin Wall, and they were introduced in 1988 and 1989. After the reunification of Germany in October 1990 the consolidated German Air Force inducted these aircraft, but in 2003 sold 22 to Poland for one Euro each! One of the two retained examples crashed and the second is on display at Laage-Rostock airport. Before handing over their MiG-29s, *Staffel* 731 of JG-73 'Steinhoff' carried out a farewell tour of the US, a MiG-29 repainted to celebrate the event being seen here. (USAF)

Valeriy shrugged and clearly did not see the case for such a wimpish departure from the plan. I chickened out of doing the roll off the top because Russian attitude indicators are fundamentally different from those in the West and I had yet to see one in operation. Their horizon bar is fixed horizontally with respect to the instrument panel – as our aeroplane symbol is – while their aeroplane symbol banks with respect to the panel. Pitch angle is provided by a drum that rotates behind the fixed horizon bar.

In my experience it is asking for trouble to just leap into the air when faced with something that is very different from what you are used to. I like to get my head round the issue first and form a specific plan of how I am going to tackle it. In this case, having flown plenty of line-astern close formation in fighters, it seemed to me that the little aeroplane of their display would look like the rear view of your leader's aircraft against the natural horizon as he rolls and pulls round the sky ahead of you. That meant all I had to do was use my stick to 'control' my leader's bank angle remotely from behind (how many times did I wish I could do that over the years!). That way if I wanted 'him' – actually me, of course – to fly wings-level or change bank angle, I knew just what to do with my ailerons.

Once I got R/T clearance to start, Valeriy got on with it and after the usual external checks with his crew chief on intercom we were ready to 'John taxi'. The intake door indicators (a pair of vertical strip indicators showing 0 to 100%

at the bottom right of the main centre panel) showed them fully shut. Taxiing was no problem and the nose-wheel steering was easy to use in both modes. After we lined up Valeriy did his checks, let the brakes off, engaged reheat and said 'John fly'.

Perhaps because I did not want to get left behind I started rotation at 185kph (100kt) but overdid the pull and Valeriy momentarily checked my back stick, saying 'No' as he did so. Once airborne, because of the brief to hold 13 alpha below 30° nose-up, I didn't quite capture 15 before the need to roll under the low base. In the debrief Valeriy said that looking through the periscope makes it hard to assess pitch attitude once the nose is raised, and that I would have been OK in the front seat. Nice guy. He also said un-stick was early at 200kph. I was looking at alpha once I started rotation so I had no idea.

We had planned to carry out the handling assessment between 1,220m (4,000ft) and 4,500m (15,000ft) near Boscombe. The cloud stopped that and after a frustrating period of no manoeuvring, we came out on top at just over 3,650m (12,000ft). The enforced instrument flying enabled me to adjust to what I felt were generally larger stick displacements and slightly heavier forces than those of a typical UK military aircraft. It reminded me more of the F-15.

Despite the scope for confusion with the attitude display, my plan to 'control my leader into doing what I wanted' worked well, and I found the aircraft very stable and easy to fly on instruments. By comparison, the Sea Harrier would have to be described as a bit touchy, but the SHAR did not use auto-stabilisers above 250kt, whereas the MiG-29 does, and they have been well optimised.

Just after we became visual on top I heard 'Valeriy fly'. A bit peeved, I studied my kneepad, as I was not expecting this. I should have known better. Out of the corner of my eye I saw the stick flash to the right-hand side of the cockpit. Looking up I was just in time to see three very quick rolls before the nose was yanked hard up. Valeriy then rolled inverted and again pulled hard. As this happened there were two loud bangs and thumps through the airframe, very reminiscent of engine surges in a Sea Harrier.

Just as I thought 'so much for the donks', I heard 'John fly' and realised that Valeriy had communicated with me in a way that needed no words. He had shown it did not matter if I was a bit rough on his aeroplane and had demonstrated for good measure what the intake doors sounded like as they slammed shut decelerating through 200kph (108kt).

Valeriy then had the patience to sit through my simple speed reduction at idle power from 400kph (216kt) until the alpha limit, at which

point I had my first feel of the stall warning system restricting rearwards movement of the stick. Approaching 30 alpha slowly, the stop could be felt tapping away at the stick and trying to nudge it forward. The aircraft was by now descending rapidly in a fairly flat and easy to control attitude. I accelerated and repeated the deceleration, this time using lots of lateral stick applications as we slowed. There was excellent control response.

As briefed, when I got to the limiter Valeriy showed we could pull through the stop to stick hard back. This needed 17kg (37.4lb) of pull. There was no problem and the aircraft remained under lateral control for some 15 seconds or so. Because the cockpit gauge was pegged at its max 30 reading, I later asked Valeriy what value we would have reached. He said flight test data showed 45/47°. For comparison, you can hold a Harrier in the stall at full back stick but the alpha would be 18° at most.

Flight test people know that incomplete data, or data noted under non-steady conditions, can be wildly misleading. For example, the speed/ alpha relationship during a deceleration means nothing without knowing the power, weight and flight path angle at the time. Despite this I was keen to get some feel for the g available at low speeds. A couple of snatches of back stick, into

BELOW *Luftwaffe pilot Oberstleutnant Johann Keck flew the MiG-29 under operational combat conditions and in engagements with Western fighters. His assessment report on the capabilities of the aircraft makes grim reading for pilots of aircraft such as the F-16, F-15 and F/A-18, against which he claims the MiG-29 is formidable and outclasses its opponents in several respects. Superior in dogfights, it turns at 28°/sec against the 26°/sec for the F-16 Block 50, and, he believes through experience, is impossible to defeat inside a radius of four miles. (Via David Baker)*

ABOVE **The ultimate development path for the MiG-29 was always going to be the 3D thrust-vectoring Klimov engine, which no other aircraft in the world has demonstrated in an operational combat platform. Incorporated as a commercial add-on to procurement of the MiG-35, this combination of superb aerodynamic design and flexible manoeuvrability buys a completely new way of waging air-to-air combat. If adopted by future high-g designs, possibly unmanned, it may return the warfighter to World War One-era close-in, eyeball-to-eyeball dogfighting – perhaps with its pilot on the ground.** *(MiG)*

heavy buffet and held long enough to peak the g, showed about 4g and 5g at 400 and 500kph (only 216 and 270kt!). These pulls were done at the low power needed to set the speeds in level flight so the wing had to be providing most of the g. In similar circumstances a Sea Harrier might have pulled half that.

We then did some tailslides that were a total non-event. In the brief Valeriy had said to 'favour the right throttle' during the pitch down, so for the first one I led a little with the right throttle as I slammed to full reheat, with the result that the nose did try and move a little to the right. I suspected this was due to gyroscopic precession from the engines at those high pitch rates. Then Valeriy did one and I watched him slam only the right throttle to full reheat, followed at once by the left one. I repeated it

again using this differential slamming technique for a completely straight drop through.

I then looked at some combat reversals from steep climbs. Pulling into a 50° climb from 400kph (220kt) I rolled right at 240kph (132kt) and pulled to a wing over back downhill. I repeated the manoeuvre waiting until 200kph (108kt) before reversing. I did it a third time leaving the reversal until 150kph (81kt). There were no problems, despite this silly low 500kph (270kt), and I was free of buffet all the way round. The second was planned to start from 300kph (162kt) in reheat but, with the burners on, it ran away from me and I did not get the pull going until 350kph (189kt). It went over the top at 15 alpha and 160kph (86kt). We were in and out of cloud between layers but I noticed that we went over the top below 8 and recovered above 5. However, in these circumstances I was clearly not getting anything like accurate data.

By now I realised that the intake doors seemed to spend much of their time in the 40% or 50% area and that there was no obvious kick as reheat lit, just a smooth push. Both things were unexpected so far as I was concerned. When instructing on Jet Provosts at Cranwell, I sometimes failed to demonstrate a good stall turn to students as it was easy to get stuck halfway round. Not so in this MiG. I pulled the nose up as for a tailslide but at 150kph (81kt) applied and held full left rudder. The nose slid round without hesitation and the wings could be kept at right angles to the horizon. I centralised the rudder as soon as we were pointing straight down and there was not so much as a wobble. Minimum speed going round at the top was 40kph (22kt). The whole thing inspired great confidence in the aircraft at low speed.

Valeriy was now pressing to return to Farnborough, but I managed to hold us in a couple of orbits as we started our descent because I wanted to give time for two Hawks from Dunsfold to join us. Chief Test Pilot Chris Roberts with BAe photographer Geoff Lee in the Hawk 100, plus Warton test pilot Phil Dye in the Hawk 200 single-seater, slid in just as we entered cloud.

Back at Farnborough, I did one orbit for pictures before the circuit to land. After the sort of manoeuvres I had been flying, drifting round the corner at 300kph (162kt) felt very easy and as if we were in the middle of the flight envelope. I only felt there was a job to be done when, on very short finals, I realised how little I could see. So I said 'Valeriy fly' but he ignored me. Happily at that time I used to fly a Ryan PT-22 from the rear seat that also needed you to look out both sides of the nose as you flared, so I just pressed on and the MiG seemed to know how to land on the numbers.

After touchdown Valeriy took it and applied the brakes and they were very impressive – but then, my bike used to stop better when I used the front brake as well as the rear one. It reminded me that the only Hunter Dunsfold ever fitted with a nose-wheel brake showed that a nose-wheel brake was worth as much as streaming the braking parachute.

When we taxied in there was quite a collection of people waiting to meet us. I climbed down the ladder and one of the journalists, a middle-aged lady, was the first to speak. She said I looked glum and asked whether the flight had been a disappointment. I suggested that if, at her age, she had just experienced the best lover of her life but at the same time knew she would never enjoy him again, she might not grin either. To everyone else I remarked that when I grew up I wanted to be a MiG test pilot.

MiG-29 specifications and performance[1]

	MiG-29 (9.12B)	MiG-29UB (9.51)	MiG-29M (9.15)	MiG-K (9.31)	MiG-29S (9.13S)	MiG-29SMT (9.17)	MiG-35D (9.61)
First flight	1977	1981	1986	1990	1990	1997	2007
Engine	2 x RD-33 Srs 2	2 x RD-33 Srs 2	2 x RD-33 Srs 2	2 x RD-33K	2 x RD33 Srs 2	2 x RD33	2 x RD33MK
A/B thrust[2]	40,899N	40,899N	40,899N	46,081N	40,899N	40,899N	44,124N
Length	17.32m	17.32m	17.32m	17.27m	17.32m	17.32m	17.31
Wingspan	11.36m	11.36m	11.36m	11.99m	11.36m	11.36m	11.99m
Height	4.73m	4.73m	4.73m	4.73m	4.73m	4.73m	4.5m
Wing area	38.056m²	38.056m²	38.056m²	43m²	38.056m²	38.056m²	n/a
TOW	14,900kg	14,600kg	15,300kg	15,570kg	15,300kg	16,850kg	17,500kg
MTOW	18,000kg	18,200kg	20,000kg	18,210kg	19,700kg	n/a	23,500kg
Ordnance	3,200kg	n/a	n/a	4,500kg	3,200kg	4,000kg	6,500kg
Internal fuel	3,630kg	n/a	3,630kg	4,460kg	3,850kg	4,835kg	4,800kg
T/W ratio	1.11:1	n/a	n/a	1.06:1	1.09:1	n/a	n/a
Max speed[3]	2,400kph	2,230kph	2,400kph	2,300kph	2,400kph	2,450kph	2,100kph
Mach limit	2.25	2.25	n/a	n/a	2.25	n/a	n/a
Ceiling	18,000m	17,500m	17,750m	17,400m	17,000m	n/a	17,500m
Climb rate	330m/min	330m/min	n/a	260m/min	300m/min	n/a	n/a
Range[4]	1,500km	1,500km	1,500km	n/a	1,500km	2,100km	2,000km
Max range[5]	2,900km	–	2,900km	3,000km	3,600km	3,300km	3,000km

Notes: 1 All parameters are in metric units. **2** Afterburner thrust for each engine. **3** At 11,000m. **4** On internal fuel. **5** With internal plus three external tanks. **n/a** = not applicable.

Acronyms and abbreviations

A – Amps.
AAM – Air-to-air missile.
AC – Alternating current.
ADC – Air data computer.
ADF – Automatic direction finder.
ADI – Attitude director indicator.
AEKRAN – Fault identification and readout display.
AESA – Active electronically scanned array.
AFCS – Automatic flight control system.
Ah – Ampere hours.
AMRAAM – Advanced medium-range air-to-air missile.
AOA – Angle of attack.
AP – Autopilot.
APU – Auxiliary power unit.
AWACS – Airborne Warning and Control System.
bar – Unit of barometric pressure.
BVR – Beyond visual range.
C – Centigrade.
cm – Centimetres.
COC – Angle of attack and limiter control system.
CPI – Combined pressure indicator.
CRT – Cathode ray tube.
DC – Direct current.
°/sec – Degrees per second.
DME – Distance Measuring Equipment.
ECP – Engine control pump.
ECU – Engine control unit.
EFIS – Electronic flight instrumentation system.
EPM – Electronic protection measures.
F – Fahrenheit.
FCS – Fire control system.
FOD – Foreign object damage.
ft – Feet.
ft² – Square feet.
ft/min – Feet per minute.
g – Measure of gravitational force.
g/cm³ – Grams per cubic centimetre.
g/sec – Gravitational force per second.
GPS – Global positioning system.
HDD – Head-down display.
HMS – Helmet-mounted sight.
HOTAS – Hands-on throttle and stick.
HP – High pressure.
hp – Horsepower.
hPa – Hectopascals.

HSI – Horizontal situation indicator.
HUD – Head-up display.
Hz – Hertz.
I – *Istrebitel* (fighter aircraft).
IAS – Indicated air speed.
ICAO – International Civil Aviation Organisation.
IFF – Identification-friend-or-foe.
ILS – Instrument landing system.
in – Inches.
IRST/LR – Infrared search and track/laser rangefinder.
IRSTS – Infrared search and track system.
izdeliye – Type.
kg/m² – Kilograms per square metre.
kHz – Kilohertz.
KIAS – Knots indicated air speed.
KLIVT – *Klimovskiy vektor tyagi* (Klimov vectoring thrust).
kN – Kilonewtons.
kPa – Kilopascals.
kp/cm² – Kilograms per square centimetre.
kph – Kilometres per hour.
kt – Knots.
kVA – Kilovolt amps.
kW – Kilowatts.
lb – Pounds.
lb/ft² – Pounds per square foot.
lb/in² – Pounds per square inch.
lb/in³ – Pounds per cubic inch.
LCD – Liquid crystal display.
LERX – Leading-edge root extension.
LH – Left-hand.
LP – Low pressure.
m – Metres.
m² – Square metres.
MHz – Megahertz.
MiG – Mikoyan and Gurevich.
mil-power – Military-power segment of engine control system performance range.
mm – Millimetres.
m/min – Metres per minute.
MPa – Megapascals.
mph – Miles per hour.
m/sec – Metres per second.
N – Newtons (unit of force).
NATO – North Atlantic Treaty Organisation.
NH – Speed of the high-pressure compressor.

NKAP – *Narodnyy Komissariat Aviatsionnoy Promyshlennosti* (People's Commissariat for Aviation Industry).

NL – Speed of the low-pressure compressor.

NORAD – North American Aerospace Defense Command.

OKB – *Opytno Konstrooktorskoye Byuro* (Experimental Design Bureau).

OKO – *Opytno Konstrooktorskoye* (Experimental Design Office).

PEC – Personal equipment connector.

PFI – *Perspectivniyy Frontovoy Istrebetal* (Perspective Frontline Fighter).

PTO – Power take-off.

PVO – *Voyska Protivovozdushnoy Oborony* (Air Defence Forces).

RAD ALT – Radar altimeter.

RAM – Radar-absorbent materials.

RCS – Radar cross-section.

RH – Right-hand.

RHAW – Radar homing and warning receiver.

rpm – Revolutions per minute.

sec – Seconds.

SHORAN – Short-range air navigation.

SIF – Selective identification feature.

Sistem – State Research Institute for Aircraft Systems.

STOL – Short take-off and landing.

TACAN – Tactical air navigation system.

TAS – True air speed.

ABOVE A Royal Malaysian Air Force MiG-29N and a Sukhoi Su-30MKM (top) fly in wingtip formation over the South China Sea on 24 June 2014. *(US Navy photo)*

TFX – Tactical fighter experimental.

TsAGI – *Tsentralniy Aerogidrodinamicheskiy Institut* (Central Aerohydrodynamic Institute).

TsNII-30 – *Tsentral'nyy Nauchno-Issledovatel'skiy Institut* (30th Central Scientific Research Institute).

TVC – Thrust-vectoring control.

UHF – Ultra-high frequency.

V – Volts.

VAC – Volts of alternating current.

VDC – Volts of direct current.

VG – Variable geometry.

VHF – Very high frequency.

VIWAS – Voice information and warning system.

VOR – VHF Omnidirectional Range.

VSTOL – Vertical and/or short take-off and landing.

VTOL – Vertical take-off and landing.

VVI – Vertical velocity indicator.

VVS RKKA – *Voenne-Vozdushnye Sily Raboche Krestiyanskoy Krasnii Armi* (Air Force of the Red Army of the Workers and Peasants).

W – Watts.

Index